DO NOT REMOVE CARD FROM POCKET

Mead Public Library
Sheboygan, Wisconsin

ASCENT

Also by EDMUND HILLARY

HIGH ADVENTURE

NO LATITUDE FOR ERROR

SCHOOLHOUSE IN THE CLOUDS

NOTHING VENTURE, NOTHING WIN

FROM THE OCEAN TO THE SKY

With George Lowe

EAST OF EVEREST

With Sir Vivian Fuchs

THE CROSSING OF ANTARCTICA

With Desmond Doig

HIGH IN THE THIN COLD AIR

Also by PETER HILLARY

A SUNNY DAY IN THE HIMALAYAS

With Graeme Dingle

FIRST ACROSS THE ROOF OF THE WORLD

ASCENT

Two Lives Explored:
The Autobiographies
of
Sir Edmund and Peter Hillary

DOUBLEDAY & COMPANY, INC.
GARDEN CITY, N.Y.
1986

Library of Congress Cataloging-in-Publication Data

Hillary, Edmund, Sir.
Ascent: two lives explored: the autobiographies
of Sir Edmund and Peter Hillary

Previously published as: Two generations. 1984.
Includes index.
1. Hillary, Edmund, Sir.   2. Mountaineers—New
Zealand—Biography.   3. Hillary, Peter.   I. Hillary,
Peter.   II. Title.
GV199.92.H54A37   1986   796.5'22'0922 [B]   86-16600
ISBN 0-385-19831-0

To Jim and Phyl

Contents

Maps

ASCENT

Introduction

THIS IS THE story of two generations of mountaineering adventure–a period of massive changes in equipment, in technical climbing skills, and in attitudes to the mountains. Some aspects of climbing have remained the same–fitness, enthusiasm, acceptance of discomfort, and energetic motivation. But there have been many variations too–we have entered the era of the prima donna, where the influence of the media is overwhelming, where commercial backing is available for even the grandest and most expensive projects–and yet strangely enough where the purist has emerged, lightly laden, carrying no oxygen, dispensing with the strong backs of Sherpas, alone or with a small team pushing relentlessly on against hardship and unseasonable weather, the one aim being to travel fast and free and, one hopes, to succeed.

It is the story of my life and part of the life of my son, Peter. Over the years much has changed but the challenge has still remained. There has been joy and sadness, the excitement of achievement and the regret of tasks uncompleted. My son and I have much in common but in other respects we are very different. Both of us suffer from an uncontrollable restlessness. We have each experienced our moments of fear and looked on the face of death. I am a relic of Victoriana, brought up with an obsession for work and responsibility and easily persuaded. Peter is more concerned with doing his 'thing' and doing it well, and he is much tougher. Whether our efforts have resulted in success or failure is of little consequence. Both of us believe we have accepted our challenges and done the best we could. That is all you can ask of anyone–that at least you have tried.

Ed Hillary

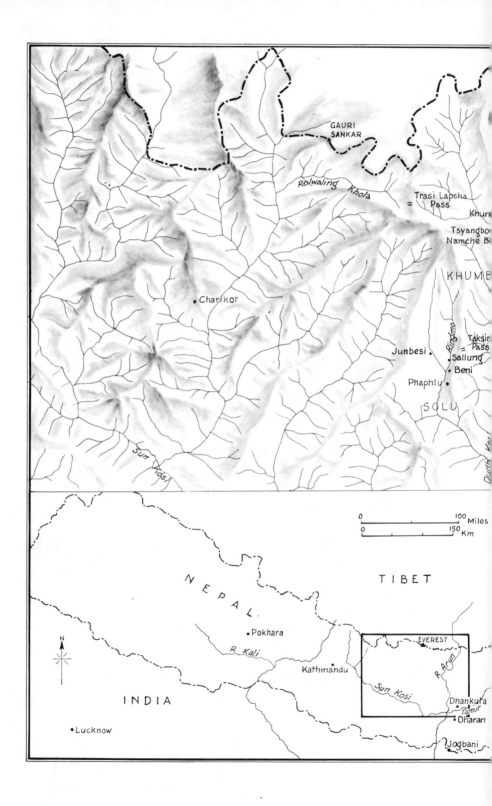

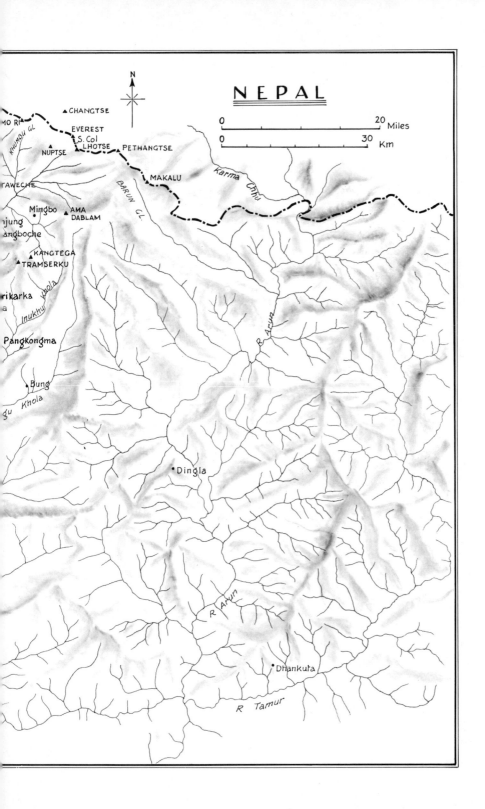

NEPAL

N

▲CHANGTSE

EVEREST
S.Col
NUPTSE LHOTSE PETHANGTSE

TAWECHE MAKALU

Mingbo ▲AMA
DABLAM

njung
angboche

KANGTEGA
▲TRAMSERKU

rikarka
a

Pangkongma

•Bung

•Dingla

•Dhankuta

R Tamur

0 _____ 20 Miles
0 _____ 30 Km

KHUMBU GL.
BARUN GL.
Inukhu Khola
gu Khola
R Arun
Karma Chhu

ONE

Edmund Hillary

1

Youth

I WAS A RESTLESS, rather lonely child and even in my teens I had few friends. My father was a man of rigid principles and any straying from the path by me was usually severely punished. Not that I believe my behaviour was irresponsible, but I had a stubborn temperament and would often refuse to admit to errors – at times because I didn't think I was to blame. This infuriated my father who would take me to the woodshed and thump me until his anger or his arm weakened. But I rarely, if ever, gave in.

And yet, strangely enough, I had a considerable respect for my father. I admired his moral courage – he would battle fiercely against society or the powers-that-be on a matter of principle and he also had the ability when in the mood to make his children laugh – and there was nothing I enjoyed more in life than laughing. My mother had a more gentle disposition, although strongly principled too, and we relied on her for the warmth and affection that all families need.

We lived in the small country town of Tuakau, forty miles south of the city of Auckland, and my father was editor of the local newspaper, the *Tuakau District News*. As a hobby he took up beekeeping and he very much enjoyed its activity and freedom. When a strong disagreement developed between the editor and his directors, my father retired from his journalistic life and increased his beehives until they became an economic proposition – but life as a beekeeper was always marginal financially. At an early age my brother and I became involved in the beekeeping and worked very hard in weekends and school holidays. I think we thoroughly enjoyed this work and never felt any particular envy for our fellow pupils who spent their holidays in their cottages at the beach. The beekeeping existence was hard work but it was challenging too. We had great enthusiasm and thought nothing of the long hours we spent on the job. Weather was the big gamble—it could result in a bumper crop or a failure, but it taught us a very philosophical attitude to life.

My mother had been a teacher and she encouraged me energetically in my primary school years. I seemed to progress remarkably well and became almost the child genius of the Tuakau district school. I graduated at the age of eleven, two years younger than normal. The crunch came when I started attending the big high school in the city. Auckland Grammar was one of the most highly regarded schools in New Zealand and I felt completely lost. Small in size and immature in outlook I hated every moment of my early high school life. Only when I started to grow rapidly and became able physically to hold my own with my contemporaries did school life become just bearable. I was constantly being caned, not for disciplinary reasons, but usually because my homework was inadequate. I had usually tried hard and considered this unjust. Probably I was a difficult student and would have experienced the same problems at any school but I certainly developed the firm view that physical violence was often both unfair and useless as a deterrent.

One of my good moments at school, and certainly one of the turning points in my life, came when I was sixteen years old. By then I was tall and lean and fairly strong. It must have been a good honey season because my father agreed that in the winter holidays I could go with a school team to Mount Ruapehu. I had never seen snow before and there had been unusually heavy snowfalls in the mountains—it was the most exciting time I had ever spent. I loved the skiing and the clambering around the mountainside; I revelled in the cold crisp air and the freedom to do almost anything I wished. I soon developed a taste for the mountains that has never left me.

Over the next few years I graduated from high school and spent a couple of unsatisfactory years at university. I had no friends and did not excel at the academic existence. I lost myself in reading books and in dreaming of great adventures. I played little formal sport but greatly enjoyed skiing and the weekends I spent tramping around the local Auckland hills.

By the time the war started in 1939 I had dropped my university activities and was working full-time with my father on the bees. Beekeeping was a reserved occupation so I didn't have to go to war—just produce food. After a couple of years I became rather bored with this and persuaded my father to release me and let me go into the air force. I trained as a navigator and was posted to Catalina flying boats in the Pacific on search and rescue. My war effort was a very modest contribution but the air force probably gave me the best holiday I had ever had. The work was so much easier than it had been with the bees and I was constantly seeing new places and doing interesting new things. I even found time for climbing in the mountains and started to develop some of the skills which proved useful to me in later years. In the Solomon Islands I did a lot of boating and crocodile hunting and finally completed my air force career by getting blown up in a speed boat and severely burnt.

After the war I returned to the bees, but I devoted every spare moment to the mountains. For five years I had a marvellous time and climbed many of the great peaks in the Southern Alps of New Zealand. I was never a highly efficient technical climber, but was strong and vigorous and full of enthusiasm. Perhaps the most important result was the friendships I made—people like Harry Ayres and George Lowe became the first real friends I'd ever had.

In 1950 my father retired and my brother and I took over the bee business. I made my first trip to Europe and with two fellow New Zealanders climbed in the Austrian and Swiss Alps. Our objectives were not the great routes of today, but we were fit and very energetic and we rushed furiously up a large number of enjoyable peaks.

The year 1951 was a major turning point for me. Four of us, all New Zealanders, made our first visit to the Himalayas, in Gahwal. We flew across the Tasman Sea from Auckland to Sydney and then travelled by ship to Colombo in Ceylon. The ship was loaded with young Australians and New Zealanders and a very cheerful and happy atmosphere prevailed. We off-loaded in Colombo, said goodbye to our new friends, and then travelled by train the full length of Ceylon and India—up through Madras and Calcutta and then along the Gangetic plain into Gahwal. From the hill station of Rhanikhet we trekked over the hills to Joshimath and Badrinath revelling in the superb mountains we could see in every direction. There were no restrictions on travel in border areas in those days and we went up-valley towards

Tibet and climbed for week after week on the virgin mountains along the Tibetan border. It was a marvellous experience to be alone in a great mountain area which few had visited and where none had climbed.

We returned to Badrinath with a considerable sense of achievement and then crossed back through torrential monsoon rain to Rhanikhet. A letter was waiting for us, an invitation for two of our team to join Eric Shipton's British reconnaissance expedition to the south side of Everest—the sort of chance that you could only dream about.

Earle Riddiford and I descended to Lucknow, purchased supplies of food and then travelled by train across northern India to Jogbani. Shipton had gone on ahead leaving a message for us to follow. We were very fit and driven by a powerful urge to catch up with the main team. We shot through Dharan and Dhankuta; walked rapidly up the Arun valley crossing a number of flooded side streams; we were ferried across the Arun river in a big dugout canoe and then raced up the hill to Dingla. To our relief Shipton and his party were there—they had been held up by difficulties in recruiting porters.

To me Shipton epitomised all that was best in mountaineering and to have the chance to work with him and become close friends was the experience of a lifetime. In continuous monsoon rain we battled our way over high ridges and flooded rivers. We descended into the valley of the Dudh Kosi and headed north. The weather cleared as we reached the pass above Surkya and for the first time we looked up-valley to the peak of Khumbila standing above the villages of Khumjung and Khunde. We were approaching the heart of the Sherpa country.

Little was known about the south side of Everest. In 1921 George Leigh Mallory had peered around the corner from the Lho La and reported that the route looked impossible. In 1950 Tilman and his party had made the first approach to Everest from the south up the Khumbu Glacier. From their furthest point, surprisingly far from the mountain, they too indicated that the chance of climbing Everest from the south was minimal. We therefore had little hope of success, just planning to confirm the impossibility of the route and then to head off exploring in the vast untouched area of mountains to the east and west.

We established our Base Camp below the great Icefall and the route still looked unclimbable. As a last effort Shipton and I ascended to 19,000 feet up a ridge on Pumo Ri. The higher we went the more we could see of the Icefall and the valley above— the Western Cwm. And the further we went the clearer it became that there was in fact a potential route—through the terrifying Icefall, up the Western Cwm, steeply up the Lhotse Face to the South Col, and then on to the summit. We descended, stimulated by our discovery, and confident that the following year a British expedition would attempt this new route. We arrived back in Kathmandu full of hope, only to discover that Swiss expeditions had been granted permission for two attempts in 1952. It is surprising how much we resented this news, as though we were the only ones who had any right to the mountain.

In 1952 the British Everest Committee decided that a team should be sent to the Everest region for training purposes, so I found myself back in Khumbu again. In many ways it was more fun than attempting Everest—we climbed many mountains, crossed new passes and explored unknown valleys. But always our minds kept turning to the Swiss expedition—how were they doing? In May we returned to the Khumbu. The Swiss had come down off the mountain, we learned. Two men, Lambert and a Sherpa called Tenzing Norgay, had reached 28,000 feet on the South-East Ridge before turning back. It was a mighty effort but they hadn't succeeded—there was still a chance for us.

The Swiss were back again in the post-monsoon season, September to November 1952. The weather was colder and windier and they had a difficult time. With considerable determination they pushed up on to the South Col at 26,000 feet and then on to the South-East Ridge. But the wind was just too strong—they were beaten back and retreated off the mountain battered and disheartened.

So now our chance had come again. Eric Shipton was appointed expedition leader and he invited me along as a member of the team. Then came the bombshell! I read in the newspaper that Eric had been replaced as leader by someone who was completely unknown to me; his name was John Hunt. I was seriously considering withdrawing from the expedition when I received a letter from Eric explaining the change and asking me to transfer my loyalty to Hunt. With some doubts I agreed.

I had never felt very much at home with the opposite sex but over the previous couple of years I had developed a considerable enthusiasm for a local Auckland girl called Louise Rose. Louise was a musician, friendly, cheerful and very energetic, and she was quite a bit younger than me. But we had much in common and I guess there was some significance in the fact that she was also the daughter of the president of the New Zealand Alpine Club. I had known Jim Rose well for several years before I really became aware of the bright young thing who seemed to rush in and out of his house on odd occasions. Louise loved the mountains, although she was not a forceful climber, despite her strength and energy.

I can remember taking her and some friends for a training climb on Mount Ruapehu. We were practising on a long, steep ice slope and I was down below shouting out instructions. Then Louise slipped and came hurtling down the mountain on her back with her feet and sharp crampons held high in the air. She was coming straight at me and I had two alternatives—to receive the ten points of her crampons in my stomach or to step aside. I glanced quickly downwards; the route below was rough but she would probably survive . . . I stepped calmly backwards and watched her shoot by. I rushed down to join her and she lay smiling up at me, bruised but undamaged and only a little mortified by her error. I determined that I would get to know her better.

Some months before I left for Everest Louise had crossed the Tasman Sea to Sydney to take up a two-year course at the Sydney Conservatorium of Music. I had sadly felt her absence from Auckland and this seemed an excellent opportunity to see her again. I crossed to Sydney a couple of days early and spent the time visiting Louise. The weather was superb; we walked over the Harbour Bridge, swam at Bondi, strolled through the Botanical Gardens, and listened to evening open-air concerts. It was all pretty harmless but it remains one of the happiest periods I have ever spent. It was with some reluctance that I said goodbye and carried on to India and Nepal. Despite my great inferiorities and my concern about our difference in ages, for the first time I felt that something might ultimately develop between Louise and myself.

The expedition gathered together in Kathmandu and I met John Hunt for the first time. He proved a forthright character with a good deal of charm and I soon accepted that he would handle the expedition, and me, rather well. I also met Tenzing, our sirdar, and liked his warm, friendly spirit. For a Sherpa he was tall and strong and I could see why he had been such a successful mountaineer.

For seventeen days we trekked across country with hundreds of laden porters and as we got higher our fitness improved and so did our acclimatisation. At 13,000 feet we reached the monastery of Thyangboche and we thrilled to the sight of Everest thrusting up above the great Nuptse/Lhotse Wall. For a couple of weeks we rushed around the hills climbing 19,000 and 20,000 feet peaks to help our adjustment to altitude. I was pleased to be given the task of taking a team up the Khumbu Glacier to set up Base Camp and force a route up through the Icefall.

We established our Base Camp at 17,000 feet on rock-strewn ice and although it wasn't a comfortable place it was readily accessible to the Icefall. Then we tackled the Icefall itself, seeking out a safe route through the multitude of crevasses and ice walls, and the all-too-frequent and tottering ice pinnacles. Hacking steps, fixing ropes, wriggling through ice cracks, suspending rope ladders, we made a route up this shaky 2,000 feet. At times we'd climb up the route in the morning and find our tracks wiped out by icefall the previous night. It was exciting climbing and always underneath we had a feeling of tension and danger. It was a good moment when we pitched our tent on a wide ice block at the top of the Icefall with most of the problems behind us.

John Hunt came up with some companions to check over the route and together we tackled the difficulty ahead—a wide crevasse on the lip of the Western Cwm. We had a long aluminium ladder with us and we pushed this slowly across the gap. Always eager to be first, I teetered my way across with the blue depths of the crevasse underneath me. Then it was up into the Western Cwm, zigzagging backwards and forwards to dodge huge crevasses, and finally reaching 21,000 feet. Here we established our Advance Base Camp.

For several weeks we worked on the mountain, carrying dozens of loads up through the Icefall to Advance Base Camp, and pioneering the route up on to the Lhotse Face. Every afternoon we had a fall of snow and each morning we had to restamp our way up the valley. It was constant hard work and progress was slow. A camp was established half-way up the Lhotse Face and then in one exciting day Wilfrid Noyce and Sherpa Annullu pushed their way up the last thousands of feet to reach the South Col at 26,000 feet.

The way was open, but first many loads had to be carried to the South Col. We had fourteen high-altitude Sherpas and all of them must be got to the col with a load. Charles Wylie was in charge of the group but we knew we couldn't afford to fail on this try. Tenzing and I rushed up to the Lhotse Face camp to support him. Next day we started upwards with Tenzing and me breaking trail. The Sherpas were not using oxygen and travelled very slowly but with determination. Finally the crest of the ridge came closer and Tenzing and I dropped over and down to the South Col. One by one the laden Sherpas joined us and our big carry had succeeded—we had fourteen loads of thirty pounds each on the South Col.

It was now May 22nd and time was rapidly turning against us as the monsoon snows could be expected by the end of the month. On May 24th Bourdillon and Evans, the closed-circuit oxygen team, with John Hunt and two Sherpas in support reached the South Col, but they had been very slow and we doubted if they would push on the next day. So it proved and on May 25th when Tenzing and I climbed up to the camp on the Lhotse Face there was no sign of activity on the mountain above us. Next morning Tenzing and I carried on and soon we saw tiny dots high above us on the South-East Ridge—it was Evans and Bourdillon heading for the South Summit and Hunt and Da Namgyal carrying loads up the ridge. Hunt's party stopped at about 27,350 feet and made their way slowly down, but Evans and Bourdillon disappeared into the clouds.

Tenzing and I reached the South Col in fast time and welcomed a very weary John Hunt. Then we waited for Evans and Bourdillon. Finally they appeared above the South Col, desperately tired and going very slowly. They had reached the South Summit at 28,700 feet, higher than anyone had ever been before, but now they were exhausted. The way had been opened towards the summit; it was up to Tenzing and me to complete the job.

May 27th wasn't a good day because of very strong winds. Tenzing and I remained in camp with our support group, George Lowe and Alf Gregory, plus a couple of Sherpas. The rest of the party made their way slowly down the mountain. Next morning we were thankful when the wind had eased and we set off upwards. Carrying loads of forty to fifty pounds we slowly ascended the snow couloir and reached the South-East Ridge. We soon came on the dump of supplies left by John Hunt and heaved these on our backs too. Everyone had then at least fifty pounds and I had over sixty. We started looking anxiously for a camp site but nothing appeared. Then Tenzing headed off a little to the left and waved that he'd found something. We joined him and there it was—our camp site at 27,900 feet—a sloping ledge under a rocky face. Certainly not ideal, but better than anything else we'd seen.

The support group dropped their loads and we waved farewell as they descended the ridge again. For several hours we dug out two small snowy ledges and then pitched our small tent across them. Then we crawled inside. Fierce gusts of wind would periodically sweep across the mountain but mostly it was calm. We melted lots of snow for sweet drinks and ate quite a substantial meal. During the night we had enough spare oxygen to breathe for two periods of two hours at one litre a minute—a small supply but enough to let us sleep peacefully. The rest of the time we were cold and miserable and only hot drinks made life worthwhile. The thermometer in the tent showed −27°C (−17°F) not really cold, I suppose, but cold enough in the thin air at that altitude.

Early in the morning we made slow preparations for departure and then left our tent at six thirty a.m. We climbed laboriously upwards, first on to a rounded snow dome and then along a sharp, flattish ridge. The route now led up the long, steep slope towards the South Summit. The snow was soft, deep and unstable and we didn't like it very much. It was a relief when the angle eased off and at nine a.m. we stepped on the South Summit.

The ridge ahead looked formidable but not impossible. On the right side the snow overhung in cornices above the huge East Face. On the left the snow capped a rock face dropping 8,000 feet down into the Western Cwm. I led off along the ridge, keeping on the left and chipping steps just above the rocks. Our pace was slow but steady. Half-way along we came to a rock step forty feet high—we'd seen it from down below, but could we get up it? I noticed a crack between the rock and the snow sticking to the East Face. I crawled inside and wriggled and jammed my way to the top. Lying there panting I felt a glow of triumph—maybe we were going to make it after all. Tenzing slowly joined me and we moved on. I chipped steps over bump after bump, wondering a little desperately where the top could be. Then I saw the ridge ahead dropped away to the north and above me on the right was a rounded snow dome. A few more whacks with my ice-axe and Tenzing and I stood on top of Everest. It was eleven thirty a.m. on May 29th 1953.

2

Maturity

IT TOOK ONLY three days to come from the top of the mountain down to Base Camp and all the way I felt a sense of satisfaction at our success, but no great surge of overwhelming joy – after all, we'd only just climbed a mountain, hadn't we? I considered that the mountaineering world might be pleased at our effort, but as for the general public – I didn't know that they'd be terribly interested. It wasn't until we were half-way out to Kathmandu that I started to realise just what a big public reaction there had been. And then I received a letter saying I'd been given a title. I simply couldn't believe it as I didn't regard myself as title material.

When we reached Kathmandu we were overwhelmed by our welcome and there was the same sort of hysteria down in India. All of us flew to London and the reaction there was just the same. Several times a day we'd attend formal receptions and my diet was largely smoked Scotch salmon and champagne – certainly a change from my normal fare. The expedition was invited to a garden party at Buckingham Palace and afterwards we were taken inside to the royal quarters to meet the Queen and the Duke and other members of the Royal Family. It was a very pleasant and relaxed occasion and when I was asked to kneel on a low stool I realised that this was it – I was going to be knighted. The Queen was given a sword and she tapped me gently on each shoulder and that's about all there was to it. Sherry was brought around and we chatted in very friendly fashion. I admired the way the Royal Family were able to make us feel completely at home – there was no nervousness or stiffness at all – and I've rather admired the Royal Family ever since.

It was agreed that George Lowe and I should return to New Zealand for a couple of months before going back to England to undertake an extensive lecture programme. My thoughts immediately turned to Sydney and I organised it so that we could spend a couple of days there on the way back to Auckland. It was marvellous to meet Louise again and I now had the courage to ask her if she might consider marrying me. She seemed agreeable about the idea, although we didn't arrange any particular date.

George and I flew into Auckland for the most terrifying reception we'd had yet. There was a huge crowd and somehow it was different being welcomed by your own people. We did a series of successful lectures throughout New Zealand and everywhere we went there was the same lively enthusiasm.

I'd been wondering what I should do about Louise when I was lecturing overseas, but her mother solved the problem for me. "Take her with you!" I telephoned Louise in Sydney and she was very happy to agree and caught an early plane back to Auckland. We were duly married and so started the happiest twenty-two years of my life.

In September 1953 we returned to England and commenced a concentrated series of lectures. I talked all over Great Britain, France, Belgium and Scandinavia and even in Iceland. I found it such a pleasure either to have Louise along with me or to know she'd be there when I came home. In December we flew the Atlantic to the U.S.A. and Canada and did an exhausting series of lectures there too. It was our first visit to the U.S.A. and we didn't find it easy at first—we were constantly dealing with the very rich and socially acceptable and that wasn't really our type of scene at all. In later years I have spent a great deal of time in the U.S.A. and developed a deep affection for the country and its people.

We arrived back in New Zealand in February 1954 and I had only six weeks to organise a house and my business affairs before heading back to the Himalayas. I don't really know what Louise felt about my sudden departure—over the twenty-two years we were together she never once tried to persuade me against some project or expedition. If that's what I wanted to do, then she was happy that I should do it. I imagine she did get rather lonely at times, but she was a very self-sufficient person in many ways—she loved her music, her tennis, and her many friends. I realised I was pretty selfish the way I continually rushed off on expeditions, but I must have been a restless person to have around the house and maybe there were times when Louise was happy to see me go for a while.

I was leading a New Zealand Alpine Club expedition into the Barun valley to the east of Everest and we experienced both success and disaster. Two of our members fell down a crevasse and I broke a couple of ribs in the process of getting them out. Jim McFarlane got severe frostbite to his hands and feet. Even though my ribs were causing me trouble I persisted in a reconnaissance of Makalu and at 22,000 feet I collapsed and had to be carried down the mountain. I had a healthy headache and for several days was pretty muddled mentally and I suffered from extreme dehydration. When I reached Base Camp I was rather uncomfortable for a few days then started to recover rapidly, although still very weak. We never did quite know what had happened to me, but later on our physiologists came to the conclusion that I'd had a case of cerebral oedema (sort of water on the brain which can afflict one at altitude). Jim McFarlane and I returned to India while the rest of the expedition went on to climb some fine peaks, including the impressive Baruntse.

I had several very happy years back in New Zealand building my house, adding two children to our family, Peter and Sarah, doing a bit of beekeeping, climbing a few mountains and even lecturing in Africa and England. But an exciting project was looming up over the horizon. Vivian Fuchs was organising the Trans-Antarctic expedition—to cross from the Weddell Sea, through the South Pole to McMurdo Sound and I was invited to lead the New Zealand part of the expedition which was to lay depots for Fuchs from McMurdo Sound south towards the Pole and to carry out an extensive scientific programme. I was loth to leave Louise and our two young children for sixteen months but the temptation was great and, as usual, I succumbed.

In the southern summer of 1955–6 I made my first visit to the Antarctic continent when I accompanied Fuchs into the Weddell Sea. For a frustrating month we were stuck immovably in the pack ice with our small ship creaking and groaning under the pressure. Then we escaped to the open water again and made our way down the coast to the southernmost corner of the Weddell Sea. Time was now very much against us and we desperately unloaded all our supplies on the ice and left behind a small team to build a base and get things organised. I returned from the Antarctic not entirely happy about the way our expedition had been run, but with a lot more knowledge about what not to do. I resolved that my expedition would be more efficiently planned and organised.

On December 21st 1956 our New Zealand expedition headed into the Southern Ocean aiming for McMurdo Sound. We had done everything we could to make our journey a success. A good party had been selected, ample supplies of food and equipment had been collected and we had well-trained dog teams. Now it was up to us. We tossed our way through the Southern Ocean then pushed through the pack ice into the Ross Sea. Soon the smoky volcanic summit of Mount Erebus was appearing over the horizon and we knew we were approaching McMurdo Sound.

We chose the site for Scott Base on Pram Point looking south over the Ross Ice Shelf. Our construction team swung into efficient action and our base huts were rapidly erected. By the time our ship departed we were in good shape with a well-equipped base and our two small aircraft in operational order.

Our plan had been to ascend the Ferrar Glacier up to the Polar Plateau but our reconnaissances had shown this route was impossible for vehicles. We did an aerial flight further south and examined the Skelton Glacier. It seemed much more feasible and I sent two dog teams up to test it out. Using our small aircraft we established depots of supplies at the foot of the Skelton Glacier and up on the Polar Plateau. As the long winter night approached we were well prepared for the travelling we expected in the following spring.

Winter in the Antarctic is long, dark and cold but we suffered very little. We had a comfortable and warm base and a very busy programme. Perhaps it was only the separation from our families that was the greatest strain. But unlike the early explorers we had effective radio communications and twice a week I would telephone Louise and learn all the latest family happenings and problems. Each time when I hung up the telephone a wave of loneliness would sweep over me and I'd have to crush the desperate desire to be back with my family. What was it that made me rush off and leave them? I wondered.

As the dim light of the returning sun started peeping over the horizon our tempo increased also. Our simple Ferguson farm tractors were being rapidly converted for long-distance travel and our sledges modified for their heavy loads. In the coldness of early spring we did exploratory journeys out over the sea ice to test out men and equipment. Then the time arrived for our southern journey.

On October 14th 1957 my party and I set off from Scott Base with three farm tractors and one Weasel bound for the Polar Plateau. Very few people in McMurdo Sound had any confidence in the travelling ability of our tractors, and our neighbouring Americans and most of the New Zealanders at Scott Base openly doubted that we would go fifty miles out on the Ross Ice Shelf before having to be rescued. But the more opposition we got the more determined I became to prove them wrong. One of our members, Peter Mulgrew, was just as stubborn as I was and his confidence helped me.

Our journey across the Ross Ice Shelf started off very slowly indeed—only six miles were covered that first day and to our embarrassment our tents could be seen from Scott Base. But then we started to improve—twenty-three miles, thirty miles, thirty-two miles and then thirty-eight miles. On the sixth day we drove for thirteen hours and covered a massive fifty miles—pretty good going with our top speed of a little under four mph. We had reached our depot at the foot of the Skelton Glacier.

Ahead of us now was the great iceflow of the glacier, peppered with steep slopes and deep crevasses. For 100 miles it climbed up to 8,000 feet where we had established the Plateau Depot with our Beaver skiplane. Would we be able to make it with our simple tractors?

For day after day we battled our way upwards through drifting snow; breaking through the crust of innumerable crevasses; being battered by constant strong winds. Whenever the sun appeared I'd hastily work out our position with the sextant and then turn the tractors back on to the right heading. Slowly we made height and reached the snow fields at the head of the glacier. Dense fog surrounded us but we still pushed on—we knew we must be somewhere near the depot.

Suddenly the mist began to thin and we emerged into clear visibility. I looked anxiously ahead and there on the horizon several miles away was a tiny black triangle—a tent. It was the Plateau Depot.

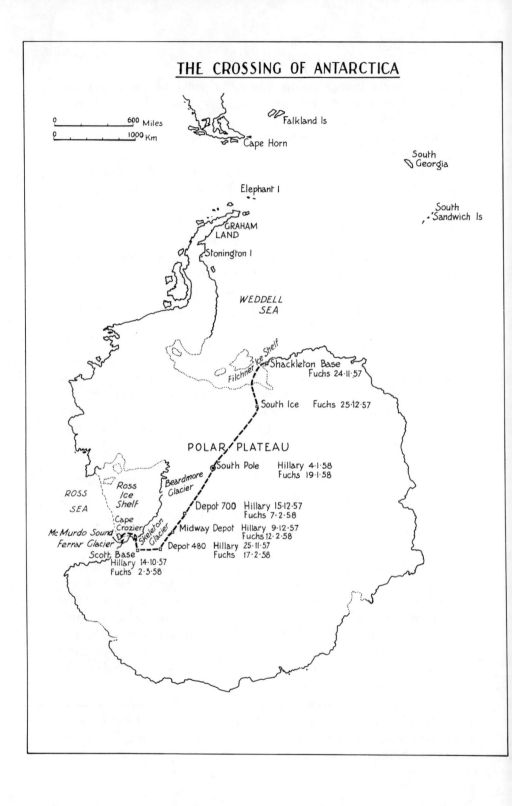

THE CROSSING OF ANTARCTICA

0 — 600 Miles
0 — 1000 Km

Falkland Is
Cape Horn

South Georgia

Elephant I

South Sandwich Is

GRAHAM LAND

Stonington I

WEDDELL SEA

Filchner Ice Shelf

Shackleton Base
Fuchs 24·11·57

South Ice   Fuchs 25·12·57

POLAR PLATEAU

South Pole   Hillary 4·1·58
Fuchs 19·1·58

Beardmore Glacier

Ross Ice Shelf

ROSS SEA

Depot 700   Hillary 15·12·57
Fuchs 7·2·58

Cape Crozier

Midway Depot   Hillary 9·12·57
Fuchs 12·2·58

McMurdo Sound
Ferrar Glacier

Skeleton Glacier

Depot 480   Hillary 25·11·57
Fuchs 17·2·58

Scott Base
Hillary 14·10·57
Fuchs 2·3·58

I have never felt more relieved or excited. Alone in my vehicle, in an unaccustomed outburst of emotion, I shouted and sang at the top of my voice. Despite all the doubts of others, and ourselves, we had made it. We were still 900 miles from the South Pole but that was one of the best moments I can ever remember. Even the summit of Everest was no more exciting.

Heavily laden we carried on south, at times bumping over rock-hard sastrugi and at times struggling desperately through deep, soft snow. We had frightening encounters with crevasse areas and almost lost several vehicles in the process but in the end we reached Depot 480 — 480 miles from Scott Base. We spent nine days here repairing and checking over our vehicles while the Beaver aircraft flew in load after load of supplies. Then we pushed on again and experienced the same variety of conditions as before — hard surfaces, deep snow, and always crevasses. Six hundred miles from Scott Base we established Midway Depot and soon after that had an appalling time with a large area of crevasses. I travelled, ate and slept crevasses, wondering every moment when we might strike another group of them, and I felt under considerable tension. Then a few miles further on the Weasel, which had been having continuous mechanical trouble, came to its final and irrevocable end and we abandoned it where it stopped.

We drove on with the three Fergusons towing a total of eight tons of supplies and for two days we had nothing but bad weather, crevasses and deep, soft snow. It was a great relief to enter a wide, shallow basin and in the middle we established Depot 700. This was in a sense the end of the journey, the last depot for Fuchs' crossing party, but I had other plans. I'd kept enough fuel in reserve and I wanted to carry on the 500 miles to the South Pole.

That 500 miles was a challenge every inch of the way. We had a number of bad crevasse areas but worst was the deep, soft snow. At times we had to relay loads and our fuel was being consumed at a dangerous rate. To increase our speed we stripped everything that wasn't urgent off our sledges and pushed on with the minimum of gear. We drove desperately on for very long hours and our fuel supplies got lower and lower. We were so tired we could hardly keep our eyes open. Another worry was my sextant which was proving erratic, and I had the terrible thought of getting lost in this vast, open space. Racked by hopelessness and despair but still grimly determined we drove stubbornly on and on January 4th 1958 we reached the American Pole station which had been completely established and supplied by air. We were the first team to travel overland with vehicles to the South Pole—and we had twenty gallons of petrol to spare, enough for about fifteen miles of travel. It had taken us eighty-three days to cover the 1,200 miles from Scott Base.

I returned to New Zealand in the middle of March 1958 to be reunited with my family. I had been invited to England to take part in the celebrations and lecture tours, but I had no desire to leave home. For a year I returned to beekeeping and our third child, Belinda, was born. This was my last involvement with the bees—I haven't even looked in a beehive since 1959.

For a number of years I had been planning a new Himalayan expedition—a combination of high-altitude physiology, mountaineering, and an investigation of that elusive creature—the yeti or Abominable Snowman. The opportunity to get support for this cause came in 1959 when I was in America and became very friendly with the senior executives of Field Enterprises Educational Corporation, publishers of *World Book Encyclopedia*. They expressed interest in my new project (largely the yeti part of it, I suspect) and agreed to put up the necessary finance. So once more I returned to expedition organising.

In September 1960 a large team of us gathered in Kathmandu with eighteen tons of supplies and a ten-month programme ahead of us. First we trekked into the remote Rolwaling valley which by repute was the home of numerous yetis. We talked to many of the local people, obtained bear skins which the Sherpas believed were those of the yeti and found impressive tracks in the snow. Over the Trashi Lapcha pass in the Khumbu area we examined yeti scalps and bony fingers, and interrogated lamas in the monasteries who were said to have seen yetis with their own eyes. It was all very good fun, and interesting too, but at the end I came to a very definite conclusion. All the evidence had a perfectly rational explanation and the yeti, alas, was only a strange, mythological creature.

There was much to do on the expedition. Up the Mingbo valley at 19,000 feet we assembled an insulated hut and here for six months an elaborate physiological programme was undertaken. During the winter four members of the party made the first ascent of the formidable Ama Dablam, much to the annoyance of the Nepalese authorities who had not granted climbing permission. It was only by a desperate appeal to the officials in Kathmandu that I persuaded them to refrain from expelling our expedition from Nepal. At 15,000 feet in the Mingbo valley we built a small airfield and a Swiss Red Cross plane flew in many loads of rice for the Tibetan refugees who were fleeing across the border—and they flew in supplies for us too.

Then came our major effort—an attempt without oxygen on Makalu (27,825 feet/8,481 metres) as the culmination of our physiological programme. Little was then known about man's ability to perform physically and mentally at extreme altitudes for any length of time without oxygen, and there were even fears of permanent brain damage. Certainly little physiological research had been carried out at such altitudes. Our route to the mountain was a difficult one—150 loads had to be carried over three passes at around 20,000 feet, probably the biggest high-altitude carry ever undertaken. After an enormous effort our Base Camp was established in the Barun valley. Slowly we put in camps up the mountainside, getting loads into position. The Barun had never been kind to me—at 23,000 feet I suffered from cerebral oedema and had to retreat miserably down to Base Camp. But the assault went on. At 27,000 feet, only 790 feet from the top, Peter Mulgrew collapsed with pulmonary oedema and the whole effort of the expedition had to be devoted to getting him down the mountain. Severely frostbitten and close to death he arrived out in Kathmandu. Many months of hospitalisation followed before Peter fully recovered—but both his feet had to be amputated. It was the end of his climbing career, but he went on to become a highly successful businessman and a world-class yachtsman.

Back in Khumbu we carried out one last successful task. The Sherpas had asked us for a school in Khumjung and I had agreed. We brought in an aluminium building from Calcutta and assembled it on a flat area near the village. From Darjeeling we recruited an experienced Sherpa teacher. On June 12th 1961 we had the formal opening of the school, the first in the Khumbu area, and unknown to me it would prove to be the start of a new way of life.

I had agreed with Field Enterprises that at the conclusion of our expedition I would bring my family to America and spend the year there lecturing on behalf of World Book Encyclopedia. I flew to Chicago with my young family and we settled into a comfortable house in the suburbs not too far from O'Hare airport. Each Monday morning I flew out of the airport to a different city and returned on the Saturday afternoon. During the course of the year I gave 106 banquet lectures in eighty different cities. It was an interesting experience in many ways and I certainly learned something about American cities and the ordinary, worthy American citizen. However, it was an energetic programme and I was happy when summertime approached and a good long holiday was possible. Sears Roebuck, the huge American merchandising operation, had asked me to join their sports advisory staff and they agreed to assist me with a vehicle to drive across the country to California, up into Alaska where we'd make a film, and then back down through Canada to Chicago.

So, like thousands of American families, in June 1962 I loaded up our big Ford station-wagon, hitched on our collapsible camper trailer and headed west. The children were seven, six and three at the time and settled down very comfortably in the back of our large air-conditioned vehicle. We camped our way across the United States mostly in National Forest campgrounds and enjoyed the enormous variety of the scenery. In California we headed north through the redwood forests, through Oregon and Washington States and up to Vancouver in Canada. Here we loaded our car and trailer on a boat appropriately called *Princess Louise* and travelled up the Inside Passage to Alaska. In Alaska we were met by a film team and spent several weeks touring around the country as film stars. The weather was apparently unusually good for Alaska and we had a superb time in that beautiful country. The film director even hired a train for us to travel from Anchorage to Fairbanks and we loaded our vehicles on board and stopped out in the wilds at any interesting stream to fish for salmon. It was the sort of trip that could never happen again.

We said goodbye to our film friends and headed down into Canada, through the Yukon and ultimately to the beautiful scenic drive from Banff. Then it was east past Calgary and across the wide open plains with their ripening wheat. Almost sadly we turned south again down towards Chicago and home. It had been a marvellous experience and one we were never likely to forget. Louise wrote a book on this trip called *Keep Calm If You Can* and it was very successful.

The next ten years was a wonderful period for me. In the Himalayas I built a dozen schools, a hospital, a number of bridges and water pipelines, and even an airfield at Lukla. My expeditions climbed the formidable summits of Kangtega and Tramserku and almost climbed Taweche. We drove a jet boat up the Sun Kosi to Kathmandu and I led another expedition to the Antarctic which climbed the superb peak of Mount Herschel.

But more than anything it was a very happy time for my family. Together we camped, swam and skied. We walked up to Everest Base Camp and drove through central Australia. I built a cottage on the West Coast cliffs only an hour away from home and we could sit and watch the great ocean breakers rolling in. Louise wrote two more books and played her viola whenever she had time. They were good days.

We had the usual teenage problems with our children, but Louise was very patient and loving and I was frequently away. Peter and Sarah displayed a good deal of self-centred and rather bloody-minded independence. On the few occasions that I was sufficiently provoked to thump Peter he certainly didn't like it, but I can't say it made any difference to his behaviour. I was the one who ended up feeling miserable. Peter didn't enjoy his high school days although he did quite well academically. He was very much an individualist and heartily disliked team games such as football or cricket. Like his father before him he spent a couple of unsuccessful years at university. He became an excellent skier and learned to fly. So, even though he lacked professional qualifications, it looked as though he might have some sort of interesting career ahead of him.

Sarah had very firm views about many things and even at quite an early age was fond of saying that her parents lacked maturity – and that her grandparents did too. She was a good student with quite a lot of artistic ability, but she could be an awful pain in the neck at times. It was rather amazing how she improved over the years. I suppose that Belinda was our only ideal child, friendly, cheerful, intelligent and co-operative – she was a pleasure to have around. She handled me very firmly and I loved it.

No doubt Louise and I were inadequate and indulgent parents, although we tried our best. I still haven't discovered the secret of success in this field and it's too late now. Certainly Louise gave the children all the affection they could ever want, but this obviously isn't enough. Being young is a miserable business on the whole, because the young don't really know what they want themselves. And being a parent can be pretty trying too.

For a long time the people in the Solu district had been asking us to build them a hospital. There were 20,000 people within a day's walk and plenty of health care was needed. At the time New Zealand had a prime minister who was very keen on foreign aid and the Government agreed to help with the Solu hospital at Phaphlu.

Louise and I decided to do something we'd always wanted to do—take the family and spend the whole of the year in Nepal. Belinda could do correspondence lessons, she'd be sixteen years old and she was an excellent student. Peter and Sarah would benefit from the experience and Louise could learn Nepali, an ambition she'd had for a long time. It seemed a great idea and we planned accordingly. In January 1975 we flew to Kathmandu, rented a house, bought a little car and settled in. Louise started learning Nepali and I made a few trips to Phaphlu and started work on the Solu hospital—it looked like a wonderful year for all of us. I was fifty-five years old and Louise was forty-four—I just couldn't understand where all the years had gone.

The coronation of the King of Nepal was due in a month's time and as Louise and I had been invited to some of the official functions we felt we must be there. But after the coronation it was agreed that Louise and the three children would trek into the Everest area and visit all their Sherpa friends. Louise was really looking forward to this.

Louise and I thoroughly enjoyed the King's coronation—particularly the last event, a private dinner with Prince Charles and Lord Mountbatten at the British Embassy. Prince Charles was delightful company in his cheerful and bluff way, but Lord Mountbatten was incredibly entertaining. He firmly believed in UFOs and had us in fits of laughter with his innumerable stories. When an Admiral of the Fleet relates story after story it is a little difficult to say, "That's all rubbish, old fella", and of course none of us did. But it was a great evening—one of the best dinners I've ever had.

Sarah duly returned to university in New Zealand and Peter headed off into India with an old school friend, full of plans to see as much of the country as he could. I returned to Phaphlu to get the Solu hospital project really rolling and was looking forward to Louise and Belinda joining me in due course.

3

Sorrow

If my life finished tomorrow I would have little cause for complaint—I have gathered a few successes, a handful of honours and more love and laughter than I probably deserve. In a sense my life has been strung together by a series of friendships—Harry Ayres, George Lowe, Peter Mulgrew, Mike Gill, Jim Wilson, Max Pearl, Mingma Tsering—and most of all, Louise—the list goes on and on and I would have been nothing without them.

Nothing Venture, Nothing Win, Edmund Hillary

I WOKE EARLY on the morning of March 31st 1975. Louise and Belinda were joining me at Phaphlu and I was filled with excitement. I quickly prepared the tents and sleeping-bags and then waited impatiently for the small Pilatus Porter to appear over the great ridge to the west. Time passed and there was no sign of the plane—was it the usual delay by Royal Nepal Air Lines? A cancelled flight, or maybe bad weather, although it was superbly clear at Phaphlu.

At nine a.m. I heard a sound approaching—it wasn't the Pilatus, it was a helicopter—and I felt a deep sense of foreboding. The helicopter circled over the airfield and then gently touched down. I went to meet it and my good friend Elizabeth Hawley, looking tired and drawn, stepped out. "I'm terribly sorry, Ed, but Louise's plane crashed on take-off."

"Are they alive?" I asked.

"I don't think so."

I wandered up the hill to where Louise's parents were standing in the sun with the great mountain behind them. I told them the news and, despite my pain, I admired their courage and strength.

We flew back to Kathmandu in the helicopter and I was numb with sorrow all the way. Louise and I had sometimes talked about death – but I was the one taking most of the risks and it was *me* that was meant to die – not Louise. "I want to go to the crash site," I told the pilot. He kindly tried to dissuade me, but I knew that if I didn't go I would never forgive myself. We circled near the Kathmandu airport and slowly descended to the paddy fields where a ring of people were surrounding a burnt and battered wreck. I waded across a small stream and over to the site of the crash – to the last resting place of the two people I had loved most.

Kathmandu
April 5th 1975

My dear and special friends,

It isn't possible to write to you all at present so Peter Mulgrew has kindly offered to share this letter among you.

It is now five days since Louise and Belinda died in the plane crash and I hope you will forgive me if I share some of my pain with you. When the Pilatus failed to arrive at Phaphlu I had a terrible premonition of disaster – when a helicopter approached I knew that something dreadful had occurred. We landed beside the little that remained of the crashed plane – hardly more than a mile from the Kathmandu runway – as the bodies were being gathered from the wreck. Thank God it must at least have been sudden and immediately over.

People have been wonderfully kind and good and Phyl and Jim Rose have been unbelievably calm and strong. We've had messages from kings and prime ministers and tears from our Sherpa and Nepalese friends. I think you know how much Louise has meant to me and Belinda was so kind and joyous.

The arrival of Sarah with Peter Mulgrew has been a great blessing. She is a dear girl and stronger in spirit than I believed possible. I will stick around as long as she feels she needs me. Peter is somewhere in India – we haven't yet been able to locate him.

On Monday we go back into Phaphlu for a while to start work going again on the hospital. Whatever else happens I feel the task must be finished. Sarah, Mingma and I will then walk up to Khumbu and mourn a little with our friends.

What will happen then I don't quite know. Life must go on, I suppose, and Sarah says she will come with me to London and the U.S.A. to help do the tasks I have promised to do. I only hope I have the courage to carry through what has to be done.

Sometime I must return to New Zealand and give Sarah and Peter a home again—poor substitute though it may be—but it may take a little time before I can face that. It is so easy to die but God knows if I'll have the courage to go on living.

Love to you all. Your friendship has meant everything to Louise and me.

Ed

We went back into Phaphlu and worked on the hospital. A little altar had been made in the cookhouse with pictures of Louise and Belinda, and every day new *kartas*, the white Nepalese ceremonial scarves, were draped over the altar, with its crimson and white rhododendrons, and butter lamps were lit.

In the evening I walked alone on the airfield with the great mountains behind—and my sorrow seemed to ease a little—or at least nobody could see my tears.

In Solu and in Khumbu there were ceremonies and sadness; many *kartas* and mountains of flowers. And the 'burra sahib' had to act like a 'burra sahib', even though his heart was broken.

As I left Kathmandu airport Mingma said, "Will you ever return?"

My family and I found sanctuary with friends in Geneva and the mountains of Chamonix. We lost ourselves in the wonders of Paris and London and New York. My autobiography seemed to be doing well and I talked on TV and radio—and talked and talked!

With our friends from Sears we canoed down the Buffalo river in Arkansas and we were glad for the friendship, and the beauty, and the peace in our tents at night. I still wasn't sleeping well, despite masses of pills, but I wasn't often now having the ghastly nightmares reliving that awful day—the horrifying scene on the paddy field—or the cremation beside the river the same night, beautiful in a way but terrible too. Now I just lay and thought dully for hour after hour. I couldn't forget the American Civil

Aviation adviser who asked me to identify my family, and I said no, I couldn't. Of course I knew which they were—but how could I say, "Yes, that's my daughter and that's my wife"?

Finally we could escape no longer from the task I most feared—to return home. We flew south across the vast waters of the Pacific, back to New Zealand.

Auckland

June 19th 1975

Well, I've been back in Auckland for five days and for me it has been a pretty grim experience. Without Louise the house—beautiful though it still is in the winter's sun—is just like an empty tomb. I'm much the same way of course—empty and sterile. I'm struggling slowly on trying to get things in order and bolstering myself up with pills when the pressure becomes too strong.

On Saturday the kids and I went to our beach cottage at Anawhata for the first time. I'd shied off doing it before—it was so much Louise . . . she'd taught me to love the West Coast and we'd worked so happily on the cottage and argued so cheerfully about so many things.

We walked along the wide sand of Piha beach on both days and it was still as peaceful and beautiful as ever—and I had the same feeling of loneliness, and even sadness, that I felt even when Louise was there.

On the beautiful brush-clad cliffs thrusting out over the great waves of the Tasman Sea we spread the ashes of Louise and Belinda and I knew that was where they would want to be. I resolved that when my time came I too would wish my ashes to be thrown in the same place.

In the middle of August I left New Zealand again to return to the U.S.A. and Nepal and continue with the Phaphlu hospital construction. I was obsessed with the idea that if there was to be any reason at all in the whole dreadful business, then the task must be completed. Peter and Sarah, on the surface at least, seemed perfectly cheerful and the talk was mostly about flying and skiing and motorbikes. But underneath I suspected they were shattered as I was.

At the airport Peter handed me a letter to read on the plane.

Dear Dad,

      Go on your way to U.S.A.
      and take with you this poem.
      It's from my heart
      Right from the start
      My feelings with words I'll show 'em.

      The trees that grow over
      The grass by the shore
      The waves that are lapping
      And leave with a roar,

      Then up like a bird
      Up high in the sky,
      My love is all taken,
      A harsh lullaby.

      Meero Ama ra
      Meero behini,★
      They both have dispersed
      To leave only ashes.
      Into tears we have burst.

      Our friends are beside us,
      They all hold our hands
      And yet we are lonely
      With feet in the sands.

      The waves they are washing
      And deeper we sink,
      So now we must struggle
      To flee that last brink.

      I look all around me
      I'm deep in the sand
      The work that surrounds me
      Must now be well planned.

      Behini ra Ama,
      You are to me
      The wonderful waters
      That fill up the sea.

★*Meero Ama* is Nepalese for 'my mother', and *meero behini* means 'my younger sister'.

My thoughts are still on you,
My love is still strong
But my want to be living
Is nearly all gone.

The strength that I'm needing
The will that I lack,
Both are in hiding
And hard to fetch back.

It's you that have shown me
From you I have learned
That life has its high sides
Which aren't easily earned.

Farewell meero Ama,
Bye bye Lindi Loo,
The time is for leaving
And saying adieu.

Love Pete

In Kathmandu the monsoon rains were still pouring down and no flights were available. Mingma and I decided to walk in to Phaphlu with a hundred porters.

September 6th 1975
Today we reached Chyangma. We've had lots of rain—it's been fullscale monsoon—but we are well organised and not suffering too much. The rivers are in great flood but the bridges have been satisfactory. All our loads are well packed and there is no sign of them getting wet. I have to admit that my legs have been pretty tired but they ultimately get me there. It's only two more days to Phaphlu—an easy one to Seta Gompa tomorrow and then a massive day over the Lamjura Banyang and right through to Phaphlu.

I got increasingly weak up to the Lamjura Banyang and over the other side. All my leech bites were badly infected and so was my shin, which had lost all its skin—but I didn't think it was only that. At Phaphlu I had severe head and back aches and life was pretty hellish. I was still suffering from deep depression and

didn't care too much if I lived or died—as long as the pain would
stop. For a week or so I was pretty sick and certainly very
miserable and uncomfortable. Then I started getting stronger
and eating more.

On September 19th it was still appalling weather, but a helicopter managed to sneak in and deposit our construction team at
Phaphlu. This made a tremendous difference and with better
weather we saw enormous progress with the building. Life certainly became a lot more bearable when we were making exciting
progress both with the hospital and at the airport.

By the end of December the Phaphlu hospital was virtually
finished. My brother, Rex, and his construction team had done a
remarkably good job. There was 10,000 feet of floor space in five
buildings: an accommodation building for staff, a kitchen, bathroom, classroom complex, a medical centre, a large building
with several medical wards, and another building where the
relations of patients could stay. We had good plumbing, with
flush toilets and showers, two solar heating systems, and an
excellent X-ray machine. It was now up to our volunteer doctors
and the local staff to make full use of the hospital.

On May 1st 1976 the Prime Minister of Nepal performed the
opening ceremony. We had plenty of distinguished guests—the
Minister of Finance and his wife; the Minister of Health and his
wife; the Director General of Health; the New Zealand and
British Ambassadors and many more besides. In typical Nepalese
fashion we had to hire a large helicopter to fly in the Prime
Minister and his Cabinet. In the evening I had organised a lively
cocktail party and then we all had an excellent dinner cooked by
Angpassang. We'd gone to a lot of trouble with the accommodation and the Prime Minister's quarters in the large classroom
looked particularly pleasant.

The following morning we had a simple breakfast at Lama
Tawa's new hotel and then, right on nine a.m., all the officials
helicoptered back to Kathmandu. We were left with a new
hospital, quite a few patients, and for me anyway a feeling of
sadness and anticlimax. Our hospital task was finished—what to
do with my life?

The only reasonable alternative seemed to be to lose myself in
a flood of activity, to keep the Himalayan work going, to get

involved in new projects and essentially to try to create a new life–it wouldn't be easy but somehow I must shake off at least part of my depression and sorrow.

For many years we had shot movie films on most of our trips, rather amateurish efforts perhaps but we had the advantage of Dr. Mike Gill who had a natural talent for the game and we produced some pretty good stories for very little money.

In 1973 all that changed. For in that year began the saga of 'The Adventure World of Sir Edmund Hillary'. The idea sprang from the fertile imagination of an Auckland businessman who suggested we put together a series of films that would do for the mountains and rivers what Jacques Cousteau had done for the undersea world. I was not, fortunately, involved in the production or financial aspects of the company: my job was to provide the ideas and lead the expeditions. Only one completed film emerged from 'The Adventure World'. It was called 'The Kaipo Wall'. Set in the primeval forests and mountains of the south-western corner of New Zealand, it was a journey in canoes and rubber inflatable boats down a wild river to the sea, down the coast on foot, and then inland up the Kaipo river to make the first ascent of a huge granite precipice forming a 4,000-foot cirque at the head of the valley. I had no difficulty in persuading my mountaineering friends to take part, and I soon put together a group consisting of Mike Gill, Jim Wilson, Graeme Dingle, Murray Jones and my son Peter.

It was certainly a magnificent adventure. The rivers came up in high flood; Ding and Jim paddled their way down seemingly impossible rapids that we had not even known were there, high in the mountains we were nearly blown off the face of the earth in the kind of devastating storm that makes the New Zealand Alps one of the most rugged locations in the world. And we made the first ascent of the Kaipo Wall. Unfortunately it proved very expensive and when the company tried to sell 'The Kaipo Wall' it became clear that they would be lucky to recover costs, let alone make a profit.

Despite the financial problems that seemed to be involved in filming I had developed an enthusiasm for the game and at the beginning of 1976 I decided to produce two half-hour films on a much more modest scale.

Lying sixty miles off the coast of Auckland is the large island of

Great Barrier, a most beautiful place where my family and I had often camped in the past. Its lonely white sand beaches and wild headlands made it one of the most attractive places I know. At the north end of Great Barrier were a number of 200-foot-high rock pinnacles rising out of the sea. Certainly nobody had ever climbed them and the central pillar wouldn't be easy to get up. Giant waves rolled in for thousands of miles across the Pacific Ocean from South America; how would we even get a footing on the pillar?

It was a great challenge and great fun. We hired a substantial motor launch with an owner who knew these waters and then motored round the coast to the north pinnacles. We anchored here, rolling heavily in the big swell. I pumped up a twelve-foot rubber inflatable and then rowed a load of my friends and their equipment to the pinnacle. The great waves dashed against the rocks and it was a terrifying place to be, but finally we got the hang of it. At the top of the wave one of the climbers would leap ashore and scramble to safety while we dropped away underneath him. Soon all the climbers, cameramen and gear were ashore and then the battle with the rock commenced. Murray Jones did most of the leading and after a considerable struggle the whole team reached the top. Two months later we had a completed film, and pretty good I thought it was too. I was now eager to start the next one.

This time I planned to use jet boats on some of the lively mountain rivers in the South Island of New Zealand—the Hurunui, the Clutha and the Kawarau. Jon Hamilton agreed to come with us, bringing one of his own boats, but for Jim Wilson I would need to purchase a second boat myself. So I sent Jim a cheque for $2,000 and told him to buy the best boat he could for that price or less. As it turned out you can buy very little for that price or less, and we ended up with an ancient fourteen-foot jet boat which had spent the latter years of its life as a fishing boat on the West Coast. Even on flat water it had a strange wave-like motion which it may well have acquired from its many years at sea, and it handled very badly indeed in white water. Jim drove it with great courage, hurling it at big rapids that he should never have thought of attempting. But the combination of Jim and his shaky boat produced some tremendous footage. We managed to tip our inflatable boat over in the big Cromwell rapid and I nearly drowned, so the whole adventure had its share of excitement.

When New Zealand Television put 'The Kaipo Wall' and our two shorter films together as a series, the reception from the public was enthusiastic to say the least. We really felt that we had it made—the only thing was we weren't making any money. Someone suggested that the thing to do was to go where the big money was—to New York—and sell the series to one of the big networks. Our agent in New York said it would be much more effective if I personally went over so, with some reluctance and a good deal of trepidation, I agreed.

After the ten-hour flight over the Pacific I had a stopover in Honolulu, and I sat out on my balcony in the sun, as Mike Gill had told me I should get a sunburnt flush of glowing health on my face before arriving in New York. I can't really stand it in the sun, so after a while I turned on the air-conditioning and crawled into bed. The flight on to New York was delayed and my agent picked me up, still more dead than alive, on the morning we went to the advertising company's office. They'd shown the films around to TV people and it was agreed that 'The Kaipo Wall' was about seventy-five per cent finished, but they thought it might be necessary to have an American producer involved. I asked if he could come to New Zealand and they said why not? I didn't ask who was going to pay for this gentleman.

They asked me to do a videotape presentation for showing to other people and other networks and after a gulp I just sat down and babbled on for ten minutes about the whole adventure project. Then they played it back and I was rather impressed; I didn't even look too bad, not fat and flabby but sort of robust and reddish, so the sun in Honolulu must have helped. Then they dropped the bombshell—they only wanted a one-hour presentation to C.B.S. (instead of the two hours originally requested). After lunch I did a hasty reshuffle of notes, feeling slightly demoralised.

I arrived at C.B.S. at three p.m. and gave my presentation to three men all of whom looked complete city types who could well have done with a bit of that Honolulu sun. The TV screen wasn't adjusted properly and jumped all over the place, but they didn't seem to care. I think I did about as adequately as I could, but missed the warm feeling of a sympathetic audience. The

C.B.S. men were certainly friendly and relaxed but said that all decisions were made by committees and that it might take a month—and that was that! I returned to my hotel feeling a vast sense of anticlimax and wondered why the heck I'd travelled 10,000 miles and spent $3,000 just for that. My New York agent and the advertising people said they thought the reaction had been promising—you could have deceived me. But then I wasn't a hardened TV network man.

I rang Mike Gill in New Zealand and he was a bit more practical. "Looks like it's back to the drawing board," he said very philosophically. Of course, he could afford to be philosophical—I was the one who had spent the money.

On my United flight back to the West Coast I read a western by my old favourite, Max Brand, called *Dead or Alive*. It was quite a while since I'd read a western but I rather enjoyed this one, particularly when the decent young hero is shot up holding the canyon against the villains while his companions get help. The Doc says, "What a lark *this* kid has had before he cashed in!" Of course the hero survived, but I thought to myself, despite all my problems, what a lark *I've* had too, for a long time.

In due course C.B.S. turned the films down and my New York agent said he planned to try N.B.C. "What are the chances?" I asked him. "About fifty/fifty—the same as the others," he told me. I didn't believe him and of course I was right. N.B.C. turned the films down too. It was a couple of years before we finally managed to break in on the tough U.S. market.

4

Ocean to Sky

O F ALL THE journeys I have undertaken the one that has left the most vivid memories in my mind is our trip up Mother Ganga in 1977 from the Ocean to the Sky. There was such enormous variety, ranging from tropical mangrove swamps to ice-clad mountains; from sophisticated, highly educated Indian aristocrats to simple, good-hearted peasant folk.

For a number of years I had enjoyed jet boating in the company of far more expert friends, particularly Jon Hamilton, probably the world's most successful jet-boat river explorer. In 1968 we took two jet boats to Nepal and although we sank one of them we succeeded in driving the other up the violent rapids of the Sun Kosi river for 200 miles from the Indian border to the outskirts of Kathmandu. It was a superb journey with good companions, wild water, remote but friendly people, and success at the end.

It was such a good journey that I constantly thought of doing another, bigger venture, and slowly the idea grew of taking the boats up the biggest and holiest river of India, the Ganges, or Mother Ganga as it is known. A number of people had floated down the mighty Ganga but as far as we knew no one had ever been right up it, so it would be a first—an interesting attraction to any explorer. Early in the 1970s Louise and I were in New Delhi to get support for the Ganga adventure, and we decided we would show Jon Hamilton's hair-raising film of his journey by jet boat up and down the Colorado river through the Grand Canyon to some of the senior Government people in Delhi. It was the worst possible move we could have made. The audience were filled with horror at the ferocious problems overcome and at the end of the film the senior general present said rather sadly to me, "Only supermen could handle boats like that and I have few supermen."

So for a period the scheme went into abeyance, although Louise and I often talked about it, as she had decided that this was an adventure that she could undertake too. After my family disaster in 1975 I lost heart for a while, but slowly the idea re-emerged and I started sounding out people in Delhi to gain permission for the plan. Early in 1977 I received positive support from the Indian Government and with growing enthusiasm I planned to undertake the journey in the latter half of the year. The many tasks to undertake helped shake me out of the depression that had gripped me for the past two years and I worked with enthusiasm at raising funds, organising the boats, selecting the team and finalising arrangements with the Indian Government and official organisations.

Jet boats are simple enough craft: ours were sixteen feet long, made of tough fibreglass, and contained a powerful V8 engine driving not a propeller but a sophisticated three-stage pump. They could reach speeds in excess of forty-five mph and operate in very shallow water and they were unbelievably manoeuvrable. Our three top drivers were all from New Zealand, Jon Hamilton, Mike Hamilton and Jim Wilson, but we also had a number of Indian expedition members who made valuable contributions with their wide knowledge of their country and its customs— Harish Sarin, Mohan Kohli, Joginder Singh, and our very successful liaison officer, Bridhiv Bhatia.

Our plan was a straightforward one. We would commence our journey in the Bay of Bengal, travel up-river through the Gangetic plain, enter the foothills with their violent rapids and push foward as far as we could. When the river became too rough for further jet-boat travel then we would take to the mountain road and walk up to Badrinath, one of the holy mountain towns of Ganga. From Badrinath we would climb up into the glaciers and complete our journey on the summit of a snowy peak, one of the original sources of water for the great river. And so our journey would be a 1,600-mile trip 'from the Ocean to the Sky'.

We had tremendous support from various Indian Government agencies. Air India transported us from Sydney to Bombay; the Indian Shipping Company conveyed our three jet boats from Christchurch to Calcutta; and the Indian Government Tourist Agency organised accommodation and transport for us in India. The Indian Oil Company provided us with all our fuel and I spent several hours with some of their officials examining maps and deciding where the most suitable refuelling spots would be. Without fail fuel was waiting at the selected locations and the support of Indian Oil could not have been more expertly handled.

The New Zealand members of the expedition flew by Air India from Sydney to Bombay and as we were travelling first class we had a most luxurious and enjoyable time crossing the oceans in our Boeing 747. Continuous champagne and delicious Indian foods were hardly the common diet of most expedition members, but we certainly made the most of them. Our luggage and ourselves arrived in Bombay on schedule and without losing a bag or a person–although Peter Hillary and Murray Jones wandered away from the airport in Perth and nearly missed the departing flight.

We transhipped to Delhi to be greeted with a crowded press conference and already we could sense the growing excitement that our expedition was engendering in India. One charming and beautiful young reporter asked us very firmly why there were no women members on the expedition. I found the question difficult to answer and had to explain that I didn't know any expert women jet-boat drivers. I had the feeling that my reply was weak and unconvincing.

We flew to Calcutta and then drove down beside the Hooghley river (a major outlet of Ganga) to the new port of Haldia. Here our three boats had been unloaded and it took us some days to uncrate them, fill them with oil and fuel, erect awnings for protection against sun and rain and carry out trials on the calm water inside the docks. The Hooghley emerged into the Bay of Bengal about thirty-five miles down-river and that's where we planned to start our journey–on the sandy beach at Ganga Sagar where Ganga meets the ocean (Sagar).

On August 24th 1977 with our tanks topped full of petrol we passed through the lock at Haldia and out into the Hooghley for the first time. It was a bright, sunny day but a brisk wind lifted a sharp chop on the broad waters of the river. To the north, over Calcutta, heavy black clouds hovered on the horizon. Crashing from wave to wave we made our way down-river with our speed limited by the choppy conditions. We reached the east bank of the river and whipped along in shallow water passing many fishermen casting their nets. We turned a headland into rough

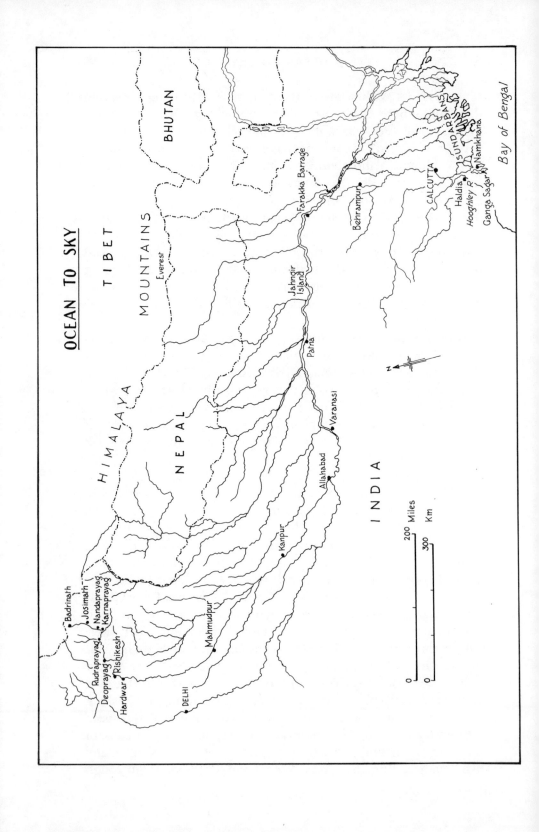

water again and then saw the long, low sandspit of Ganga Sagar pushing out into the ocean. The waves were breaking on the shore and I could see no easy place for a landing. Then ahead of us we saw a small estuary leading into land and we dived over the bar and up into the still, shallow water.

A few hundred yards away amongst low trees was a modest building—a temple, we were told, and the home of the ancient *pujare* (priest) who traditionally farewelled those redoubtable souls who undertook the long religious pilgrimage from Ganga Sagar along the sacred banks to the headwaters of the river.

It seemed right for us to undergo the same procedure and when we approached the old man with our request he was very happy to co-operate. He came down to our beached craft carrying his supply of coloured powders, coconuts and various religious trinkets and started chanting his prayers. On the bow of each boat he marked coloured powder and broke a coconut, and on our foreheads he put a coloured mark too. As we pushed our boats off shore and climbed back on board I felt a warm sense of how appropriate it had been. We were starting up the holy river and the right prayers were going with us.

With a sense of growing excitement we crashed out over the bar and our boats were thrown high in the air. Then we were bashing through waves up-river with our journey really under way. The dark clouds had come down to meet us and we were soon drenched with monsoon rain. The heavy drops stung our eyes and cheeks and we were forced to drop our speed. Dusk was falling as we reached Haldia again and, soaking wet, we waited impatiently for the lock to open and let us through into the dock. That night there was a new feeling about our group, a feeling of contentment and satisfaction. We'd touched the ocean and had started up-river—we had 1,600 miles of Ganga ahead of us.

As it approaches the Bay of Bengal Ganga splits up into a large number of channels (of which the Hooghley is one of the most important). These channels pass through an enormous area of low islands and mangrove swamps called the Sundarbands. A large area of the Sundarbands is classified as a tiger sanctuary and before heading for Calcutta we planned to enter the Sundarbands and hopefully sight some of these creatures.

Next day we crossed the river and drove up a side channel and after an hour arrived at the big village of Namkhana. The Forest

Department of West Bengal were organising this part of our trip and they were greatly concerned about the possible danger if we should try to sleep in our jet boats or on a sandy mangrove island. They had brought along several large launches and they towed us with these deep into the Sundarbands. For several days we searched the delta area, roaring up narrow side streams and bumping over wide open stretches of water swept with waves. We saw hordes of crabs and shellfish, many birds, and even some deer—but not a sight of a tiger. This vast area was almost wholly deserted with only the odd fishing boat anchored in the middle of wide streams. Periodically, we were told, when a fishing boat was tied up at night, a tiger would swim out from the shore, lean over the side and scoop the fisherman to his doom. In the previous year seventy fishermen had been taken in this fashion.

By the end of a couple of days we had lost all hope of seeing any tigers and when we returned at the end of a long day of ducking and diving around the narrow streams and clambered on board the big launch for a meal, our only ambition was to return to the Hooghley and set off up-river.

Suddenly as we morosely munched our meal there was a cry of "Tiger!" We rushed to the side of the boat and there several hundred yards away was an animal swimming across the broad river. In a matter of seconds we were over the side of the launch, into the jet boats and racing down-river. The tiger, for tiger indeed it was, was startled at the noise of the boats and turned back to shore and safety. Jim Wilson's boat was in the lead and we shouted to him to head through the narrowing gap between the tiger and the shore and so turn the creature back into deeper water. But Jim was not foolish—he had no desire to have an angry tiger climbing over the thwarts—and instead passed the tiger on the outside edge. A few more lurches and the tiger was ashore and loping up through the soft mud to the mangroves above. It was quite small, thoroughly wet and singularly unimpressive. Well, that's our tiger for the trip, we thought, and keeping a keen eye on the bank we turned to return to the launch. Next moment there was a deep roar and on the bank above appeared a most magnificent tiger. Huge in size, brightly striped, and in perfect condition, it looked on us with scorn and then slowly made its way along the bank, disappearing at times behind the brush, then reappearing again in full sight. For half an hour we caught sight of this magnificent animal and no one suggested we attempt to go ashore. And then it was gone and we saw it no more.

"You are very lucky, sir," said the chief forestry officer, "rarely does anyone see one tiger let alone two. It is indeed a very good omen for your journey up Mother Ganga." More than happy at our success we tied our jet boats on behind the launches and chugged for twenty-four hours out of the Sundarbands.

It was sixty miles from Haldia to the heart of Calcutta. Lashed by frequent rain showers, we raced up the river, quickly entering a heavy industrial area with many chimneys belching out smoke and frequent barges being towed up-stream. Then ahead of us we could see the giant shape of the Howrah bridge and we were soon speeding in to the Man of War jetty and the huge crowd awaiting our arrival. Not often have such a damp and disreputable crew been welcomed by such a large and enthusiastic gathering. Beautiful girls spread rose petals in our path as we walked up the jetty and we entered a huge crowded tent for our official reception. We were barely a hundred miles from Ganga Sagar but already we were being treated as though we had completed a long and heroic journey.

For two days we completed our preparations in Calcutta and then we were off again. There were few people to watch our departure from Man of War jetty and to our relief we felt that maybe the crowds would be something of the past. We shot under the Howrah bridge and there was a mighty roar of welcome. Thousands of people lined the bridge and on the banks above were tens of thousands more. The city of Calcutta is very large and for mile after mile people were gathered in their hordes, waving and smiling with incredible enthusiasm as we swept in towards them. One of our senior Indian members estimated that we must have passed at least two million people. It was the warmth of the reaction that was so astonishing—there was no doubt that our expedition had captured the interest of the people of India. It had become a pilgrimage with which they readily identified themselves.

For hour after hour we swept up the river. The continuous masses had now departed, but every village or small town had its solid group of waving and cheering people. All India Radio was following our passage almost minute by minute, so everyone knew when we might appear and they were ready for us. Our first refuelling spot was eighty miles up the river at the small town of Nabadwip. I was aghast as we approached the landing stage—there must have been 30,000 people gathered on the bank and around the landing barge and official dais. We swept in and tied up and there was a deafening roar as I stepped off the boat. A small official group was gathered on the dais to welcome us with a large group of armed policemen supporting them. A strong bamboo wall separated us from the crowd.

I was warmly welcomed by the local magistrate and other senior officials who also had their families along. One child thrust forward an autograph book and rather foolishly I signed it. Immediately there was a sigh from the huge gathering and a small movement forward; it was clear that everyone of them wanted an autograph too. The bamboo wall started cracking under the pressure.

The police responded immediately, pushing forward their rifles against the mob, which was laughing and cheerful at this stage. Then one of the policemen got rather carried away. In front of the crowd was a large, respectably dressed young man and with virtually no provocation the policeman rammed the butt of his rifle into the man's chest. The reaction was understandably violent—the man was livid with rage and started haranguing the crowd and stirring up their anger against the police.

The situation was looking decidedly grim and I had mentally chosen a path for myself from the dais to the boats if the position should further deteriorate. The chairman of the welcoming committee was also very concerned. Would I, he asked me, mind going over to the angry man and shaking him by the hand? Somewhat nervously I agreed. I crossed the dais to the bamboo wall, tapped the man on the back and when he turned around I grabbed his hand and wrung it firmly. Immediately his anger dissipated and he laughed with joy and shook my hand vigorously. The situation was eased, but I was glad to get on to the pontoon and finally on to the first boat to be refilled with fuel and then safely out in the middle of the river. With my departure the turbulence died down and there was no trouble in refilling the other two boats and we duly departed up-stream.

All afternoon we travelled and then well into the evening until a further 100 miles had been covered. In the darkness we eased our way into the bank at Behrampur, weary and damp, having covered 180 miles—our longest day's trip on the whole journey.

We spent the night ashore in simple but adequate accommodation. It had been a tough day and my one desire was for a good night's rest. But first I had another problem to meet—a very angry and unreasonable son. Peter by this stage had become an enthusiastic and accomplished mountaineer, very accustomed to making his own decisions and following his own plans. For the last couple of weeks he had been forced to shake thousands of hands and sign thousands of autographs of people who wanted to meet not mountaineer Pete Hillary but merely the son of 'the famous Sir Hillary'.

Peter was quite frank about the fact that he didn't like it very much and he suggested to me in some wrath that maybe he should withdraw from the expedition. I could appreciate his reaction, but I was hardly sympathetic. Peter had wanted to join the trip and I'd gone to the trouble to organise that. If he left now it would certainly cause unfavourable comment—but I was too tired to argue. "If you want to chicken out now," I told him, "go ahead." Peter departed in his not unusual fury and I fell into bed.

We were away at a leisurely hour next morning, leaving the miles rapidly behind us. After a restful night's sleep Peter had regained his good humour and was still with us. By mid-afternoon we emerged into an enormous open river—the main flow of Ganga— and ahead of us was the giant Farraka barrage with its 102 gates spanning the river and controlling its huge volume of water. Gate number ninety-two had been opened for us and despite the fierce current we charged through without difficulty and were soon up-stream of the great barrage.

For day after day we pushed on upwards, refuelling in small towns and camping at night on grassy stretches beside tiny villages. We found it astonishing that in the Gangetic basin with its enormous population there were so many pleasant and open tree-clad locations where tents could be comfortably pitched. The local villagers were universally kind and welcoming and we felt very much at home in their presence.

Each day we passed fleets of country boats battling their way up-river under sail, for the prevailing wind at this time of the year seemed always vigorous and against the current. The boats had

huge, tattered sails billowing in the wind and they were incredibly
beautiful. In one place I came alongside in the jet boat and
clambered aboard a sailing ship. It was a different world, free
from roaring engines and petrol fumes. Only the creak of the
mainsheet, the flapping of the sails, and the gurgle of water
around the bow filled our ears and it was superbly peaceful. I
wished I could sail on for ever.

The river was several miles wide and in a number of places
rocky islands thrust against the current. The granite island of
Jahngir was one of these and it was covered in towers and temples
like a fairy castle. We went ashore and were warmly welcomed
by the Hindu priests and shown everything we wanted to see. I
had always believed that Hindu temples were prohibited places
to non-believers like ourselves, but this was certainly not our
experience on Mother Ganga. Everywhere, we were taken into
the temples as though we belonged there – and maybe for our
journey on Ganga we had indeed become Hindus ourselves.

The wide river had many tricky sections. Its monsoon waters
were muddy and fast flowing and it was difficult to follow the
deep channels and dodge the shallow sandbanks. At least once
each day a jet boat would run aground on a sandbank at thirty
mph and come to a violent halt. At times a passenger or two
would be hurled over the front of the boat and dropped in the
shallow water. And many of us had bruises and cuts from impacts
with the front of the cockpit.

On September 8th after covering 800 miles we arrived in the
city of Varanasi and distance-wise at least our journey was half
over. Varanasi (or Benares) is one of the oldest and certainly the
holiest of all cities in India. It is here that by choice most Hindus
would prefer to die. As we approached the city we saw the
right-hand bank was lined with minarets and domes, stone walls
and steps, and myriads of temples. But the left bank was free of
buildings, with grassy fields and thorny bushes. We were met
at the entrance to the city by a group of dignitaries including
the Commissioner of Varanasi. His ancient launch was tied up
at the steps and he was anxious for me to come on board and
be formally conducted up the river. The Commissioner and I
boarded the craft and then all the officials streamed on too. The
boat was jam-packed with people inside and they even covered
every inch of the roof. We pulled out from the shore and slowly

made way against the brisk current, swaying uneasily with our top-heavy load.

Jim Wilson, always alert for the welfare of his friends, drove alongside in his jet boat and was aghast at the unstable nature of the official launch. "Why don't you and the Commissioner come along with me?" he shouted across the water. The Commissioner was willing and I was eager. We scrambled across the mob, dropped down the side of the launch, and were soon in the stability of the jet boat. Next moment the motor roared with energy and we were cruising at thirty mph, leaving the launch far behind.

The Commissioner had arranged for us to stay on the city side of the river, but we could see that we would never be free from crowds and have little peace. He was quite agreeable to our camping on the open side and that's what we did, pitching our tents on the grass fields amongst the thorn bushes, with a magnificent view of the city across the river.

We had been a little concerned that the priests and local people and even the thousands of visitors might resent the sight and noise of our jet boats rushing up and down the holy waterfront, but to our relief we were welcomed with great warmth and friendliness. The city even insisted on having a special *puja* (religious ceremony) for us so that we would carry on up Mother Ganga with the blessing of Varanasi to guide and protect us. We drove our three boats into a large area of steps and hitched them safely to the shore. A large group of smiling Indians gathered around and then the *pujare* appeared—a tall, slim, muscular young man with tangled hair and a look of wild energy. He started a vigorous chant and a band behind him took up the refrain. It was an incredible scene—flaming butter lamps, the tinkling of bells, blossoms floating on the water. For half an hour we were transported into a different world, a world of religious fervour, of deafening sound, of the importance of Mother Ganga, and the acceptance of our journey as a sacred pilgrimage.

When I crawled into my tent that night the music and the chanting were still ringing in my ears. I felt stimulated and revived; for a time at least the sadness of the previous two and a half years had vanished from my mind. Life was worth living again and the challenges were all ahead of us.

We spent four days in Varanasi and then carried on up the river again for ten days. We passed through great cities and camped beside peaceful little villages. The kindness and generosity of the country people overwhelmed us. In the village of Mahmudpur the banks were being rapidly eroded by the river and all night great chunks of earth plopped into the water. The villagers were very cheerful but very poor, too. They had fields of ripe corn and we asked them if we could buy some for our pot. They insisted on giving us all we needed and refused to take any payment. I think that all of us from our affluent society wondered if we would have been so generous to passing visitors.

On September 22nd the river changed markedly; it twisted and turned and there were frequent small rapids. Out of the haze loomed the foothills of the Himalayas and our excitement grew. By mid-afternoon we arrived at the town of Hardwar, 'Gate of God', and knew the wild white water was immediately ahead of us. Behind us lay 1,300 miles of river.

At the head of the town the river was barred by a massive barrage with the water cascading over the top. It was no place for us. We swung our boats around and pulled into the left bank where the main city lay. A large crowd quickly gathered as we discussed the problem of getting beyond the barrage–the only answer seemed to be to drag the boats out of the water. A well-dressed gentleman with a quiet but confident manner pushed through the crowd and introduced himself. He was the engineer in charge of the barrage. We explained our problem to him and he waved his hands vigorously. "No problem!" he told us. "You can come up the canal." Flowing from the left side of the barrage was a deep canal to supply water and sanitation to the town, but it was four feet higher than the main river. "No problem!" he said again. "We can remove some of the large boards holding the side of the canal in place and you can drive your boats up." With a feeling of deep thankfulness for this generous engineer we unloaded our boats and then drove them in forceful fashion up the foaming little river that now filled the dry watercourse. The retaining boards had indeed been lowered and a steep flood of water poured down. But could our boats get up?

Mike Hamilton made the first run. At top speed he hit the racing water, sliced dangerously sideways and was then up and over. There was a tremendous cheer from the crowd. Then it was Jim Wilson's turn. Calmly and confidently he hurled himself at

Everest and Lhotse rise above the monsoon cloud.

The sun returns to Scott Base after the long Antarctic winter.

Mingma Tsering, Ed and Angtemba, 1963.

Louise, Mingma and Ed receive scarves of welcome from villagers.

Building Bakanje school in 1970.

Ed and Louise in Kathmandu during the King of Nepal's coronation celebrations.

Belinda, Peter and Sarah in the bazaar in Kathmandu.

the speeding water, hit it dead centre and smoothly rose over the crest. I was driving the third boat, but decided it would be safer to have Mike take it up. By now the canal had dropped substantially in depth and the water flowing down was much lower. Mike drove firmly forward but alas the water was too shallow; he hit the steel edge of the hinged retaining board and came to a crashing halt. His boat stalled and drifted backwards. But next moment Mike had the engine going again and he charged a little further to the right where the water seemed a fraction deeper. With a lurch he was over the top and all of us were safely in the canal. The last boat had a healthy dent in its nose and some fibreglass repairs would be necessary.

We spent that night in Hardwar and it was happy enough, although I became rather irritated at the constant succession of people demanding autographs. How I pined for one of our peaceful camps on the grassy river bank! In the morning Jon and Mike Hamilton worked on repairing the damaged fibreglass, but it was mid-afternoon before their task was completed and the boats reloaded. As we said farewell to the huge crowd the skies opened and down came torrential rain. Driving along the canal was painful in the extreme and a few of the team suggested we might spend another night in Hardwar. I had no intention of doing this and Jim and I fumbled our way up the canal through a sheet of water and then roared once more out into the open river. Miraculously the rain cleared and we drove furiously up the fast-flowing, clear water, sideslipping around sharp corners and charging up lively rapids. This was delightful mountain water, cool and fresh, and most exciting travelling. As darkness approached we reached the town of Rishikesh and pulled into the bank for the night.

From here on we could expect a succession of big rapids. We removed the awnings which had protected us well from sun and rain, for they could be a danger if a boat should tip and someone get tangled in the lines. Rishikesh is a town of many *ashrams* and a succession of 'holy' men, mostly Indian but many foreign, came down to the boats to wish us well, but expressed their confidence that we wouldn't get very far. We thanked them for their blessings but hoped their fears didn't prove to be correct.

Then with a roar, a succession of cheers and a mass of hearty waves we were out in the river and heading up-stream. The first main rapid was five miles away, we had been told, but we were barely around the first corner when we saw big water ahead of us. I could feel my stomach muscles tightening and a shiver of fear running down my spine. I was travelling in Jim Wilson's boat. Not only was he a particular friend, but he was also the least experienced of our three main drivers and I almost felt it was my duty to travel with him. Jim and I had one thing in common, a terror of the wild water ahead, but Jim had a forceful courage too and I basically felt confidence in his natural ability.

We cruised up to the heaving water, searching for a safe line through. Then Jon was away, leaping to the left close in to the cliffs and then smashing his way out into the middle and up between a line of great rocks. It had been almost too easy, but that's the way Jon made things appear. Jim and I followed along behind with screaming engine and spray everywhere, the huge surges of water whipping by. Then we too were up and the tension eased.

A mile or two further on there was another rapid, a bit easier this one and we passed through with little difficulty. Five miles out we could hear the mighty roar of heavy water and turned the corner to see a terrifying sight—great heaps of water pounding down in huge waves with cross currents and flying spray. Could our boats handle something like this?

Evening was approaching so we decided to leave this rapid until morning and camp on the white sand beside the river. It was a beautiful place with ample supplies of driftwood and not a soul around. In the chill of the evening we sat around a blazing camp fire and talked about mountains and rivers and food—but never about the great rapid above us. The roar of the water wafted us peacefully off to sleep.

The morning was clear and sunny. We had decided that some of the party would carry loads of gear along the bank to the top of the rapid. Only two of us would travel in each boat. Jon nosed into the bottom of the rapid but was tossed back by great stopper waves. "There's only one way to go," he told us. "First into the right bank, then straight across the river and up the left bank and then somehow escape out through the middle."

We watched as he made his run, at times almost disappearing out of sight in the hollows between the waves and then being tossed high with spray surrounding him. We could hear the scream of his engine above the roar of the water, but then in brilliant fashion he was over the top in calm water and speeding easily to the bank.

Then it was Jim's turn, and mine, and I could once again feel the grip of fear. With a grim face but strong hand Jim took us up the right bank, competently and well. It was time to cross. We headed through the surging waves and were tossed high in the air. Jim's foot slipped off the accelerator and the boat rolled sideways down a huge surge, completely out of control. "This is it," I thought, "next roll we'll go under!" But Jim had quickly recovered, he restarted the motor, got us under way and we were soon in the shelter of the left bank, somewhat shaken but safe for the moment. He turned the boat up-river again, hugging the left bank, keeping out of the giant waves in the centre. The water was very fast and the engine was screaming with full power. Ahead of us were big rocks—we must get out in the middle. Jim swung right over a huge wave, the bow shot into the sky and we were drenched with spray. Somehow we held on the crest of the wave and then slowly inched our way over. The surface flattened, the waves grew less, and we were at speed again and charging happily into the right bank. We were through!

We carried on up a deep and beautiful gorge, overcoming many rapids and having some difficult moments. In one rapid, to our horror, Jon actually disappeared from sight and then reappeared completely waterlogged and having turned 180° while under the surface. Somehow he started the motor again and limped into the bank. It took us a couple of hours before the boat was thoroughly dried out and we could carry on. Ahead of us now we saw a small mountain town perched on the side of the cliffs. It was Deoprayag, a very holy place, where two large rivers meet. Pushing out into the water like the prow of a boat was a rock step and everywhere were crowds of people. We were waved in to the rock and I was invited to come ashore. The crowd gathered around me and I had flowers placed around my neck and a local priest performed a *puja* for our safety and welfare on the rest of the journey. Then we roared up-river again through gorges and rapids to reach an adequate camping site on a sandy beach. It had been a long and tiring day with much tension and we were very happy to crawl into our sleeping-bags.

For four more days we battled on up the river and each day had its share of frightening moments. The first day it was the fierce rapid at Rudraprayag but there were a dozen other too. The second day the Chute was our greatest challenge and once we had overcome it we felt that nothing more could stop us. On the third day the river became rougher and rougher and we were battling every inch of the way. We reached another of the river meetings at Karnaprayag and gasped in wonder at the huge crowd waiting to welcome us. Where in all these barren hills had they come from? A little further on we had our second swamping—Jon this time also—and only by luck and quick reaction did he get his boat safely to the bank.

For a long time Peter and Murray Jones had been restless and impatient. They weren't expert jet-boat drivers and they felt they were just passengers in this wild white water. I had tried to point out that even their help with unloading and reloading the boat was valuable, but this simply wasn't enough. They wanted to be out leading the field in an environment where they knew they could excel—the mountains. Finally I agreed that they should head off, go up into the hills, carry out a reconnaissance, and let us know what they could find. They departed with great enthusiasm—and I have to admit it was with some relief that I watched them go.

The fourth day was the end of the road for the jet boats. Only a few hundred yards from the town of Nandaprayag we came around a fierce corner and saw the end of our journey ahead of us: crossing the river was a vertical waterfall ten feet high, we could go no further.

Somehow it wasn't too much of a disappointment—we had known we would get stopped somewhere and we had got further than we had ever hoped. We were 1,500 miles from the ocean, had covered 200 miles of white water and were 3,000 feet above sea level. It was a fair effort and now we could carry on the last hundred miles on foot.

Free from the stress of the white water we walked cheerfully on up the pilgrim road. Always below us was the wild river and we increasingly realised that we could have gone no further. The road zigzagged steeply up the great mountainside and we camped at night on little grassy patches beside the road. On the third day we reached the important town of Joshimath, a large military encampment, and we were warmly welcomed by the Indian army.

Here we diverted from the main road and climbed a side track to the small village of Ghangaria at 10,300 feet, on into the famous valley of flowers and up to the sacred lake of Hemkund at 15,000 feet. We climbed a couple of thousand feet and then struck fresh snow as we started on the Golden Staircase of 1,064 carefully fashioned stone steps leading straight and steep up the mountainside. The lake was in a beautiful position, cradled amongst the mountains but cold and misty. In traditional fashion most of our expedition dived into the frigid water and emerged with great rapidity. I satisfied myself by splashing the freezing water over my hands and face. We descended to Ghangaria again and next morning returned to the road and climbed slowly up the switchbacks to reach the sacred town of Badrinath at 10,000 feet. Our journey was now nearly over. We had still to reach one of the glaciers and climb a snowy summit, but already I could feel a sense of sadness that our long adventure was drawing to a close.

On October 10th the chill of approaching winter was gathering around us as we climbed slowly with heavy loads up the mountainside. Across the valley was the superb summit of the 21,000 feet Nilkanta and other great mountains reared their craggy heads into the sky. Weary from the long pull, we established our Base Camp on a rocky ledge at 15,000 feet, the terminal iceface of the glacier only 500 feet above us. We felt no sense of urgency—maybe it was the altitude—but the vigorous drive we had displayed in the lower valley seemed to have gone for ever. I had planned to move very slowly above Base Camp to give time for ample acclimatisation, but foolishly I allowed myself to be overruled by the more vigorous members of the party. Next morning the fittest team set off to pioneer the route up to a High Camp at 18,000 feet, while the slower of us carried loads up and dumped them at 16,500 feet. We were driving desperately and unnecessarily on, although many of us were clearly showing the effects of altitude. Let's get it all over and done with seemed to be our aim.

On October 12th we set off to establish our High Camp. The first section was very easy, big, rounded, red slabs, but then we reached grey, steeper rock with rather more exposure. The route now lay up a long snow and ice gully down which we had suspended a 500 foot safety rope. Some of the party picked up loads from the dump and they must have been carrying at least seventy-five pounds. I was carrying only forty-five pounds, but

this was more than enough for me. I kept thinking to myself,
"What's an overweight, broken–down, fifty–eight–year–old doing
wandering around up here?"

We started up a steep snow slope and then a long traverse out
to the left–it was quite exposed. The slope eased off and ahead of
us was a long glacier valley with deep, soft snow. It seemed to go
on for ever and I was having the greatest difficulty in dragging
one leg after the other. I was making frequent stops now for rests,
but would then struggle slowly on. It was a tremendous relief to
come over a small crest and reach the site of our High Camp at
over 18,000 feet. I was too tired to enjoy it very much but noticed
how beautiful the snow field was and I was impressed with the
two graceful peaks on the other side. It took me a long time to
stamp out a flat place for my tent and then pitch it. With enormous
relief I crawled inside my sleeping–bag and left all the main tasks
to the others. I didn't eat much dinner, just sipped some warm
drink.

I was warm all night but had a succession of ghastly dreams.
Some of the others hadn't slept well either and it was decided to
have a more–or–less rest day. Peter and Murray were much better
acclimatised and decided to plug steps through the soft snow
towards the peak, Akash Parbat. I crawled out of my tent with
the idea of helping them but felt so weak that I quickly returned.

The day passed slowly and I was most uncomfortable with
headaches and backache. In the evening I was very miserable
and Dr. Mike Gill checked me over but couldn't find too much
wrong except a tenderness in the small of my back. He gave me a
small injection for the pain and after a short while I just passed
out.

I came back to life very slowly. The light was dim and I realised
I was inside a sleeping–bag. But most noticeable was the fact that
I seemed to be bumping over rocks and outside I could hear the
muted sound of voices. I started mumbling and the movement
stopped. The sleeping–bag was opened and a face looked in. I
don't really know what he said, but I have a feeling it was,
"Christ! He's alive!" I wondered where I was and was able to
look around. I was below the glacier, below the steep snow
slope, even below the long snow gully. I was bumping over the
highest of the rocks and that's what had brought me back to life.
Stretching up from my bag were two long climbing ropes with a

couple of fellows hanging on to each, and below me was another rope. All my companions were smiling—it looked as though they'd given me up for dead.

They continued on, moving me down, and my mind got clearer and clearer. I even tried to walk after a while on the easier rock, but I was very weak and had to be half-carried. Then we reached a fairly flat place and Mike said, "This will do for the camp." It was about 15,500 feet.

Slowly the whole story came out. In the morning they'd found me in my tent, out cold, and Mike knew things were pretty desperate and that I probably had a cerebral oedema. I had to be got down as quickly as possible. They left me in my sleeping-bag inside my tent, attached the ropes, and started dragging me down the slope. When it steepened, all the effort went into checking me from sliding down into the valley. They'd done a marvellous job in very difficult conditions and I was appropriately grateful.

Meanwhile Murray Jones had headed off down to Badrinath at great speed to try and organise a rescue helicopter. We heard the sound of one churning around in the valley below, but there was no way it could get to us, as the mist had swept in and we couldn't see a thing. Darkness was falling and Peter arrived up from Base Camp with a tent and food. We all crawled inside and were really very cheerful and I slept a good deal of the night.

Early in the morning we heard the sound of a helicopter again and quickly crawled out of the tent. It was fine and clear but there was a dusting of fresh snow on the rocks. I was much more stable now. The helicopter moved expertly over to the slope and rested one ski on the rock. The door opened and a hand beckoned. Mike firmly pushed me inside and then jumped in after. In a few seconds we were floating out over the valley.

We circled down to Badrinath and landed beside a big group of army officers and some civilians. A line of chairs was set up and I crawled out of the chopper and was carefully assisted into a seat. I was feeling much better now at this lower altitude and I was aghast when they told me I was to be taken to a hospital far down on the plains. All my money, passport and papers were in Badrinath—what would the expedition do without me?

But the commanding officer was quite insistent. Orders had been given at the highest level. So Mike and I got into the helicopter again and spent two long days in the heat of Bareilly before I was declared fit enough to be returned to the expedition. While Mike and I were in the plains, the climbers had come into their own and completed our pilgrimage by climbing Na Parbat and Akash Parbat where they sprinkled the summit with holy Ganga water blessed by the *pujare* at the river's mouth.

For my own part, I seemed as intelligent as I ever am, but there was no doubt that my memory had been affected by the cerebral oedema. And always hanging in the back of my mind was a slight feeling of depression. It had been a great trip—I'd never had a better—but I had the feeling that I'd never be quite the same again.

5

Some same, some changing

AFTER THE OCEAN TO SKY journey I spent a few days in hospital in Auckland but they didn't seem to find any major problems. I worked on the book and the film of the trip in somewhat lethargic fashion, but once this was done a constant feeling of depression made me feel restless and dissatisfied. I decided to head back to Nepal, to do some work on my aid projects and then drift off with a few companions into some isolated valleys and see if I couldn't straighten myself out.

I walked in from Kathmandu to Solu with just a few Sherpa companions—Mingma Tsering, Angtsering and Pemma. They were some of my oldest Sherpa friends. I'd stayed in their homes, knew their wives and children, and had relied on their common sense and good judgement on many expeditions and construction projects. After Everest their lives had changed too, just as mine had. Their standard of living had greatly improved and Mingma had become a very important man throughout the Sherpa community. But still they clung to their old, reliable social customs and religious beliefs. They were tough and hardy men but incredibly generous and kind to their friends. We didn't talk about it much, but they certainly appreciated the new opportunities for their children to go to school and their families to get medical treatment. They looked after me like a favoured and rather helpless child, although in some ways, I suppose, I was a sort of father figure.

I was aghast at the destruction of forest and the consequent erosion which had taken place on a massive scale, even in the few months since I had passed through here last, and threatened the economy of the whole region. I passed a Government Agriculture Centre but couldn't see any sign of tree plantations. The hills were getting more and more barren with only scrub and second growth remaining.

The ordinary Nepalese peasant seemed to have little concern about the forest destruction. With increasing population pressure it had become a matter of survival—more land must be cultivated and more trees cut for houses and cooking and heating. The future seemed remote and unimportant and only the small proportion of the enlightened in the population were desperately aware of the need to encourage re-afforestation and wise agricultural practices.

We continued up the Dudh Kosi valley, checking schools and bridges on the way, then we shot to the right up the valley above Lukla following airy traverses and high passes before plunging down through azaleas, rhododendron and pine to the floor of the Inukhu valley. We passed the monastery ruins and abandoned yak-grazing pasture of Lungsamba and a little further up the valley came upon a huge, overhanging rock closed in by a wall with a window and a door. Inside in the dim light we saw three big religious figures, very old we were told, but recently repainted by a down-valley lama. It was certainly a very impressive place with a strong atmosphere of mystery.

We climbed up a steep rise in the valley and I was enthralled by the dense juniper and the great peaks—it was just as the approach to Everest had been in the old days. Then we came to the summer village of Tarnak, eight houses and many potato fields, but all were now deserted. During the monsoon we were told there were 150 yaks here and 600 sheep from Bung. The views of the great peaks, wreathed in cloud, were magnificent, but I was content just to drift through this wild country and try to absorb some of the peace of its seclusion.

Mingma and I started along the high yak route to Pangkongma and it was pretty impressive. There was a bitter wind blowing and we crossed pass after pass at 14,500 to 15,000 feet. Then we sidled above the Inukhu gorge with quite unbelievable drops down to the river. It was a very spectacular route, although I soon developed a headache from the wind, the glare, and the altitude. After one very long day we couldn't find a suitable camp site on the ridge, so we plunged down 700 feet on the Dudh Kosi side over rock and slippery ice to a very isolated ledge and there we pitched our tents. We were at 14,300 feet and I felt mighty lonely.

I still had a headache in the morning and felt rather weak.

There were heavy clouds in the valleys below and over many of the peaks, but we went on and on along the ridge with enormous drops on either side. There was plenty of firewood but no water, so we had to wait for breakfast until we had dropped a few thousand feet in height on a little pass above Pangkongma village. My headache had largely gone now, unless I coughed vigorously.

We climbed down to the small village of Setuk, then on down a precipitous track to the Inukhu river and the bridge we had fixed there some years before. It was in a bad state of repair and we measured it all up for new timber. There aren't many homes in this steep desolate valley but a thousand feet above the river was the house of an old Sherpa friend, Passang. Passang was a young and vigorous man who had worked for us on many occasions. His house and farm were perched very steeply on the mountainside and he produced barely enough food to supply his young family. A few months each year on one of our construction projects gave him the spare cash to make all the difference between a poverty-stricken existence and a barely tolerable one.

With true Sherpa hospitality Passang welcomed us with great warmth and insisted on supplying us with a chicken. Pemma made it into an excellent stew and I enjoyed that meal more than any I'd had for a long time. I admired the expertise of the Sherpas in turning damp, smoky branches into raging fires—and I enjoyed our strange mixture of porters moving in and out of the fog, Tamangs, Kamis and Sherpas.

For some reason I had a terribly restless night with little sleep. A series of morbid and depressive topics ran through my brain. In my dreams I wrote letters, gave speeches and delivered advice, none of it very happy or constructive, and I kept wondering what the hell I should do with myself. What I did was descend 7,000 feet through Sherpa villages and then down into the large isolated Rai village of Bung. In the floor of the valley the beautiful Hongu river was spanned by an incredibly awful bridge. It seemed a good place to carry out a construction project. It wouldn't be hard to put in a couple of steel wire ropes, I thought, as the rock was so solid, but getting the new timber would be more difficult. The chairman of the local Sherpa village was extremely keen on the idea. He'd get the timber himself, he told us, if the people in Bung wouldn't agree.

Our camp beside the river was very pleasant and warm and

I could comfortably sit outside. I also had the last couple of shots of my remaining Scotch and felt pleasantly numb and content. Maybe life wasn't too bad after all. Pemma roasted a superb chicken and roast potatoes too; with real chicken soup before and some apricots and custard afterwards. I ate so much I had to lie on my back to recover. We had a good fire and lay around talking until seven thirty p.m. – pretty late for us as we were often in bed by six p.m. Treks of 6,000 feet downhill, then up a couple of thousand to cross an impassable gorge, and down again to wander along the Arun river ensured I was so tired I had no difficulty in sleeping.

But even though I'd lost a lot of weight, my age was beginning to tell and I realised I'd probably never be particularly fit again. Altitude seemed to be worrying me more too – each time I slept over 14,000 feet I developed severe headaches. Most of all I felt I'd lost some of my basic enjoyment of energetic walking. Grinding up steep hills at six a.m. wasn't enjoyable any more (maybe it never had been? – but I'd been a bit more competitive in days gone by).

I decided that I just had to accept that I was getting older (fifty-eight) and losing heart a bit, and I didn't seem to have such a strong grip on life. I'd been trying to run away from things and it hadn't worked very well. However miserable I might feel at times, there had been good moments too – and hopefully they might remain so. I knew that most people thought I was battling on in great style – but few of them knew just how I felt underneath it all.

From one year to the next my major objective in life became my aid work in Nepal with the Himalayan Trust. With the completion of the Phaphlu hospital there seemed no end to the tasks to be undertaken.

A severe earthquake had shaken loose the rock lining of Khunde hospital, so there was much work to do improving and enlarging the building. My brother Rex, who is an experienced builder, was the leader of our construction team in 1978 and worked energetically in co-operation with local carpenters and rock masons. The accommodation for the volunteer doctor and his wife was rebuilt and enlarged and the kitchen and storage area greatly improved. A separate building was also constructed for storage of tools and building materials, with a large room for charcoal which was now our main source of fuel.

In the following year Peter, Murray Jones and I headed off to reconstruct the difficult bridge in the depths of the remote Inukhu valley. We crossed the Taksindu pass and dropped steeply down to the village of Manedingma where we received a warm welcome from the school children as this was one of our schools. We enjoyed an excellent meal around a blazing fire, after plenty of good *arak* from a local Sherpa friend.

Next morning it was an early departure and we plunged steadily down to the Dudh Kosi river and then up the long rocky stairway to our customary breakfast place. On we went for hour after hour, up the long, steep valley to Pangkongma, and I was vastly relieved finally to reach the village and establish our camp. The school was still closed after the winter but by chance a new teacher had arrived that day and he quickly opened up the shutters. I thought he looked a handsome but lethargic young man.

The precarious rope and plank suspension bridges of Nepal are famous, at first sight unnerving to Western eyes, but generally more effective than they look and absolutely essential for man and beast in that terrain of great gorges and ridges, with fast-flowing, icy rivers in the depths of precipitous ravines. Keeping the bridges in good repair was a pretty tricky job, demanding a head for heights, some elementary mechanics, a lot of willing labour and a bit of good luck.

We left camp at six thirty a.m. and clambered up the steep slope to the pass at 10,500 feet. From there the track edged along the Inukhu valley with a precipitous drop towards the river below. We descended a thousand feet to a farm and house on the edge of the bluff where Gallu lived—he was a good friend and had worked for us on many occasions. Mingma came out of the house looking very disturbed. "Gallu dead!" he said shortly. Finally the story came out.

With several local people Gallu had gone down to India to work on a bridge near Darjeeling. One Sherpa girl from Cheremi had slipped in the swift-flowing waters. Gallu had tried to save her and fell in too and both were drowned as neither could swim. Gallu had left six children—three from his brother who had died and Gallu had married his widow—and three of his own. I wondered how the family would survive, but Gallu's wife seemed remarkably calm and philosophical. She still had the farm; the children would help; and she would just have to work harder, she told us. I admired her courage and asked Mingma to give her a good donation in memory of our friend Gallu.

Somewhat subdued, we plunged down the steep walls of the valley for 2,000 feet to the Inukhu bridge which was in a spectacular position spanning a narrow gorge a hundred feet above the river. I examined the bridge and was concerned about the condition of the east cantilever and the central span, but the west cantilever was in good condition. Obviously the bridge was mainly being supported by the two steel wire ropes we had slung across some years before.

We pitched our tents on tiny ledges in the gloomy depths of the gorge – a place where the sun hardly ever reached – but there were ample supplies of dead firewood and in the evening the light from our blazing fire sparkled over the great damp rock faces. The only sound was the quiet rushing of the river below.

Mingma and ten local people started work very early next morning, lowering and carrying timber down the precipitous east bluffs to the bridge. To replace the east cantilever we would have to suspend the central section from the steel wire ropes, a difficult and dangerous procedure. Attaching a block and tackle to the centre of each wire rope in turn, we winched the central section up into the air until it was hanging completely free from the cantilevers at each end. I kept hoping the wires would take this extra strain and as a safety factor we slung a heavy rope from the cliffs above along the line of the bridge. Anyone moving on the bridge would snap a karabiner on to this rope and at least have some protection if the bridge were to collapse.

Then we stripped the planking off the east cantilever to reveal the rotten timbers beneath. We cleared away all the heavy rocks holding down the end of the cantilever and tipped the old beams over the side to fall a hundred feet with an almighty crash to the stream bed below. The short lower cantilever appeared very solid, so we used this as a firm base. We slid out two rows of twenty-six-feet-long eight by three inch beams (four beams to the row) and this brought the cantilever up under the suspended central section. We moved the tons of rock back on to the land end of the cantilever to weight it firmly down and then lowered the central section back into place. We were delighted when it was clearly stable and secure. Then we nailed on eight by one and a half inch planking with heavy six-inch nails and the east cantilever was virtually complete. Hitched on to the safety line, Peter and Murray had been flitting backwards and forwards over the bridge and the whole process had gone very smoothly.

During the night I spent a lot of time worrying about the tricky business of replacing the central span, but finally came to what I felt was a safe conclusion. Once again Mingma and his gang were up very early lowering the three largest thirty-six-foot beams down the cliff. Then Murray and Peter hitched on their safety harness and started prising off the floorboards out above the middle of the gorge. When we reached the central crossbeam hanging from the steel wire ropes we cautiously slid a thirty-six-foot beam on its side across the gap and then through underneath the other half of the planking to the far side. We repeated this with a second beam which made a safe walkway across.

Then the rest of the planking on the middle section was stripped off and plunged down into the river. Next came the tricky part—the three old central beams were cautiously hauled back to the bank and tipped over the side. The third new beam was slid out, making a wide walkway—in fact Murray thought we should leave the crossing this way, but with the beams flat it was just too whippy. I nailed chocks into place each end and then we tipped the beams up on to their edges as they were much stronger that way. Now we nailed a new floor in place—heavy work with six-inch nails in tough timber—but it was finally complete and a very impressive floor it made. It had been a long, tough day and we were happy to have a substantial dinner and crawl into our sleeping-bags.

Next morning we had an easier day ahead of us. Murray and Mingma stripped the flooring off the west cantilever and I was pleased to see that the beams were very sound. New flooring was then nailed into place. Peter and I constructed light rails on either side of the bridge with number eight fencing wire and vertical battens and the job was completed. It certainly wasn't a Golden Gate bridge, but it was a simple and effective crossing for laden men and yaks in the depths of a narrow, rocky gorge.

Murray and Peter headed off up-valley with plans to reconnoitre and maybe climb the virgin mountain Ku Sang Kang. Peter was now twenty-four years old and though his university career (like his father's) had not been particularly successful he had quite a lot to show for his life. He was a professional ski instructor in the winter; he had a commercial pilot's licence; and in more recent years he had become a very competent technical mountaineer with many tough climbs to his credit in the New Zealand Alps and in Yosemite. Himalayan climbing was now his major ambition and in September 1979 he and three companions planned the first ascent of the West Face of Ama Dablam, 22,300 feet. I had grave doubts about the safety of this formidable route with its overhanging ice, but made no comment until Peter asked my views. I told him of my concern about avalanche danger on the route but Peter was full of confidence. He had watched the face on many occasions, he told me, and had never seen an avalanche sweep down. I argued no longer. I too had never actually seen an avalanche falling down the face, although they must come down sometimes, I felt, judging from the debris at the bottom. However, it was Peter's own decision.

I have always believed that whether you're young or old you have the right to risk your life in a challenge—as long as you aren't taking a gamble with an unwilling person's life at the same time. I don't think there is anything very clever about killing yourself off, or even about having a fall and surviving. It can be an admission of lack of experience or inefficiency in some form or another. But I do believe that if you approach the matter in a reasonably sensible fashion you at least have the right to try yourself out on even the most hazardous of objectives.

A few months later we were back in Solu Khumbu again and Rex and I completed a school hostel at Junbesi. Peter and his party had gone quite high on Ku Sang Kang but just missed reaching the summit. Now they were turning their attention to Ama Dablam. I made a brief visit up-valley to Khunde and wrote a note to Peter.

October 19th 1979

Dear Peter,

I laboured up the Namche Hill yesterday and was pleased to receive your letters. You seem to be making good progress on Ama Dablam and I certainly wish you well—it is a pretty hairy-looking route. Take it easy—there's not much point in wiping yourself out.

I'm afraid I still won't be able to come up and see you. I'm only here today and I'm certainly not fit enough to grind up to 15,000 feet and down again. It is quite important that I get back to Phaphlu as HMG now wish to take over Solu hospital and the Director of Health flies in on October 26th to look things over. The Chief District Officer at Sallari has been rather difficult in many ways and I won't be sorry to get rid of the hospital, even though we've put a lot of sweat and blood into the operation. I feel a little sad about your Mother and Lindy— they were so involved in it all. However time passes, I guess.

I returned to Phaphlu to join Rex and to discuss the handover of the hospital. The Director of Health flew in to Phaphlu on October 27th and with him he had a note from Elizabeth Hawley. There'd been an accident on the West Face of Ama Dablam. One of the party was dead—she didn't know who—and another badly knocked around. Despite my appointment with the Director of Health I knew I had to get back up to Khunde and find out if Peter was alive. Would the plane take me there? The pilot was agreeable and off we went, over into the Dudh Kosi valley and up towards Khumbila. In twenty minutes we had covered the four-day walk and were making our approach to the airfield at Tsyangboche. Refusing to believe the worst, I trudged over the hill to Khunde hospital. I was welcomed with a hug by the volunteer doctor's wife. "It's O.K., Ed. Peter is pretty badly knocked around but he's still alive. The chopper will be down in a few minutes."

Ten minutes later we heard the sound of a helicopter as it churned its way up the valley and settled in a cloud of dust beside the hospital. Peter was there, looking pale and frail—a broken arm and several other minor fractures. They'd had a terrible three days descending the mountain. There was room for me on the helicopter and we flew back to Kathmandu, and that night he was operated on at Shanta Bhavan hospital. He had been very lucky to survive—and still believed the West Face could be climbed. It was just the luck of the game, he said. I had no comment to make. Such decisions must be up to him.

The annual raising of funds was largely my responsibility and as this involved $U.S. 100,000 to $U.S.120,000 per year it proved a considerable burden. With the assistance of friends in Canada, the U.S.A. and New Zealand I did many lectures to service clubs, schools and other organisations, and we were helped substantially by companies, foundations and individual contributions. For a number of years the External Aid Division of the New Zealand Government had been a firm supporter of the Phaphlu hospital and increasingly the Canadian International Development Agency (C.I.D.A.) had subsidised the funds we had successfully raised in Canada. Our projects were very small compared to the millions of dollars spent by the United Nations and national aid projects but it is doubtful if many of them had such careful supervision of the money spent as our Himalayan Trust. The foreign members of our teams had their air fares paid and were supplied with food and tentage in Nepal, but their time and effort was a voluntary contribution. We had substantial donations of materials from many companies and we greatly benefited from the free labour supplied by the local people. I became a little desperate about how long we could keep it going as inflation pushed up the costs and the difficult economic conditions made people a little more reluctant to donate. One thing was fairly clear—if anything should happen to me there was a very good chance our whole project would collapse.

In March 1980 my first task was the formal handing over of the Solu hospital at Phaphlu to the Nepalese Government. The Minister of Health flew in from Kathmandu for the ceremony. Establishing this hospital had been a five-year exercise in co-operation between the Himalayan Trust, the Nepalese Government and the local people, who had contributed a tremendous amount of work towards its construction—more than 10,000 man days of free labour. Over five years the Himalayan Trust had supplied foreign doctors to administer the hospital and treat the patients. Now the time had come for the Nepalese Government to assume this responsibility and run the hospital with its own Nepalese doctors. This did not mean that the Himalayan Trust was abandoning its responsibilities at Phaphlu. We would continue to finance the supply of medicines, assist with food and wages, and carry out necessary maintenance, possibly also assist periodically with short-term medical experts.

Alas, the new takeover of Phaphlu hospital did not prove particularly successful. The first Nepalese superintendent was well meaning enough but lacked the drive and enthusiasm of his

Western brethren. The hospital opened at ten a.m. and closed at one p.m. Anyone, however sick, who arrived outside these hours would have to wait until next day. And the doctor was frequently away for months at a time in Kathmandu. We discussed the matter with the Ministry of Health in Kathmandu and a decision was reached. At the beginning of 1982 a new Nepalese superintendent of Sherpa descent was installed and an experienced New Zealand doctor joined the hospital as his assistant. To date this has proved remarkably successful. The number of patients has increased enormously and with it the demand for drugs. Our problem now is not a lack of medical attention but doubts as to whether we can afford to keep the finance going.

Our building programme carried energetically on. We built an extra school building at Chaunrikarka and a new school at Gumila. In April 1981 Rex and I were back up in Khumbu with some more big projects in hand. A pleasant surprise was waiting for us: Peter had arrived from the east over a number of high snow passes with Graeme Dingle. They were undertaking a most ambitious project, a traverse of the Himalayas from Kangchenjunga to K2 which would occupy a long ten months. Peter had almost recovered from his Ama Dablam injuries and was still incorrigibly devoted to the mountains.

After a week of constant bickering the Himalayan traverse party departed, well fed and refreshed, but I wondered how they could possibly last for another eight months together. (Miracles do sometimes occur! With many adventures and a fair share of disagreement Peter and Graeme did complete their journey together, the first time such an adventure had been successfully concluded.)

In the middle of April I was invited down to a meeting of the Khumjung school committee in the house of Angtsering Sherpa, the chairman of the Khumjung Panchyatt. After the enthusiastic formalities, involving many glasses of *arak*, had been concluded an important proposition was put forward to me. Khumjung was desperately keen to have a high school in the village. Headmaster Shyam Pradhan explained that he had talked at length to the District Supervisor of high schools who explained what must be done in Khumjung to qualify it for high school status. Three new classrooms must be built, each about twenty foot square, and school desks must be supplied for 100 pupils. A rather unusual provision was that the Khumbu must raise Rs 100,000 ($U.S.8,000) and deposit this in the Nepal Rastra Bank in Namche Bazar as an indication that they had the financial backing to keep the school going. Would the Himalayan Trust, they requested, see fit to help with this project? The local people, they assured me, would do everything in their power to make the high school successful.

Khumjung school, I knew, already had more than 270 daily students and a high school would be a valuable addition. After deep thought and a few more glasses of *arak* I made the following proposition. The Trust would subsidise the local donations rupee for rupee up to Rs 50,000 and above that we would subsidise two rupees for every one rupee contributed by the local people. This meant the local population would only have to produce Rs 40,000–a very considerable sum indeed in this impoverished community. As far as the building was concerned, I agreed that the Trust would finance the cutting of the timber, its carrying up to Khunde and its hand planing. Then next year we would construct the building. The local people would be expected to carry to the site the large quantities of broken rock that would be needed and there would be much other voluntary work to be done.

The school committee was delighted. Out came more silk scarves and *leis* of flowers. More bottles of *arak* were produced and the party carried on energetically into the night.

Our journey in to Khumbu in March 1982 was different from any I had undertaken before. We left Kathmandu by truck on March 12th before six a.m. It was a clear, cool morning and the Kathmandu valley was superbly beautiful in the early morning light with patches of frost in places. The road was almost empty and we reached Banepa very quickly and then plunged down the long steep hill to the luxuriant flat a couple of thousand feet below–in the half-light it was a really gorgeous scene. We headed down the long, winding valley to Dhologhat and crossed the big bridge built by Chinese engineers. Then it was a slow climb over the ridge and down to the road beside the Sun Kosi river. At eight thirty a.m. we reached the rather scruffy town of Lamsangu.

Now, for the first time we crossed the Swiss bridge over the river and climbed slowly to the east up the new Swiss road. It was a fantastic route, very steep and with superb views of the mountains to the west. We slowly climbed upwards past the spot where the Lamsangu track arrives and then higher and higher over a big pass. Then it was down again for thousands of feet, winding round sharp corners, negotiating very rough sections above steep drops. We reached Charikot and then plunged down an incredibly rough ridge to reach our destination at Kirantichap at one ten p.m. We'd had seven hours of rough, tiring but very spectacular driving. We pitched our tents in a pleasant position just down off the pass.

We had hoped that 100 porters would be waiting for us but only fourteen had turned up. A very large Russian expedition to Everest had just passed through and had gathered up all the porters available. We'd have to wait for a day or two, we decided.

It was a beautiful night, clear and cool. I looked out of my tent door early in the morning and the huge summits of Gauri Sankar and Menlungtse were sharp against the Tibetan sky. Mingma and his Sherpas searched the villages for porters and slowly groups drifted in.

I found Kirantichap completely changed. It used to be a tiny bazaar in a dip in the ridge with several huge pipal trees shading it. It was always a pleasant place to camp with vigorous winds at times. Well, the trees were still there and so was the wind, but there were now many houses and a big bazaar. The construction work on the road had produced a dusty desert and I couldn't see what advantage it would all have. The whole mountainside ahead of us up to Namdu was scarred from the construction of the road and it was an appalling sight—it had once been so beautiful. The Swiss had gone to great trouble to build rock retaining walls but on these steep hills the erosion would still be substantial. Were the Swiss, I wondered, proud of what they were doing to this countryside? The children in Kirantichap seemed reasonably well fed and well clad, but they kept asking for pens and books and chocolates. Not quite begging—just asking, but I didn't like it.

After two days we only had forty-five porters but decided to push on leaving two Sherpas to recruit the other fifty porters we needed and then follow along behind us. For two days we travelled steadily on, camping in a beautiful site at Kabre and a less attractive position near the small town of Those. Next morning we caught up with the tail end of the Russian Everest expedition, two Russians and sixty porters, and we travelled together with them for the next few days. They proved cheerful companions and we enjoyed their company.

From the Phaphlu hospital we headed up-valley taking the new high route above Beni. The whole beautiful Ringmo valley was scarred with a big new track and the steep hill down to Manedingma was heavily cut out with wide stretches of trees destroyed. Why, I kept asking myself—the old road was just as short—why this obsession with destruction? The United Nations were largely financing this work by contributing imported grain and cooking oil. Did they realise what they were doing?

In Manedingma we were met by a large group of the locals and the teachers, plus the local mayor, the *pradhan panch*. They led us into one of the classrooms and plied us with beer, *arak*, scarves and flowers. Then the expected petition arrived. They wanted assistance to build a small house for the four teachers. The headmaster was getting Rs 325 a month ($U.S. 25) and the other teachers Rs 280 a month ($U.S. 21). Manedingma was essentially a village of hotels and that's where the teachers had to stay, paying Rs 250 a month for food and lodging—and if their hotel was crowded with foreign trekkers, then the teachers just had to sleep outside or anywhere they could find.

The *pradhan panch* asked if we would pay Rs 5,000 towards teacher accommodation and then the village would pay a matching Rs 5,000. I was appalled at the situation of the teachers and agreed; we'd pay Rs 2,500 now and then the second Rs 2,500 when the job was finished. (A month later, in Khumjung, the headmaster arrived to see us. The building was completed with only the roof still to go on. Could they have their second Rs 2,500? I was happy to pay it out.)

All the way up the Dudh Kosi river the track had been 'improved' with terrible scars and long stretches of eroded soil to show for it. Maybe the walking was a little easier and maybe the scars would heal again but I didn't believe it was needed or worth it. And without the United Nations' help it would never have happened.

I asked my good friend Mingma what he thought of the situation in his mountainous world. "Some same, some changing—but we helping," he said philosophically. Maybe he was right—at least we were trying to help.

The construction of the high school at Khumjung was one of our better efforts. To conserve the limited sources of timber we decided to use it only in the roof structure. By aircraft and on porters' backs we carried in from Kathmandu ninety bags of cement weighing fifty kilos each. By the time they reached Khumjung each bag had cost $U.S. 60. We cemented the strong rock walls together; constructed wooden trusses to support the roof, and then nailed corrugated aluminium roofing into place. The final task was to concrete the floors, all done by hand and hard work indeed.

But we were proud of the finished high school. It was long-lasting, reasonably warm, well equipped with school desks, and all the timber was varnished or painted. As far as buildings were concerned, the educational future of Khumbu was assured.

6

Tibet

I HAVE KNOWN RICHARD BLUM for a number of years. At first it was largely through correspondence but later I met him in person in San Francisco. Dick was a successful merchant banker who for a long time had trekked in the Himalayas and had built up a considerable enthusiasm for and knowledge of the Sherpas and Tibetans. Dick established the American Himalayan Foundation and with the funds they raised they supported our Himalayan Trust activities, the Dalai Lama's projects in Dharamsala and many other worthy objectives.

In the spring of 1979 Dick accompanied the mayoral delegation of Dianne Feinstein to the People's Republic of China. Their objective was to sign a Friendship City relationship agreement between Shanghai and San Francisco but also to encourage trade and transport between China and the port of San Francisco. On the flight over one of the delegation who knew Dick's interest in the mountains and the Tibetan people suggested to him that if an opportunity presented itself he should ask permission for an American expedition to attempt an ascent of Everest through Tibet. Dick thought it a great idea but had little hope of success.

Tibet, and hence the north side of Everest, had been closed to the West since 1939 and for a number of years the mountain had been left in peace. In 1950 the borders of Nepal were opened and the southern approaches were reconnoitred and ultimately climbed by our expedition in 1953. It wasn't until 1960 that Chinese mountaineers reached the summit of Everest up the historic route from the north pioneered between the first and second world wars by climbers like Mallory and Irvine, Shipton and Tilman.

The San Francisco delegation arrived in Shanghai and somewhat to their surprise received a tumultuous welcome. The

Chinese had their schedule well laid out, the committees from the port, the airport, and the chamber of commerce had done their homework well, and they moved easily from one organised and productive meeting to the next. Dick decided that things were going so well that it was worth requesting a meeting with the Chinese Mountaineering Association. A few days later he found himself sitting on a green overstuffed chair in the offices of the Association and beside him was the vice-chairman, the famous climber Wang Fu-chou who had led the first successful Chinese assault on Mount Everest in 1960. When Dick very tentatively put forward his suggestion for an American expedition he was somewhat astonished when Wang Fu-chou said he would give the request "special consideration". It was agreed that Dick should write a letter and outline his plans as soon as he returned to America. The letter was duly sent and after some exchange of correspondence the agreement was approved: an American expedition would go to the Tibetan side of Everest in August 1981.

Within a few days of Dick receiving his permission I was with him in San Francisco (by then he was married to Dianne Feinstein). Dick suggested I should join the party, not as a hotshot climber – after all I would be sixty-two years old – but more in the capacity of Chairman Emeritus. My task would be to help with publicity and fund raising and maybe a little bit of advice. The temptation was too great – a chance to visit Tibet and its monasteries; and a journey into the remote Karma valley up to the foot of the East Face. I enthusiastically agreed. What did I care that the last few times I had been at high altitude I had been severely affected? This time I would be O.K.

It was the Karma valley and the Kangshung Glacier that really attracted me. The only previous expedition into the area had been led by Lieutenant-Colonel O. K. Howard-Bury in 1921 and included the renowned alpinist George H. Leigh Mallory who was later to lose his life on the mountain.

The 1921 reconnaissance team was a very competent party and carried out a most efficient examination of nearly every side of the formidable mountain. From the divide ridge with Nepal they looked up the Icefall into the Western Cwm (the way by which the mountain was ultimately climbed) but discarded it as a potential route due to its difficulty and danger.

A thorough examination was made up the Karma valley on the east side of Everest. Mallory describes this area with great enthusiasm:

> At the broad head of the Karma valley the two summits of Everest are enclosed between the north-east arête and the south-east arête bending around from the South Peak, below them is a basin of tumbled ice well marked by a number of moraines and receiving a series of tributaries pouring down between the buttresses which support the mountain faces in this immense cirque . . . But for me the most magnificent and sublime in mountain scenery can be made lovelier by some more tender touch; and that, too, is added here. When all is said about Chomolungma, the Goddess Mother of the World, I come back to the valley, the valley bed itself, the broad pastures where our tents lay, where the cattle grazed and where butter was made, the little stream we followed up to the valley head, wandering along its well-turfed banks under the high moraine, the few rare plants, saxifrages, gentians and primulas, so well watered there, and a soft, familiar blueness in the air which even here may charm us.
>
> We had already by this hour taken time to observe the great Eastern Face of Mount Everest, and more particularly the lower edge of the hanging glacier; it required but little further gazing to be convinced—to know that almost everywhere the rocks below must be exposed to ice falling from this glacier; that if, elsewhere, it might be possible to climb up, the performance would be too arduous, would take too much time and would lead to no convenient platform that, in short, other men, less wise, might attempt this way if they would, but, emphatically, it was not for us.

During our ascent of Everest in 1953 I spent several nights on the South Col at 26,000 feet. George Lowe and I crossed the South Col and looked down the East Face into the Karma valley. It was an immensely spectacular view—a tremendous iceface pouring down to the Kangshung Glacier in the valley floor, and then the broad sweep of the Karma valley lined by giant peaks— Lhotse, Makalu, and Chomo Lonzo. I felt a great urge some day to descend into this valley and see it close at hand for myself.

Now in 1981 my opportunity seemed to have come–twenty-eight years later.

Dick Blum was overall leader but he lacked technical climbing experience, so a climbing leader was needed. Lou Reichardt was chosen–he had extensive Himalayan experience and had reached the summit of the world's second highest mountain, K2, without oxygen. The other members of the team had a wide variety of experience–Himalayan climbing, Andean ascents, new routes in Alaska and a host of difficult routes in Yosemite and elsewhere. It was a team, it was hoped, that had the potential to succeed even on the unclimbed East Face of Everest. There was John Roskelley, perhaps America's leading Himalayan climber, Jim Morrissey, the American George Lowe (not to be confused with my old New Zealand climbing partner), Dan Reid, Chris Jones, Kim Momb, Gary Bocarde, Eric Perlman and a number of other formidable climbers. My main concern was that the team also included a number of members who were perhaps not of the same high calibre technically. Time alone would tell if they could meet this challenge.

At first, fund raising proved a little slow to develop. Then I joined the team in California for a concentrated two weeks of effort. We had fund-raising dinners and fund-raising cocktail parties; masses of lectures and calls on the executive officers of big corporations. Our support grew rapidly, the expedition was becoming well recognised, and from then on there was never any doubt that the necessary money would be raised.

There was one other item that worried me a little. In the participation agreement signed by all the members it stated, "Decisions during the actual expedition shall be made collectively with the guidance of the climbing leader in accordance with American mountaineering tradition and democratic procedures." I am a firm believer that all expedition members must be given the chance to express their views, but in the end a decision must be made by someone, and that someone must inevitably be the climbing leader. Democratic procedures are all very well but they don't always lead to firm decisions–and firm decisions would be needed if the expedition was to be successful. I mentioned this to Dick Blum but he felt that it would not be a problem and everything would work out well.

We flew to the city of Chengdu by way of Hong Kong and

Canton and were warmly welcomed by officials of the Chinese Mountaineering Association who introduced our Chinese liaison officer, Wang Fu-chou, and our interpreter, Tsao Hongjun. The evening was fully occupied with a sumptuous repast which included a wide variety of Chinese food and plenty of local booze—spirits (very strong), wine (rather pleasant), and beer (very adequate). For some reason I had not expected China to be so alcoholically inclined but there was certainly plenty available wherever we went. There were a number of important speeches and our Chinese host warmly welcomed me and complimented me on my first ascent of the mountain. "Although," he told us, "the way climbed by Sir Hillary was easier than the Chinese route up the north side." I had always been under the impression that the North Col route was probably the easiest approach on the mountain and smiled to myself at the chairman's confidence. We were all happy to stagger off to bed in the best of humour.

Early on the morning of August 15th we took off from Chengdu airport for Tibet. We were soon flying through mountainous country with many snow-clad peaks usually wreathed in heavy cloud. The valleys were barren and sparsely populated—much as we had expected Tibet to be—but the large number of glaciated peaks was something of a surprise. After a two-hour flight we dipped into a broad river valley and landed on a desolate airfield at 11,500 feet. A bus and several trucks were waiting for us and our gear and we all piled on board. We still had a hundred kilometres to go to reach Lhasa and a mighty bumpy two and a half hours it proved to be. It was an exciting moment when we emerged into the Lhasa valley and saw the beautiful Potala Palace thrusting up on its prominent mound.

The next few days were devoted to purchasing local food, sorting out equipment, and visits to the great monasteries of the area, in particular Drepung, Sera and the Potala. Drepung was probably typical of them all—a huge place that used to house 10,000 monks but now has only 180. The main temples were very large with superb *thankas* (religious paintings) hanging down the walls and many magnificent Buddhist statues. But somehow the place, although beautiful, seemed rather sad and depressing with many deserted and dilapidated buildings. We were interested to note quite a large number of Tibetan families wandering around bowing before the statues of the gods and pouring ghee into the hundreds of butter lamps. There were also quite a few photographs of the Dalai Lama in prominent positions and we were told that the Chinese had greatly liberalised regulations on religious activity over the previous couple of years.

The Potala, the headquarters of the Dalai Lamas, is a magnificent place, both inside and out. In days gone by it contained 300 monks but now only eight people look after the building. The rooms of the present living Dalai Lama are superbly beautiful, although he, of course, is not there; he now lives in India. The Potala is no longer an active religious centre but has become a museum, magnificently decorated but in other ways sad and empty.

All of us felt the effects of the sudden rise to 12,000 feet altitude—I more than most—but some of the vigorous climbing members ran several miles every day to help their fitness and acclimatisation. Like all expeditions we had our problems as well—thirty loads had been left behind in Chengdu and there was some delay in getting them flown in to Lhasa. Things were pretty chaotic for a while, which irritated some of the expedition members, although I found it fairly normal for this stage of a trip.

At eight p.m. on our second night in Lhasa we had the first of what I called our Democratic Leadership Discussions. Dick Blum was away on the telephone trying to get things organised, so Lou Reichardt gathered us all together and explained the general situation. The thirty boxes were missing. Mr. Wang and Andy Harvard would stay behind (as Andy had local experience) and they'd make sure the gear came in by air and then catch us up at Kharta or earlier. If the main group got to Kharta first, they'd have to wait there until Mr. Wang arrived as he was of prime importance in the recruiting of the yaks and drivers. Lou then went on to say that this was his plan, but did anyone else have any other ideas? They sure did! Many and general were the suggestions offered, mostly in very dramatic fashion. One of the more startling ones was that Dick Blum should stay behind and that Andy Harvard should go with the main group. I wondered what Dick's view would be about that. There were all sorts of suggestions about the team carrying their own loads on from Kharta, plus the twelve Tibetan porters without their gear. I couldn't quite understand the desperate drive to get going—most of us were still not acclimatised and the monsoon rains had certainly not finished.

Lou just listened somewhat dismayed and then said he would discuss the suggestions with Dick Blum.

The discussion raged on but then fortunately Dick returned full of enthusiasm—the boxes had been located at Chengdu. Mr. Wang had decided he would go to the airport in the morning with an empty truck and get the stuff then chase after us to Xigaze. The rest of us would all go on to Xigaze together. The lively discussion died away to a faint murmur. The first Democratic Leadership Discussion was over.

One of the great pleasures for me in Lhasa was to find that Sherpa Tenzing was there. Tenzing was welcoming the groups of tourists who seemed to arrive every second day. He still looked remarkably fit, despite his sixty-six years, and was unbelievably charming and thoughtful to the foreigners. He had already been in Lhasa for some months and was getting rather tired of it, but admitted that the finance was pretty helpful to his young family who were still attending school.

On Tuesday, August 18th, we loaded up our trucks and a bus left Lhasa at ten a.m., following first the Tsang Po river and then heading off into a side valley and climbing a fantastic switchback road. The hillsides were very steep, but lining the river were narrow terraces planted with barley and other crops. Up and up we went, passing a number of ruined and desolate old towers until we emerged on the summit of a pass at 15,700 feet just after midday. There were piles of rock and prayer flags to indicate the pass and a most fabulous view down the other side to a very large blue lake. We had lunch on the pass—boiled eggs, rather oily bread, mature roast duck and bottles of beer.

Soon we were winding down to the lake at 14,584 feet. It was very large and surrounded by low green hills, well clothed in grass. We passed a large herd of zums (a cross between the yak and the cow), and drove past a number of quite large fishing boats with bundles of nets on board. The lake was alive with birds—seagulls, birds diving for fish, crows, shags and many others I couldn't identify. We could look down into the beautifully clear water as we wound along the edge, passing many villages and areas of cultivation. At one village children were swimming in the lake, so we surmised that it couldn't be too cold. As we progressed towards the head of the lake many snow-clad mountains started rising up. After much discussion we came to the conclusion that the lake was called Yangzijung, although we suffered from the problem that our interpreter was Chinese and did not speak Tibetan, so we were never quite sure of local names.

At the head of the lake there were huge grassy flats with large numbers of horses, cows, pigs, sheep and goats. We entered a broad, flat valley with snowy mountains all around and there was quite a mixture of villages, some with new houses and tin roofs, largely Chinese occupied, and many Tibetan villages with battered old mud-and-rock houses.

The valley narrowed and steepened with a tumbling, swift-flowing river below. The peaks were very close now with heavy glaciation and sharp summits. Yaks grazed on the steep pastures and Tibetan tents were dotted here and there. Our vehicles had a variety of engine troubles which delayed our progress, but we reached the crest of the pass at 16,513 feet and made a narrow, steep descent into a broad, fertile plain with many big villages in the distance.

We entered an area where there had recently been severe rain. The river below was a foaming, dirty-brown torrent and we bumped over a succession of washed-out gulleys. We climbed up a wild, grim gorge with very steep and incredibly coloured walls and soon dropped down into a wide, fertile valley with the hills around getting lower and lower. We entered the large town of Gyantse with a huge, shattered monastery perched on top of a great rock—destroyed we surmised by the Chinese. The only major Buddhist relic remaining was a large and very beautiful *chorten*—regarded as one of the best religious shrines in all Tibet.

We drove on through an enormous area of arable land. The road was flat and much easier but extremely dusty. Our bus driver was like a Grand Prix driver, battling his way through the dust, passing heavily laden trucks in most forceful fashion. Most of us were wearing face masks and this helped a little but our eyes were soon bloodshot and our hair caked with dust. Soon after nine p.m. we reached our destination—Xigaze. It had been a remarkable drive through the centre of the continent but we were all thoroughly exhausted at the end of it.

We had a day to kill in Xigaze while Mr. Wang and the thirty boxes caught up with us. In the morning we met the twelve Tibetan porters who were coming with us to Base Camp. They were strong, heavy-featured young men and looked pretty tough—but at first sight did not perhaps have the same light-hearted cheerfulness of my old friends the Sherpas.

During the day we visited the Tashi Lumpo monastery which is the most active in Tibet, with 400 monks. This is the seat of the Panchen Lama who is next in status to the Dalai Lama. Instead of escaping out of Tibet with the Dalai Lama in 1959 he remained, came to terms with the Chinese and now lives in Peking. Possibly this is why Tashi Lumpo is still intact and full of statues, *thankas* and a multitude of paintings and religious books. At six we visited one of the meditation rooms where a large group of monks were chanting their prayers and drinking Tibetan tea. Then we moved into another room where more monks were beating drums, clashing cymbals, and blowing big trumpets. It made us realise how lively the monasteries must have been in the old days. As we returned to our modest hotel a loudspeaker was blaring out familiar Western songs in Chinese—including, of all things, 'Red River Valley'. Late in the evening Mr. Wang arrived with the final truck load of supplies and we were ready for action.

At eight thirty next morning we left Xigaze with four trucks, one bus and a Jeep. We drove through a rather dry, broad valley with low hills on either side and frequent washouts which made travelling very bumpy. By ten a.m. the valley was narrowing and an hour later we were climbing steadily upwards, bumping over wide gravel fans. There were dozens of washouts and it was slow going until we reached a high pass at 14,813 feet. The road plunged steeply down the other side, out on to a green flat and then into a broader valley which contained thousands of sheep in large flocks.

Soon after midday we reached a Chinese army base and had lunch there. The commander was a very agreeable person and most hospitable. We were given chairs in the dining-room and plenty of tea. Most of the soldiers were very young—not much over seventeen years old—and they all spent four years in this isolated posting. Nowhere in this large base did we see any sign of weapons.

We set off again up a steep, narrow valley, lined with high cliffs of schist. In mid-afternoon we reached 15,000 feet in a tight valley with many yaks and yak herders' tents. Then the bus overheated and we had to stop and refill with water from the mountain stream. Most of the expedition set off up the hill on foot and when the bus was mobile again we duly picked them up. We carried on through high mountain pastures, dotted with yaks, and then out on to a high plateau and the final pass at 17,069 feet. In the distance ahead were snow-covered peaks and it was a grand and lonely scene. We descended slowly over the high plateau and then more steeply down a beautiful valley beside a sparkling river. We arrived at our destination, Shigar, just after five p.m. It was a real Tibetan town at 14,355 feet and scores of people gathered around to greet us. The hotel was rather inadequate but as I was noticing the effects of altitude I was glad to crawl early into a firm bed.

When we left Shigar on the morning of August 20th our adventures really started. We had still one more day of vehicle travel to do but the road over the high pass to Kharta was so rough that our bus could not be used. We would all have to travel by truck. So our five trucks bumped their way down to the main bridge over the river, travelling west through the bleak Tibetan landscape for an hour before striking south up an enormous shingle fan. Our road was barely a potholed track which zigzagged backward and forward as we gained slow height, mostly in low gear. At first we passed patches of green barley, primitive villages, and a couple of dozen mules laden with juniper firewood. Then the terrain became barren and steep with only yaks grazing the thin grass.

As we gained altitude we had frequent engine trouble which caused some delay, but finally we laboured over the crest of the pass at nearly 17,000 feet. There ahead of us was Mount Everest, the summit shrouded in cloud but the lower glaciers clearly revealed. It was an exciting moment and cameras clicked and whirred.

The road ahead swept down along dry, desert-like ridges thousands of feet below. After a brief lunch we rolled off the crest and down we went in a crazy ride – rocking and swaying, bouncing over bumps, brakes jamming on as we screeched around tight corners. I found it a frightening experience. Expedition leader Dick Blum was in the truck in front of me and his driver just didn't complete one turn. He came to a shuddering halt with his front wheels on the edge of a mighty drop, and it was only with

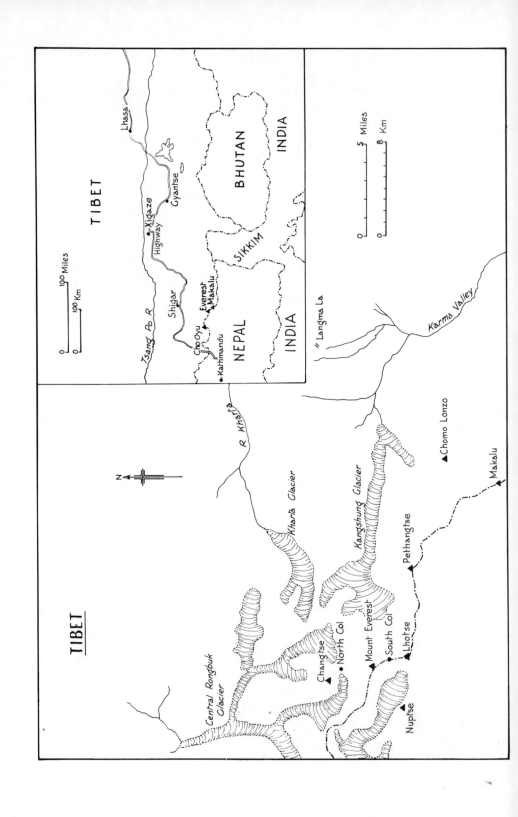

the greatest of difficulty that he was able to back off and make it around.

It was a great relief when we had completed the 4,000-foot descent and rolled out into a wide valley with green fields, many trees and a large village. Flowing down the middle of the valley was a broad stream, the Rongbuk Chhu. We turned down this valley and passed barley fields, trees, villages and the remnants of many monasteries.

Then we entered a spectacular gorge. It was an astonishing place, driving on a road jammed between the high cliffs and the raging river–the water sometimes lapping over the road. It was like being at the bottom of the Grand Canyon. After a couple of nervous hours of this, the gorge widened and we bumped across wide rocky flats or crept along a road carved out of the bluffs a couple of hundred feet above the river. At four thirty p.m. we branched to the right away from the Rongbuk Chhu and up the Kharta river. The change was fantastic, from barren gorge to a beautiful valley with foaming river and green pastures. Half an hour later we reached our destination, the village of Kharta, only a comfortable 12,474 feet altitude.

Everyone was tired and tempers rather frayed as we unloaded our five trucks. Huge piles of equipment were stacked beside the river and tents pitched in any possible spot. I noticed a rather astonishing optimism in expedition members for the action that would begin next day. Yaks, porters and expedition members would carry loads up-valley. The push would be on! I wondered about the sorting of gear, the issuing of equipment, the gathering of the yaks, the storing of the remaining gear. Next day the problem was solved for us–only seven of our promised fifty yaks turned up and a profitable day was devoted to the necessary preparations.

On Sunday, August 23rd, yaks started arriving quite early, not enough but sufficient to make a good start. It was a hectic scene, yaks snorting and twisting as their 130-pound loads were lashed into place. Jim Morrissey and I had our loads tied on a really wild creature. It buckjumped all over the place, throwing our loads to left and right. To my horror my precious duffel bag landed in the middle of a muddy pool.

Soon after noon Lou Reichardt led the main group off with thirty-seven yaks, leaving Dick Blum, George Lowe, Chris Jones and Mr. Wang to recruit the remaining animals. We followed a track beside the Kharta river and then branched to the left up a steep, rounded valley. Showers of rain came streaming down and the clouds were low on the hills. I was the last into camp. I came slowly around a great rock and there the camp lay—despite the drizzle it was a lovely scene. Many tents were pitched on the green grass beside beautiful Tsoa Lake at 15,260 feet, and the yaks were grazing peacefully on the hillside. There was an air of warm contentment—our expedition was really under way.

Over the next few days the monsoon was constantly with us in the form of heavy fog and drenching showers of rain. In poor visibility we crossed the 16,000-foot pass, the Shago La, and plunged down a rocky and vague track to the depths of a steep little river valley. We had a beautiful camp site beside a still clear section of the river amongst the forest at 13,200 feet. In one of the few spells of fine weather we saw that the stream was a tributary of the Karma river which flows down from the Kangshung Glacier and the East Face of Everest. The Karma Chhu then joins the Arun river and cuts through the Himalayan chain south into Nepal and finally into the Ganges and the Bay of Bengal.

Late on the evening of August 25th Dick Blum and his party joined us at Forest Camp with forty-two more yaks. It was very good to see them and know that we were all together again.

It rained heavily all night and next morning it was misty but showed signs of clearing as various groups moved off, climbed a muddy track through dense forest and after a thousand feet traversed along the steep north slopes above the Karma Chhu. We crossed a succession of grassy plateaux, traversed around the hillsides and descended to lake or stream-filled valleys. Out of the fog shrouding the cliffs on the south side of the Karma Chhu, a huge avalanche came rumbling down and shook the whole area. After five hours of particularly hard, rough walking we descended to a beautiful camp site in broad meadows and cooked our evening meal, a Mexican chilli soup with boiled potatoes and tuna fish. It was was very good indeed.

At seven fifteen next morning Jim Morrissey poked his head out of the tent door and yelled, "Take a look at that!" At the head of the valley were the mighty snow-covered shapes of Everest and Lhotse. What a fabulous sight! Our camp site was sunny and bubbling with excitement. And then Chomo Lonzo came clear, surely from this angle one of the most beautiful of all mountains. There was a greater air of jollity and cheerfulness than had been present at any time so far during the expedition.

Three pieces of timber spanned a milky torrent, then it was up-valley again, crossing dense juniper scrub and fast-flowing streams. After two and a half hours' travelling we reached the terminal face of the Kangshung Glacier with great sloping chunks of solid ice capped with small rock moraine. We climbed the steep and exposed scree slope to the north, the weather was fine and hot and it almost seemed as if the monsoon rains had concluded. Traversing down a narrow track above a steep slope covered with grass and shrubs, we descended into the lateral trough of the Kangshung Glacier, and after five hours' walking we reached yet another beautiful camp site at an altitude of 15,000 feet. This was a superb location with Chomo Lonzo towering up on the other side of the valley. The sun streamed into my tent and it was like a warm summer's day.

August 28th was foggy at first and, although we were hauled out of bed for an early breakfast, there was no sign of action from the porters and the yak men—so most of us returned to bed for a while. At ten a.m. the weather was much better and Chomo Lonzo, Lhotse and Everest appeared. People started moving off. It was a very long and arduous day. The tracks were not difficult but the gradual rise in height was decidedly tedious. It was seven hours before I staggered into Base Camp at 17,000 feet—perhaps one of the most spectacular Base Camps in the world. Our challenge was the mighty unclimbed East Face of Everest—and it lay straight in front of our door.

The face is a succession of great ice cliffs and deadly avalanche chutes and it certainly has little appeal to even the most enthusiastic of technical climbers. Just what odds is one prepared to take against destruction and death? But the expedition saw a potential route lying up the middle. Starting at the bottom (17,500 feet) was a rock buttress, reasonably safe we believed, which was split at 19,000 feet by a mushroom snow ridge, possibly giving a safe camp site. The rock buttress continued up to a steep and demanding ice flute between 19,700 and 20,500 feet. The line then followed a major ice buttress that rose to about 25,000 feet and was split from side to side by giant crevasses, some of which were clearly major obstacles. At the top of the buttress it is only a

thousand feet below the famed South Col, and a great ice field
stretches up to terminate below the South Summit and the final
summit of Everest. This ice field did not look easy–maybe a
traverse could be made to the traditional South-East Ridge at
27,000 feet? Perhaps straight to the South Summit at 28,700 feet?
It was almost inconceivable that a 'directissimo' could be carried
out immediately to the summit itself! There were certainly formidable challenges ahead.

I set up my little tent and had a very comfortable night. After
breakfast half a dozen of the party reconnoitred over towards the
foot of the buttress and found it hard going. They chose a site for
Advance Base Camp about half an hour back from the buttress
and numerous loads were carried across. A number of alternative
routes to the summit were examined but in the end it was agreed
that the only feasible way was up the left side of the rock buttress,
which seemed relatively safe from avalanches, although extremely
steep in places.

For several days I had suffered from headaches which didn't
seem to go away and on September 1st our physician Dr. Jim
Morrissey decided I must go down to a lower altitude. He
accompanied me a couple of thousand feet down to Yak Camp
and I certainly felt a little better there. It was pretty lonely at times
and the weather was appalling but most days one or two of the
expedition would come down to have a walk and a chat.

On the fifth day Mr. Wang and Mr. Tsao turned up and they
had a fresh leg of mutton with them which was a great treat. Mr.
Tsao proceeded with the limited supplies of condiments available
to cook a delicious meat dish–certainly the best food I'd had for a
couple of weeks. I felt much better, so on September 8th I
returned to Base Camp and it was very good to join the team and
get up-to-date on what they had been doing.

On September 2nd Chris Jones and David Breashears had
started on the buttress. After a steep introductory section they
made some progress up the right-hand side, seeking out the best
route for the subsequent ferrying of loads. Driving snow and rain
made the going difficult and after some four hours they secured
their retreat with fixed line some 400 feet up Everest–the team
was on the way.

Next day Dan Reid, Chris Jones and George Lowe regained
their high point in driving snow and poor visibility. The route

was pushed ahead over moderate ground and Dan and then Chris advanced on to a head wall that led to the snow mushrooms which were a key to the route. In driving snow they attached their rope to the high point and made a hasty retreat. They had gained about 1,200 feet in altitude—an excellent performance, although they still had more than 10,000 feet to go.

On September 4th George Lowe and Dan Reid, with Kim Momb in support, pushed the route up to the beginning of the mushroom ridge. By the time the top of the fixed ropes was reached the perpetual mid-morning snowstorm had begun. Several pitches up easy rock, made difficult by the driving sleet, led to the beginning of the lower mushroom ridge.

Dan Reid struggled up through the snow and immediately ran into difficulty with its depth and consistency. As he approached the corniced crest of the ridge he found himself sinking in the forty-five-degree slope up to his thighs. Chopping through the overhanging cornice required much time and effort. Finally he reduced the angle enough for him to belly-flop over the edge. On the other side snow conditions were just as bad and it was a full two hours before he arrived at a suitable but precarious belay point.

George Lowe attempted to continue along the exposed, wet and slippery edge but found the footing and avalanche danger to be unpredictable. Instead he headed up an iced runnel, quickly regaining the corniced crest. It was close to six p.m., still snowing, and they had at least an hour of descent on iced ropes ahead of them. He quickly dug down to solid ice, placed two ice screws for an anchoring point and then their retreat began. It was a formidable struggle before they safely reached the foot of the buttress.

On September 5th it was agreed that an early start would be made. George Lowe and Kim Momb were on the fixed ropes by eight a.m. with Dan Reid coming later in support, carrying extra rope and hardware. Enthusiasm prevailed as the weather appeared to be clearing. Their goal was to reach the next major obstacle—the upper head wall of the buttress. Contrary to the previous day, it was a pleasure ascending the fixed ropes. The sun peered through the clouds, exposing the alpine flora and spring flowers emerging from the lower mossy slopes. However, by the time the tops of the ropes were reached it had begun to snow again—an annoying and disappointing recurrence of the familiar daily pattern.

George Lowe set off to complete his lead of the previous day. He veered high, just off the crest of the ridge, to avoid avalanche danger but soon was floundering in miserable waist-deep snow and had to pound this down in order to make any sort of a track. He ended his lead at a large boulder and handed over the climbing to Kim Momb.

Kim led up a sixty-degree slope to the next horizontal section of the ridge, using an ice-axe in each hand and flailing his way along. He crawled on all fours along the ridge to displace his weight, hoping to prevent a crumbling of the corniced lip. Despite his great strength, he was cold and exhausted when he reached the end of the long lead and was only able to find a tenuous anchor point. By this time he was also beginning to have doubts about the possibility of load carrying along this ridge, which would be required in the future to attain the upper slopes of the mountain.

George Lowe followed along the rope and carried on into the lead. The wind had picked up and the snowstorm increased in intensity. Kim was suffering from hypothermia and handed over the rope belay to Dan Reid and then descended. After a marathon three-hour lead George Lowe reached a safe portion of the rock buttress and secured the rope. George retraced his steps quickly and rejoined Dan Reid within an astonishing ten minutes. Dan and George then rappelled down the rope in increasing storm.

During the next few days the monsoon snows intensified and the expedition was unable to return to the buttress. It was a period of frustration and disappointment. When I reached Base Camp again there was another Democratic Leadership Discussion. Some pretty ferocious avalanches had come down the face and some of the party had grave doubts about the route and thought the expedition should shift around to the easier north side. Others felt that another week or so would enable the snow conditions to consolidate and get safer. Nobody seemed able to make a firm decision and it was a period of great uncertainty and doubt.

Over the next four days the weather remained fairly miserable and although a small peak was climbed and a little work done on the buttress, the main activity was another Democratic Leadership

Discussion. I had been feeling pretty good and wandered around rather freely. Then, about midday on Sunday, September 13th, out of the blue I suddenly started vomiting. I lay on my bed all afternoon and suffered from strange hallucinations and considerable discomfort. Jim Morrissey did all he could for me but I had a terrible night with pressure on my chest, double vision and a completely mixed-up idea of where I was. Jim kept giving me oxygen but it didn't seem to make much difference. He was convinced I was suffering from my old complaint, cerebral oedema.

At daylight I crawled out of my tent and it was cold and clear. The mountains loomed up above me but I had no idea what they were. I couldn't speak clearly, I had a severe headache, and I was obviously in quite a mess. Jim was very concerned indeed and decided I must be got down to a lower level as quickly as possible. He asked me if I could walk and I was able to mumble, "Yes!"

Jim made rapid preparations, sorted out food and clothing into his rucksack for the two of us and organised five porters to come down after us. Then we walked slowly off for hour after hour until we reached Yak Camp (although I didn't recognise it). Jim had decided to take a more direct route to lower levels and we plunged down a huge rubble slope for what seemed thousands of feet. I was convinced we would soon meet a truck on the track and was terrified we would miss it, so kept driving on as hard as I could. Finally we descended down a small slippery stream and out on to a grassy patch beside a much larger river. It was raining and miserable but this was where we planned to meet our porters, so here we stopped. Soon the sun came out and I enjoyed the warmth and was feeling much better. I kept looking for the Tibetan porters but I was still seeing double so couldn't pick them out.

Down on the riverbed I noticed a movement—yes! there it was—the truck I had been expecting for hours. Gleefully I pointed it out to Jim. "That's not a truck, Ed. It's only a rock!" he patiently explained. "We're three days' walk from the nearest road." But I didn't believe him—I *knew* the truck was coming.

After a long time the five porters arrived and we headed off down-valley, following a narrow precipitous track high

above the Kangshung Glacier and the Karma river. I felt quite
unstable but knew we had to get down if I was to survive. My
double vision was receding and, although I still recognised
nothing around me, I knew we were losing altitude and that was
the main thing. At some stage John Roskelley joined us and we
followed a narrow zigzag track down an enormously long
shingle slide. Then we crossed a little pass out into a scrubby
basin filled with lakes and meadows and here we pitched our tent.
I still had a bad headache, but already my vision had cleared and I
could talk reasonably adequately. We were now below 14,000
feet.

Encouraged by my improvement, despite the long day, Jim
decided we would have a rest day in the same camp. I listened as
John Roskelley and Jim talked about the East Face of Everest–not
the difficulties but the danger. John had a record of fantastically
difficult climbs but he felt the East Face in its present condition
was an unjustifiable risk. It was hard not to agree with him.

On September 16th we moved on again. I still had constant
headaches and a tightness in my chest, but seemed to move
reasonably well. We climbed a long steep hill which I now
remembered from the journey in, then we diverted to the left up
a long traverse. After a tedious climb we entered a most beautiful
high valley with snow-tipped peaks all around and a sparkling
stream running down the middle. We climbed up the valley and
came to a beautiful blue lake with the remnants of an old
monastery beside it.

Camped here were two handsome Tibetan children, a boy and
a girl, with half a dozen yaks. They too were apparently crossing
the pass and willingly took some of the loads of our porters on to
their yaks. When Jim suggested that some of his load might also
be shared the porters just laughed and refused. Maybe it was our
lack of communication but those five Tibetan porters had not
endeared themselves to us.

The pass, the Langma La, rose steeply in front of us and on and
on we went. I was desperately tired and moving pretty slowly.
We'd reach one crest but there was always another one behind.
Finally we came to the top at 17,658 feet, so we'd climbed 4,000
feet that day. For quite a way we crossed in deep snow over a
series of summits and I noted how the Tibetan children almost
danced along in bare feet.

Then we started descending by a steep zigzagging track, first over snow, and then out on to rock and mud. We were funnelled down into a long steep rocky gully, very narrow with a small blue lake far down below. I heard a shout from above and looked up to see a horrifying sight. Charging down the gully with widespread horns and a tent dragging behind was one of the yaks. I looked desperately for somewhere to escape but there was nowhere. I shrank into the right-hand wall and the desperate yak rushed by, knocking me headfirst on to some boulders. Groggy, I clambered to my feet, glad that I was still alive. Then I felt something wet dripping down my neck – it was blood.

Jim rushed up to join me and anxiously examined my skull. There was a two-inch split with the bone clearly to be seen. "What next!" said Jim in despair. He had limited medical supplies but sat me down and went calmly and confidently to work – snipping off the hair, putting antibiotic in the wound, and plastering it up. The yaks were reloaded and we continued down. First around the lake, then a plunging descent of a long steep slope, and finally a long rocky traverse to a huge boulder which had obviously been a camp site before. We pitched our torn tent and scrambled inside.

About nine thirty p.m. we heard a noise outside. Another porter had arrived all the way from Base Camp – a fantastic day – and he had a bottle of Scotch whisky and some fresh potatoes from Mr. Wang, an extremely kind gesture from a very kind man.

I had a rather uncomfortable night but next morning I felt stronger and moved more energetically down the track. After an hour of walking I saw people approaching – it was two of our expedition hurrying in to join us and they had mail and messages. We talked for a while and we told them of the problems on the mountain and then saw them on their way. We carried on for hour after hour down into the Kharta valley and at last reached the village of Kharta and the end of the road. I have rarely been more pleased to arrive anywhere. But what was happening on the mountain?

With a gradual improvement in weather the team returned to the rock buttress on the East Face of Everest. George Lowe, Dan Reid and Chris Jones pushed the route up the buttress to within a few hundred feet of the top. Then they entered an area of almost vertical rock with a great deal of ice hanging down, which made the climbing not only difficult but extremely hazardous. There were many icicles in excess of twenty feet in length and weighing hundreds of pounds.

Before I had been forced to leave Base Camp John Roskelley, Kim Momb and Jim Morrissey climbed a 21,000-foot peak with a good view of the East Face, as they wanted to assess the difficulties of the upper slopes. While they were on top of this peak they were horrified to see an enormous avalanche break off the upper ice field and sweep down over a large proportion of the face—but fortunately the rock buttress was untouched. John and Kim, two of our most formidable climbers, decided that the dangers of the upper ice field were just too great and suggested that the party should transfer to the north side of the mountain. The majority of the party disagreed with this plan, so John and Kim decided to withdraw from the expedition.

The remaining members battled on, meeting considerable difficulties. On September 26th George Lowe and Dan Reid overcame the steep ice that barred the way to the top of the buttress and reached the gentler snow slopes above. "It's great up here," they radioed down, "a flat camp site and the best thing is you can walk out the tent door without being tied into the mountain." Following behind them Gary Bocarde and Eric Perlman reached their tent door by headlamp. They were all very excited as they were now established above the major technical difficulties.

But that night and the next day snow swirled into the mountain and all activity stopped. A tremendous avalanche swept down from above and along the right side of the buttress and piled snow twenty feet deep down on the Kangshung Glacier. Despite the weather, Gary Bocarde and Eric Perlman made a quick reconnaissance up ahead and at about 21,500 feet reported that there were five major crevasses, several of which would be difficult, and it could take up to two weeks to negotiate them—but it could be done, they felt. Their bad news was that the snow was still knee-deep. With cloud, wind and the new snow to contend with the party decided it would be wise to come down off the mountain next day.

Their decision on the weather and the descent proved to be the right one. The following day the storm moved in relentlessly, tearing down tents at Base Camp and dropping two feet of snow at Buttress Camp. It was a different storm from the earlier ones. The wind hammered in from the south and the temperature plummeted. At breakfast the next day Dan Reid poured water into his cup. When he picked it up a couple of minutes later the water was frozen.

They realised that they faced a new situation. The weather had improved but it was also much colder. Up high the new snow on top of the previous snow would only make conditions worse. Team morale was also at a low ebb. While some felt that the route was within their grasp others were pessimistic over the potential dangers of both the upper slope and the ropes leading up the head wall.

It was with a considerable sense of urgency that five people returned to Buttress Camp when the weather cleared. They knew they had to get back to their high point quickly and build up supplies on top of the buttress. They could only hope that the snow had hardened for, without this, all agreed that they had no chance of getting really high.

For two days they battled their way back up the buttress. Fresh snow had filled all the tracks and the camps and tents were buried in new snow. After a considerable struggle Sue Giller and George Lowe reoccupied the camp on top of the buttress and carried on for another look at the crevasses up ahead. Their heartening news was that the crevasses were simple to cross, but this had to be balanced by the fact that the snow was as bad as ever.

The next day was again clear as Reichardt and Reid hauled loads up the head wall and joined Giller and Lowe at the camp on top of the buttress. They moved on ahead for another look at the slopes above.

At the eight p.m. radio call Lou Reichardt confirmed that the crevasses were no real problem but that the snow was not improving, owing to the lack of freezing and thawing. A decision must be made today, he considered, and suggested there be another radio schedule at nine p.m.

Nine p.m. duly arrived and the radios were tuned in. "I think we should abort and call for the yaks," Lou's voice cracked over the radio. There was stunned silence in the cook tent at the

Buttress Camp. After the years of planning and the weeks of climbing, did it have to end this way? Yet when the hesitant voices from the other camps finally joined in over the radio they had to admit the logic of the decision. The first consideration was the dangerous condition of the snow slopes that led to the summit—the snow showed no signs of improving and there was still over 7,000 feet to go. No consolidation was taking place, so the climbers would be struggling through snow up to their knees, sometimes waists and, worse yet, the slopes would be prone to sudden and unpredictable avalanche.

The attempt on the East Face of Everest was clearly over. The expedition had suffered from many problems. Food had been poor and tentage and equipment barely adequate. We had too many people along, like myself, who were no longer strong climbers but had plenty to say. There was a lack of decision when decisions were badly needed. But there had been some good things too—the buttress, by far the hardest stretch of the East Face route, had been successfully overcome, despite appalling weather. It was conceivable that if better snow conditions could be obtained on the upper face then the mountain might be safely climbed. The East Face would never be easy, it would always be a gamble, but perhaps some day with the right men, the right weather and a bit of luck the summit of Everest could be reached.

Dick Blum and I travelled by Jeep and bus over the long road back to Lhasa. I was still experiencing headaches and slight difficulty in breathing and was eager to get to lower altitudes. After a reluctant wait of two days in Lhasa I caught a plane back to Chengdu and the thicker air at lower altitude felt superb. I flew on to Canton, anxious to return home, and found no scheduled flight to Hong Kong—only a charter flight leaving in half an hour. I purchased the last remaining seat, dashed out to the luggage terminal, draped my 120 pounds of gear around myself, and staggered back into the departure section. As a last gesture of kindness two Chinese policemen helped carry my luggage to the counter and ten minutes later I was boarding the plane for Hong Kong. For ten hours that night I flew south over the ocean and Australia to land in Auckland on a warm spring morning. For two weeks my head still troubled me but then the pain disappeared. The hair on my shaved scalp grew back into place and my split skull mended. It had been quite an experience, but now I was back to normal—overweight, slightly depressed, but still planning modest new adventures. But one thing was clear—Chairman Emeritus or not, my big mountain days were over.

In August 1983 an American expedition returned to the East Face of Everest. This time Jim Morrissey was expedition leader and seven members of our earlier party were the heart of a very strong team. Equipment and food were greatly improved and the weather much kinder. Taking some risk, Kim Momb climbed the old 300-foot vertical rope at the top of the buttress and the way was open to the upper slopes. In a superb *tour de force* six members of the party set foot on the summit of Everest. The East Face with all its dangers had been climbed—surely one of the finest efforts ever undertaken on the world's highest mountain.

7

Looking, looking!

FOR MORE THAN thirty years I had been visiting India, but much of my time had been spent in Calcutta dealing with the customs authorities or in New Delhi talking to Government officials. Our jet-boat expedition in 1977 gave me the opportunity to camp beside small villages in rural areas and to grasp something of Hindu religion and mythology. My many visits to the Himalayas had shown me the hill stations of India with their vibrant life and superb views. But always I had been busy, going somewhere, doing something, organising or planning, asking or persuading.

I mentioned this once to my good Sherpa friend Mingma Tsering whose journey up the Ganges had produced in him a deep affection for India (not by any means the universal reaction in Nepal). "Better some time you just go looking, looking!" he told me and I agreed. If the chance should arise I would see something of the wonders of India that I had missed—the Taj Mahal, the beaches of Goa, the Ajanta and Ellora caves, the red cities of Rajasthan, and the houseboats of Kashmir.

At the end of September 1982 I flew in to Bombay by Air India at four in the morning with virtually nothing official to do. But I planned plenty of looking, looking! Half-bemused with travel I chartered a small beaten-up taxi to take me shopping for a few items. The cheerful Sikh driver negotiated a ridiculous fee and he drove me from place to place even when all my needs had been satisfied. We even visited the Bombay seashore and he tried to persuade me to have a ride on a camel or a pony, tiny animals that would have shuddered under my solid weight. As he told me, if I didn't do many things his conscience would trouble him about the large sum I had agreed to pay him, although at no stage did he suggest that the charge might be reduced.

Mount Aspiring from the air. Peter's ski route was the North-West Ridge, running towards the photographer.

Peter making the first ski descent of Mount Aspiring, 1977.

Ama Dablam, a menacing profile.

Advance Base Camp at 17,500 feet on Ama Dablam.

The formidable East Face of Everest, a full 12,000 feet of technical climbing.

Avalanche on the East Face of Everest.

I arrived at the Bombay domestic airport in plenty of time for my flight to Dabolim in Goa but was quickly brought down to the firm Indian earth by the huge lines of passengers waiting to go through security checks. Apparently there had been a hijacking in Bombay only a week or so before and now hand searches were very thorough. Everyone's boarding ticket and carry-on-baggage ticket was stamped and scrutinised a multitude of times and it was difficult to see what useful purpose was being served. The plane left one and a half hours late but everybody, nearly all Indians apart from me, was exceptionally patient and long suffering. In forty-five minutes our Boeing 737 was sweeping down through damp post-monsoon clouds to land at Dabolim. For two hours my car drove me over narrow Goanese roads, crossing a short stretch of water on a crowded ferry, and finally bumping over a small hill and down to the luxurious Fort Aguada beach resort. It was thirty-three hours since I had left Sydney, Australia. My comfortable bedroom window looked out on the beautiful sweep of Calangute beach. I had rarely spent time in an expensive beach resort before and I decided I might get to like it. The gentle tossing of the surf lulled me quickly off to sleep.

The tiny state of Goa with less than a million inhabitants lies on the west coast of India nearly 400 miles south of Bombay. The Portuguese were the first Europeans to take over the area when Alfonso de Albuquerque landed in 1510. Goa became an enormously rich trading station and vast quantities of silk, spices and pearls were shipped back to Europe. With the administrators and soldiers came the Catholic priests and thirty years after Albuquerque there arrived the most famous figure in Goan history, St. Francis Xavier. Although St. Francis moved on to other lands, when he died his body was returned to Goa where it still remains. The Portuguese stayed in Goa for 451 years, until the Indians took over the country in 1961. My impression was of a particularly friendly and cheerful people with no noticeable disagreements between the Catholic and Hindu sections of the population.

I had never regarded India as the home of ancient Catholic cathedrals until I visited the old town of Goa. This almost deserted city, once a thriving metropolis, is largely subsiding into the jungle, although repairs are being carried out on most of the remaining churches.

The Bom Jesus Basilica towers up, its walls blackened by the damp tropical climate, but inside it is most impressive with the Basilica carved delicately in wood covered with brilliant gold leaf. In a side chapel is the huge marble tomb of St. Francis Xavier and on the top is the casket containing the saint himself with a corner cut away to reveal his head and shoulders. I do not enjoy looking at corpses, however ancient and holy they may be, but it was impossible not to admire the tomb with its fine bronze groups of figures on all four sides depicting important moments in the life of the saint.

The Sé Cathedral is an enormous structure, the largest Catholic cathedral in India, my guide informed me, and constructed in 1530. On either side of the main building were seven chapels, some were very elaborate and beautifully carved. Considering the age of the cathedral (450 years) and the local climate, the building was in a remarkably good state of preservation.

But of them all I think I preferred the St. Francis of Assisi Church and Convent. It was a beautiful building, handsome outside and superbly shaped within. In its prime it must have been a sight to behold. High above the main altar is the figure of Christ on the Cross with one arm draped around St. Francis in a warm and touching gesture.

To see such great .buildings in decline should, I felt, have created a feeling of sadness, but in a way they didn't. Efforts were being made to maintain them, the wide lawns were carefully mown, and small groups of nuns were walking briskly from one destination to another. The surrounding jungle had engulfed many churches but the main area of old Goa exuded an air of peace and tranquillity.

A walk along Calangute beach at low tide was a very pleasant experience. I enjoyed the golden sand, the high coconut palms and the lack of people and buildings. Perhaps the beach is no more beautiful than a hundred in Australia or New Zealand, but it has a character all of its own—crabs scuttling rapidly over the firm sand, jellyfish frying in the sun, myriads of delicate sea birds resting on sandbanks with the sea washing around their feet, and many half-buried fishing boats, signs of the great storms that sweep off the Arabian Sea. At one end of the beach the solid red walls of Fort Aguada push out into the bay, looking almost as strong as when they were constructed 450 years before. I noticed at high tide that the local inhabitants came in their dozens casting fishing lines from the fort terraces that centuries ago had mounted great cannon to protect the sea approaches to Goa. The mid-afternoon sun was a little hot for me, only the gentle sea breeze made life bearable. But for those who love the sun and the sea Calangute must take a lot of beating.

From Goa I travelled north to Aurangabad to see the remnants of a far more ancient civilisation.

I have always enjoyed ancient castles and forts. I can remember walking in the early morning around the old city walls of York and dreaming of the mighty battles and heroic efforts that occurred there. But I have seen few more dramatic forts than the one at Daultabad only fifteen kilometres from Aurangabad. As I approached the fort it loomed up into the sky on its 600-foot-high rock pinnacle and in every direction were massive rock walls enclosing a huge area. The entrance path twisted through several great iron-bound wooden doors covered with long spikes to make it very uncomfortable for elephants to push them down. On the wide sloping areas at the foot of the central fort were the remnants of ancient temples and buildings, including an absolutely colossal water storage tank (now empty) and rows of fortifica-tions. On the top of a high round bastion rested a large bronze gun—a monster nearly sixteen feet long—which must have been a formidable weapon against any attacker.

A few hundred yards further on I came to the moat which is at the base of the original citadel. It was forty feet deep and the rock walls above had been made smooth and unclimbable for 250 feet. There was only one narrow entrance over the moat (once a drawbridge) and steep stairs led up the side of the citadel to an eerie underground passage 150 feet long hewn out of the rock. At the top end of the passage a final obstacle was created by a great iron brazier. When fire was lit in the brazier the immense heat was sucked down into the passage by underground outlets and this made it most unpleasant for any invader trying to force a way upwards.

Close to the top of the citadel I was told was a water reservoir fed by a small natural spring and no doubt a considerable advantage to the defenders. From high up the view down the great smooth walls was incredibly impressive and it was difficult to imagine this citadel ever being stormed and overcome as it had been on a number of occasions – but mostly by cunning and stealth.

The tourist guides all give the same story. The history of Daultabad goes back to the twelfth century when it was called Deogiri, the Hill of the Gods. The actual fortress of Deogiri was constructed by Raja Bhillamraj, of the Hindu Yadav Dynasty, who had been a great general in his day. The 'Hill' was the site of the rock-hewn citadel which was understandably regarded as being invulnerable. But somehow, maybe by siege or by treachery, Deogiri yielded to enemy assault and became a possession of the Sultans of Delhi in 1308.

Thirty years later, Deogiri attained a brief period of glory as India's capital. Muhammed Tughlak ascended the Delhi throne and ordered his capital to be moved 700 miles to the southern city which he renamed Daultabad, the City of Fortune. It must have been a desperate journey for the people of Delhi and thousands died in the process. But it was all wasted effort – the Sultan regretted his decision and repenting his act of madness, ordered the whole mass of migrants to move back to the abandoned Delhi.

Despite this, Daultabad grew to be a great city and the province to which it belonged broke away from the rule of Delhi. The old citadel became too small to hold all its people and fortifications were extended well out on to the sloping plains. Great battlements laden with cannon guarded every approach.

Daultabad is still a remarkable sight. Its people have gone and so too have many of the buildings, but it is easy to visualise what it must have been, a fortress of immense power and strength, throbbing with life and vitality.

Next morning, October 4th 1982, the *Times of India* had a story about Peter who was attempting the ascent of Lhotse, the world's fourth highest mountain. Peter and his team were planning to climb alpine-style – without using oxygen and without the help of high-altitude Sherpa porters.

A four-man New Zealand expedition trying to climb Mount Lhotse, sister peak of Mount Everest, set up its fourth high-altitude camp on Friday at 7,750 metres.

Led by Mr. Peter Edmund Hillary, of Auckland, twenty-seven-year-old son of Sir Edmund Hillary, the first man ever to scale Mount Everest, the team will pitch one more camp before launching its final assault on the 8,420-metre mountain.

Far from the mountains I carried on with my examination of the historical wonders of India. How can one adequately describe the Ajanta and Ellora caves? Dozens of superb temples carved out of the living rock, some of them more than 2,000 years old.

The Ajanta caves were one of the first of the excavated cave temples. There are in all some thirty excavations whose dates range from the second century B.C. to the seventh century A.D. How this work could be continuously carried out over a period of 900 years is hard to comprehend. The early temples were simple in structure but superbly balanced, while the later temples were far more decorative with much carving, many fine statues of the Buddha and magnificent painted walls. The amount of solid rock that had to be excavated was unbelievable—one estimate was three million cubic metres—and the devotion of the Buddhist monks to the task for centuries is difficult to contemplate. In Cave 26 on the left side of the wall, starting from the left door, is the huge figure of Buddha, reclining on a couch on the verge of death. Below him are seen the wailing disciples and above the rejoicing heavenly beings waiting to have the Lord amidst them. But the face of the Buddha is magnificently calm and serene.

In Cave 1 the sanctum contains the seated figure of the Buddha, and his attendants are carved in high relief. One of the staff in the cave had a powerful electric light and he demonstrated how, when the light was shone from the front of the Buddha, his face was calm and tranquil; when the light shone from the right the Buddha's face showed a delightful, almost impish, smile; from the left the face was serious and formidable.

The Ellora caves were later in construction, ranging from A.D. 600 to 1,000 and celebrated not only Buddhism but Hinduism and Jainism as well. I will always remember Cave 10 of the Buddhist group. The statue of the Buddha was deep within the back of the dark cave but with the use of reflectors a bright ray of sunlight had been projected into the depths. The great Buddha with his calm, sweet expression was clearly outlined and the impact was tremendous. It was hard to believe that he had been sitting there in the darkness for 1,100 years.

The main Hindu temple, the Kailasa, is huge, elaborate and enormously impressive. The delicate detail must have taken vast patience and great skill. And it took 150 years to build—how could the original plan be so effectively maintained over six generations? There is so much to see in the Ajanta and Ellora caves, so much superb carving and beautiful painting. But the great figures of the Buddha with their supreme calmness and serenity are the things I will most remember.

From the superb and ancient caves of Ajanta and Ellora I moved to Jaipur and a more recent era. In 1526 Babur the Mogul, descendant of the renowned Mongol conquerors Timur and Genghis Khan, defeated the Afghan Sultan of Delhi and declared himself Emperor of India. But this redoubtable position was not easily established—for thirty years the Moguls and the Afghans fought each other and it was only in 1560 that Akbar, Babur's grandson, was able effectively to claim a firm authority over the Gangetic valley.

I had already learned a good deal about Akbar and he was clearly an emperor of outstanding ability and knowledge. Instead of crushing the Hindus, as his predecessors had done, he sought to unite them with the Moslems. His two immediate successors, Jahangir and Shajahan, carried on his policy very successfully and it wasn't until Emperor Aurangzeb that the Mogul empire began to decline. Certainly the century and a half (from 1560 to 1707) when the great Moguls ruled from Agra and Delhi was a time of greatness in India and one of the most notable periods for art and architecture in the country's history.

Jaipur was only established in 1727 but up on the high ridge behind the city was Amber—the capital of Rajasthan during the six previous centuries. The Amber Palace, built in the seventeenth century and greatly influenced by Mogul architecture, was a huge and beautiful structure, although now only filled with tourists. The vast and complicated building has much fine marble inlay work, a shimmering hall of mirrors, and a superb view down to the lake below.

The Hindu Rajputs who had ruled the various states in Rajputan for many centuries were notable warriors in constant conflict between themselves and the other parts of India. But the Kachhawas of Amber formed a happy relationship with the Mogul Emperor, Akbar, and he used the services of many of their able military commanders and some of their diplomats who were among the most astute in medieval India. In return they had little fear of being attacked. The ancient twelfth-century forts at Amber, although now in ruins, looked formidable defensive positions but the Amber Palace itself, despite the high and strong walls surrounding it on the neighbouring hilltops, did not appear as a particularly difficult military objective. The palace must certainly have been a beautiful home in which some thousands of people had lived in considerable comfort and safety.

The general manager of the Mansingh Hotel where I was staying invited a number of the local dignitaries to a cocktail party in my honour. We sat in the coolness of the terrace on the sixth floor of the hotel, the highest building in Jaipur, while lightning flashed over the hills. Her Royal Highness the Maharani of Jaipur was present with her youngest son and she proved to be a charming and beautiful lady. I was impressed with the cheerful nature of the conversation as the guests reminisced about the days gone by. All of them had travelled extensively throughout the world but they whole-heartedly agreed that Jaipur had a friendliness that was unique in their experience. By the end of the evening I was inclined to agree with them.

This does not mean that Jaipur is a Shangri-la. It is a big city with crowded streets and hordes of bicycles. I have rarely before encountered so many beggars asking for alms, touts trying to persuade me to visit particular emporiums, or taxis and trishaws desperately wanting me to travel somewhere. But atmosphere Jaipur certainly has and, despite its population of over one million, you feel very close to the deserts of Rajasthan.

I drove from Jaipur up over the pass at the Amber Palace and then along the fast road to Delhi—only 260 kilometres away. It was a most colourful journey. The women of Rajasthan wore notably bright dresses of red, green, blue and yellow and there were multitudes of huge camels dragging carts piled high with firewood, dried grass and broken rock. This was the main road from Bombay to Delhi and it was crowded with heavily laden trucks. In four hours I saw at least a dozen trucks that had been involved in accidents—some had crashed head on, others had run off the road, and some had toppled over on their backs. My Sikh driver was always calm and competent. He nodded his head in wonder at each new incident. "Too sleepy and too much drinking," he told me.

I had two days in the great city of Delhi and then drove towards Agra. I could hardly believe that after thirty-one years of visiting India I was going to see the Taj Mahal for the first time. Six miles north of Agra I reached Sikandra and now I was really in Mogul country. Here was the tomb of Akbar the Great, a huge enclosed area with a superb entrance gateway and a long pathway leading up to the massive low mausoleum. For two days I revelled in Mogul history. The Agra fort is enormously impressive with huge red sandstone double walls built by Emperor Akbar and a number of magnificent buildings. Everyone will undoubtedly have his own opinion but of all the buildings in the Red Fort at Agra I found the Hall of Public Audience the most impressive, its handsome white marble magnificently carved and the dramatic throne room built by Shahjahan superbly beautiful.

Twenty-five miles out of Agra was the ghost capital of Fatehpur Sikri—a dream in red sandstone. The story is told that Akbar was desperate because he had no son. He visited a Moslem holy man, Shaikh Salim Christi. The holy man blessed Akbar and in due course, to his joy, his wife produced a son, later to become Emperor Jahangir. Akbar was incredibly grateful to the Shaikh and in 1569 moved his capital to the village, Fatehpur Sikri. I wandered through the great empty city, visiting enormous public rooms and delightful private homes. I climbed up and down hundreds of steps, looking from high terraces down over the wide sweep of fertile plains below. In 1584, only fourteen years after moving into the great city, Akbar moved out again, the reason given being a major shortage of water. So for 400 years Fatehpur Sikri has dreamed on, abandoned and empty, but magnificently beautiful.

And finally there was the Taj Mahal—certainly the most graceful building I have ever seen. I visited it three times and enjoyed it most in the early morning when it was warmed by the rising sun and there were few people around. The story is known to everyone: Shahjahan's much loved wife, Mumtaz Mahal, died in her fourteenth childbirth and Shahjahan resolved to build a memorial to her memory. It took twenty-two years with 20,000 people working on the task continuously. But the result is exquisitely beautiful, certainly one of the great architectural wonders of the world.

I went away from Agra immensely impressed with the creative genius of the Moguls and the craftsmen they had employed. The great buildings around Agra and indeed the Taj Mahal itself are worthy of a visit from the ends of the earth.

I had been watching the newspapers closely for news of Peter's expedition. Finally in the London *Daily Telegraph* I learned:

Hillary Son's Climb Fails.

Four men buffeted by strong winds and snow, abandoned their attempt to scale the 27,890-foot Mount Lhotse in the Himalayas after climbing to within 980 feet of its summit, Nepal's Ministry of Tourism said yesterday.

The team was led by Peter Edmund Hillary, twenty-seven-year-old son of Sir Edmund Hillary, who climbed Everest in 1953.

I felt sorry for Peter and knew how disappointed he must be. It would have been good for him to have claimed his first 8,000-metre peak. Still, they had done extremely well. Without oxygen and carrying all their own loads of equipment, they had reached 27,000 feet in the difficult post-monsoon period. They had a good deal to be proud of.

I flew on to Srinagar in Kashmir and revelled in the cool fresh atmosphere. Living in the considerable comfort of a large houseboat moored at the edge of the lake, I explored this delightful valley. The Mogul Emperors had been here too and I strolled happily through three of their gorgeous gardens more than 300 years old. There was early snow on the 9,000-foot hills to the south and I snuggled comfortably into my warm bed in the chill night air.

I was driven to the ski resort at Gulmarg, first across the fertile plains where rice was being harvested and the straight road was lined with tall poplars yellowing in the approaching winter. The road climbed steeply upwards through magnificent pine forests and the vale of Kashmir shrank away below. At 8,700 feet the resort of Gulmarg looked, alas, a little shabby, like all ski resorts in the summertime, but it was fringed with snow-capped mountains and beautiful pine forests. I climbed up a few hundred feet for a sight of the great Nanga Parbat but cloud covered the distant view.

With a small group of friends I carried out a new type of trekking—water trekking. We had two *shikaras*, which were a bit like gondolas, and our team of paddlers, boss, cook and customers made a total of ten in all. We boarded our craft on the narrow swift-flowing Sind river and made a great pace down between the high banks lined with deep layers of yellowing willow trees.

At lunch-time we pulled into the bank and in a matter of seconds a table was erected, chairs assembled and food laid out—hot mutton stew, bread and cool beer. It was very luxurious travelling.

We carried on down the Sind river and then joined the much larger Jhelum, floating effortlessly along on its broad bosom. We planned to spend our first night at Manasbal Lake which is joined to the Jhelum by a narrow canal. The boats had to be dragged through the shallows into deeper water and then we paddled and poled our way up the narrow stream through villages and rice fields. Sometimes we grounded on gravel banks but finally emerged into Manasbal Lake, a sheet of glassy water, still and beautiful in the setting sun.

Half-way down the lake we paddled to shore beside an ancient garden with a magnificent chinar tree and impressive Mogul ruins. There were grassy terraces for camping and an air of great tranquillity. In moments, it seemed, tents were erected, tables and chairs assembled again and a delicious meal placed before us. Everything was quiet as we drifted peacefully off to sleep.

All next day we paddled down the broad Jhelum, passing many villages and periodically walking along the smooth banks. As we glided along, the pressure stove in one of the boats was soon in action and we lounged in great comfort, sipping the delicate Kashmiri tea and eating delicious fruit cake. In mid-afternoon the river divided a number of times and we raced down one of the swift flowing channels. Fish were jumping everywhere and masses of kingfishers were diving into the water. We emerged into an open area, free of trees, and ahead of us we could see the broad sweep of Wullar Lake. We pulled into the bank and pitched our camp on a wide grassy plain that clearly had been under water not too many weeks before. Our Kashmiri team had the tents up and the dinner cooking in no time at all—they were very expert.

A cool autumn breeze drifted over the wide flats and we were happy to eat in the protection of a large dining tent.

Next morning was cloudy and cool. One boat would remain behind, it was decided, while the other with nine on board would cross Wullar Lake. There was little warmth in the sun as we climbed on the boat and we pampered passengers huddled under warm rugs. We raced down the fast-flowing channel into the lake and grounded frequently as the water shallowed. Then we reached open water and our four paddlers had us moving along at a fine pace. Our cook was perched comfortably in the middle of the boat surrounded by his pressure stove, utensils and food. Soon he was supplying us with a substantial breakfast—cornflakes and milk, boiled eggs, toast and marmalade and hot coffee.

Wullar is a very large lake and in every direction there were numbers of fishermen, some using spears and others casting a wide variety of nets. Small fish were jumping everywhere, especially when we passed through wide patches of floating weed. For hour after hour we paddled on and slowly the distant end of the lake came closer. Cows appeared on the banks and houses loomed up amongst the trees. At eleven a.m. we pulled ashore at the end of our journey. Three days had been just enough. We had enjoyed the beauty and the comfort, but as passengers we were never asked to meet any of the problems—and even in camping a sense of personal challenge adds spice to life.

I had enjoyed Kashmir. The town of Srinagar is jumbled and untidy but the countryside is beautiful, the people friendly and smiling, the mountains abrupt and there are lakes and streams everywhere. Some day I would like to do a trek through the mountains and steep pine forests.

I flew in to Kathmandu and there to meet me at the airport was Peter, looking lean and fit after his expedition to Lhotse. It had all been great fun, he told me. They'd reached 27,000 feet and only the weather had stopped them getting to the top. I envied him his enthusiasm and pleasure. I, too, used to feel like that I told myself wistfully—but now those days were gone.

TWO

Peter Hillary

8

The family

I WAS THE OLDEST. Sarah was only eighteen months younger than me and Belinda was four years my junior. Like most inhabitants of the 'new world' my family tree had two brief stems and then a sea of separation, from our origins in Europe. We were the sixth generation to live on our land in Auckland and so, I suppose, I have learned to feel a sense of antipodean ancestry.

My memories of early Hillary family life are very happy ones. There were periods when Dad, and sometimes my mother also, were away from home on expeditions but these served to draw us together all the more when we were reunited. The best part of two decades of family activities and adventures more than compensated for those times when we could not be together. Even now with plenty of my own experiences to look back on, they were amongst my happiest times.

Being the oldest child isn't easy (as any oldest child will testify). It's as if you are a test-piece for your parents, doting and loving as they may be. With all their new-found experience, which you have provided them, their efforts with the second of their offspring will be eminently more successful and with the third child the result will be ineffable. It all seems a gross injustice. Of course you are told time and again not to be rough, you are twice the size of your sisters. "It's not fair," you reason, however obvious these truths may be. But then being the oldest has its advantages too. You can observe the turbulent progress of your fellow siblings through the ghastly ages of two and five and nine and eleven and, worst of all, fifteen, after you yourself have already been through them. You feel able to offer advice. However, if you have a demonstrative sister of similar age, as I do, you rapidly learn that you are better off keeping this invaluable experience to yourself.

Our family holidays were our most memorable times together for me. I loved the excitement of anticipation and the moment of departure generally proved so euphoric that it's a wonder the adventures themselves retained any significance! The alarm going off during the darkness of early morning and the whole family climbing into the car and driving down the dimly lit Great South Road. We would drive for several hours to Lake Taupo and for several more to Wellington to board the Cook Strait ferry.

The long car journeys were not just 'a little tiring but magnificently scenic' as they were for adults. For us they were an agonising infinity of 'Are we there yet?' and 'I want to go to the toilet' and pleading with Mum and Dad to stop at the next Tip Top ice-cream shop. The South Island of New Zealand was an interminable distance from home it seemed and it made the arrival at our destination all the more marvellous. We were the classic family on holiday. Dad at the wheel whistling 'Home on the Range' as we barrelled along at sixty mph, Mum with the road map in her lap and passing fruit and biscuits over to the rumpus in the back seat. As it was a station-wagon for most of these journeys, we often travelled with the back seat rolled forward and the three of us would be sprawled out with a variety of play things to keep us occupied. The crossings to the South Island enthralled me. Watching our car being lifted by a crane on board the ship, the deep sounding horn as we pulled out of the dock and the swells of the open sea. I revelled in the drama of the departures and looked forward impatiently to our arrival in the South Island.

Ever since I can remember I've had a deep-rooted love for the South. I've travelled about its beautiful countryside at various stages throughout my life and to this day I know more about the South than I do the North Island. I suspect it is its small and widely dispersed population, the intrigue of its not-so-distant history, the high passes over which the roads wind, the huge glaciated mountains and the lonely beauty of the South which fascinated me as a child, and that love has never left me.

Our South Island travels were always very much outdoor affairs. We would pitch our tents along the roadside at night and drive on the next day, be it to Nelson Lakes, the West Coast, the Mackenzie Country or to Otago. We would set up our family Base Camp in some scenic location and from there we conducted a series of sidetrips. One of the areas we visited frequently was Lake Wanaka and it's in that area that we, as a family, had some of our most enjoyable adventures together. With our tents pitched among a stand of poplar trees and an open fire over which to cook, we spent several weeks together in this region for many consecutive years. There were wild gooseberries to pick, picnics by the lake shore when we would build driftwood rafts and search the water's edge for pretty pebbles; one year we rafted many of the local rivers, screeching with excitement as we splashed through the rapids and later I became interested in ornithology and, with my mother's old Box-Brownie camera in hand, conducted my own bird-watching expeditions. Then there were the family hikes. There are mountains scattered all around Lake Wanaka and over the years we scrambled up many of their golden, tussock-grass-covered flanks to their rock-strewn summits. These wonderful vantage points (usually they were in the vicinity of 5,000 feet in height) allowed us to look deep into the Southern Alps to where the great peaks and brilliant white glaciers flowed. We could see the many inlets and bays around the lake shores and we could often make out our camp site far, far below. I always found these climbs most exhilarating; I loved the rushing winds, the vistas, the challenge of the ascent, but most of all the isolation, the knowledge that few others ever went to that particular spot. To me the descents were more a return to the hustle and bustle of humanity than they were the simplistic act of losing height.

Most years we visited the Matukituki valley and our friends the Aspinal family, who lived on a remote homestead in the upper reaches of the valley. The drive to the road end took about one hour from Wanaka and the mountains converged upon the road the further we drove along it. Delicate waterfalls sprayed down the bluffs to the valley floor, and far above the treeline snow fields on the mountain tops glistened in the sunlight. At an old barn there was a telephone—one of the old type with a winder handle on the side—with which we could call the homestead on the eastern side of the braided Matukituki river. Half an hour later (or what felt like an eternity to the three young Hillarys), we would see a tractor with a trailer on behind come chugging across the river-flats, driving through the water courses with water foaming up around the axles and sending clouds of steam off the engine. The two youngest Aspinal children were our ages and we became good friends and all looked forward to our riverside get-togethers each year. The tractor-ride back across the river was always a joy to us young ones. The trailer bounced along over the river boulders vaulting us into the air as we huddled on the rough-sawn wooden surface, while several sheep-dogs accompanied the tractor's journey, running along behind, barking and sprinting from side to side. The air was cold and invigorating and I remember watching the puffs of condensed breath blast from the dogs' muzzles as they loped along. I savoured the scent of hay that lay scattered on the trailer top and delighted in the clear, fast-flowing water of the river, the relentless, transparent flow that gushed over the front wheels of the tractor and which the large tread of the rear wheels scattered into the air.

Across on the other side the methodical chug of the tractor would speed up, mud flying from its tracks as it wound its way across the river-flats past herds of cattle; occasionally we would surprise a pair of paradise ducks who would fly noisily off to a more private spot. Beech forests stretched up the mountainsides from the green river-flats and the tussock reached even higher to the screes and rock ridges that led to the snow fields and the remote summits. It was a magnificent environment and I loved it.

The homestead nestled on one side of the valley in a wind-break of beech trees and exotics. Tea and hot scones would appear on the table as we entered the house and, while our parents chatted, we listened, wide-eyed, to the stories the Aspinal kids told us of huge herds of red deer roaming the mountainsides, the wild characters who hunted them for a living and who visited the homestead from time to time and how the tractor got stuck in the river not so long ago and all about the last major snow storm they had had. Before long we would adjourn our chatter in favour of the hay shed. There was just so much fun to be had in that shed amid the smell of sheep with the odd skin hanging up to dry. There were tools racked above a bench and across several sheep-pen enclosures was a great pile of hay bales. We would climb them, hide among them, make forts out of them and run and jump all over them.

Whether we stayed one day or two days, our time at the homestead was always too short and I looked forward to returning at the first opportunity. It's amusing how your appreciation of time changes as you grow older. Although time passes quickly, regardless of your age, when you are enjoying yourself I thought our six-week-long summer vacations were almost a year in length, so much did we do and see in that time.

In 1964 Dad brought his Sherpa sirdar (foreman), Mingma Tsering, back to New Zealand for a holiday. The concept of a holiday was well and truly beyond Mingma, a man who is at his happiest when busy working. Wherever he went in New Zealand he continually found things to do, whether it was mowing lawns or collecting useful pieces of farm equipment for his home at 13,000 feet in Nepal. It was during Mingma's visit that Dad decided it would be a good opportunity for us to attempt to climb a large snow peak called Mount Fog in the Matukituki valley. We had often talked of scaling this mountain, as it stands out clearly when you look across Lake Wanaka to the west. I was about ten years old at the time and Dad decided that he and Mingma would take me with them. I was so excited at the prospects of this special adventure I felt I could hardly wait to get under way.

The whole family drove up the valley to an old corrugated-iron musterer's hut where we stopped and had an early evening meal. We bade farewell to Mum, Sarah and Belinda and the three of us headed off up the mountainside. We must have looked a sight—one very large man in front, a small boy and the short, squat figure of Mingma behind. Following a sheep track, we made our way up the bracken-covered flanks of the valley to the tussocks where we scrambled on, paralleling a deep ravine that cut into the face. In the soft evening light we found a small shelf on which we erected a nylon tarpaulin and nestled down in our sleeping-bags amongst the alpine grasses. I remember I felt thirsty. Dad found our water supply was finished and it was too dark to collect more from the ravine, so he rummaged around in his pack and produced one of two precious cans of beer. Nowadays I would be delighted to have beer as a substitute for water in such a place but for me at the age of ten beer was a nasty taste you drank under sufferance. We all had a sip to quench our thirsts before lolling off to sleep. Early the next morning we climbed up above the tussock line and on to a ridge which we traversed until we reached a large snow face. It was this snow face that we had seen from Lake Wanaka on our previous excursions. We planned to make an ascending traverse of the face to just below the summit, which was a steep pile of loose rock. I was all togged up with dark glasses and someone's oversized leather boots and woolly mittens. I really felt the part. But walking upon an inclined snow surface was new to me and I spent much of my time suspended on the rope between Dad and Mingma, kicking and scratching to find purchase on the snow. With frustrating ease they would drag me up the slope and back into their steps. Eventually we reached the base of the rocky summit pyramid. It wasn't difficult, but the risk of falling rocks was high and Dad was concerned it would be dangerous for me. We began skirting around its base looking for an alternative.

It was all thoroughly exciting this climbing business, I decided. Kea birds (large alpine parrots) flew around making their raucous cry, the valleys swept away below us and I could see lakes and roads and even Wanaka township in the distance. That day the sky was a special blue and everything was wonderful.

We couldn't find a way to the summit that Dad thought would be suitable for me so, a little disappointed, I was guided back across the snow face to the ridge. In the evening light we descended through the bracken to the old musterers' hut where Mum and the two girls awaited us. I was very tired but the pleasure of that day has remained with me.

Hillary family adventures covered the spectrum of outdoor activities, from New Zealand's coastline where we swam, snorkelled and fished, to the mountains of the Himalayas where we trekked, climbing over high passes, and lived in the tiny hamlets on Nepal's border with Tibet. Our visits to Asia were important parts of my early life and education, where I learned of the inequalities that exist in the world and saw how destitute much of the world's population is and yet realised that there is still happiness there, an energy for survival and a love of life. I found that the hill country people enjoyed a certain quality of life, although on a standard of living index they were amongst the poorest people on earth. If nothing else, they had fresh air and water. Our Asian excursions exposed for me many of the commonly held fallacies in Western society, preconceived ideas regarding race and colour and language and philosophy and nationality. I learned that there were other ways of conceptualising things and, whereas other civilisations had weathered the millennia, the West's self-proclaimed successes had, thus far, only made a brief debut in history. Our family developed friendships with many people in the Himalayas which was a marvellous opportunity for fitting in to the communities and developing a range of relationships right down through the scale of our young family.

The Himalayas never fail to earn new enthusiasts for their dramatic alpine beauty, hillsides covered with flowering shrubs and trees and, scattered here and there, the tiny villages and broad-smiling mountain people. Loose rock walls surround the potato fields to keep the large, hairy yaks away from the crop and lying among the fields are the two-storeyed, mud-plastered houses. Downstairs is for the yaks and upstairs, in the smoky atmosphere of the living-room-kitchen-cum-bedroom, is where the people live. I remember one night, after crawling into my sleeping-bag upon the floor, looking across the room at the fireplace. A low ceiling of smoke hung a short distance above the floor and my prostrate body; the Sherpas seemed oblivious to the thick air and, enjoying the warmth of the fire, they talked as they prepared food, the light of the fire flickering upon their faces. The scene intrigued me. They were so at home and so comfortable here despite the rigours. One of them noticed my gaze and grinned back at me. He offered me some potato and chilli.

As we were involved in aid work – in the building and operating of schools and hospitals – there was a great deal of co-operation from the local communities. It was quite a humbling experience to see how grateful they were and to receive their thanks for facilities I had never given a thought to in my own society and whose presence I had accepted without question. It made me appreciate so much more what I had at home, the simple pleasures that we often take for granted: hot showers and holidays, the time and facilities for learning and inquiry into any personal interests and freedom from the most time-consuming and mundane chores – carrying water from a water hole, collecting firewood and digging fields by hand.

During these visits to Asia I noticed the reverence with which the local people treated my father. They called him 'burra sahib' (head man or big man) rather than just 'sahib'. I suppose I have been aware, ever since I can remember, of the public approbation accorded my father but, perhaps more than anywhere else, I felt aware of his influence and prestige in the Himalayas. For me, all this fame and acknowledgement produced a quandary in my mind, as the same man was just my father!

In 1966 Dad took my mother and me, aged twelve, up a small peak called Kala Pittar. It stood to the west of the Khumbu Icefall and the first ascent route of Everest. After the clamber to the top we rested and looked about us from our magnificent vantage point. I remember the breathlessness of the thin air, the cold, the imposing pyramidal bulk of Everest and the steep, dark rock of its South-West Face. Although I couldn't envisage the problems of such a gigantic climb I could relate the difficulties I had had reaching Kala Pittar's 18,000-foot-high summit. I think that for the first time I really appreciated an inkling of what Dad had accomplished when he climbed Everest . . . seeing the mountain myself and feeling in awe of it. On this occasion I was glad to descend, as I had a high-altitude headache and as we lost altitude on the way down the throbbing in my head ceased.

As a student I was a rather serious character. Although I didn't lack friends I often felt lonely and at fourteen and fifteen years of age when everyone else was spending their Friday and Saturday evenings in the grip of adolescent social activities, I, more often than not, found myself at home. I would go for long walks with a friend or by myself. That is not to say I was a loner, for I desperately missed some type of group companionship. Adolescence was spent with just a few friends with whom I frequently engaged in lengthy and in-depth conversation. I day-dreamed a lot. The school curriculum and sports did not provide the stimulation and excitement I sought. I was always cynical about team sports, particularly the first fifteen rugby team; the camaraderie they enjoyed seemed a trifle nauseating to me, and their pounding up and down a muddy paddock hurling their sweaty bodies at each other was all rather undignified and contrived . . . even if it did make a man out of you. There was another school-age bugbear that plagued me: the frequent reference to my being the son of Sir Edmund Hillary. At times I wondered if I even existed as an individual and during the school holidays when I took a job to make some pocket money I used pseudonyms. This often proved most amusing when my father's name came up during smoko or while getting a lift home from a fellow work-mate. I would smile and answer with the appropriate grunts and affirmations until the conversation drifted on to other topics.

During my schooldays the family became ardent skiers and I became obsessed by the sport. I sought the steepest slopes, the narrowest gullies and the worst snow. I joined forces with a group of like-minded young men and we terrorised the ski-field for several years with our antics. All the while my standard of skiing improved and I became involved in ski racing which enabled me to be excused compulsory house football and hockey at school during the weekends. Then I and another school friend, Nigel Lewis, became interested in rock climbing which rapidly turned to mountaineering. We made a few low-key visits to Mount Ruapehu, the active volcano where I did most of my skiing, to climb the three main peaks of the rambling mountain. By this stage I knew what I wanted to do with my leisure time: I wanted to ski and to climb and to do plenty of it. I was sixteen and I was finding secondary school claustrophobic and frustrating. In the classes I enjoyed and with the masters I respected (which had nothing to do with their prowess with the cane) I was as much a model student as I could be, but with the classes where I considered the teacher incompetent or overly restrictive I made my feelings known. This inevitably brought me to the notice of our headmaster, an elderly and very distinguished gentleman. He was not at all happy about my demonstrative views; however, I felt they were warranted and refused to budge. He told me he was disappointed; he thought I was a person who kept notes on any events that went on about me and that I thought about things carefully. I had a considerable respect for my headmaster and from that day on I have kept a notebook for my jottings and thoughts.

At the end of that year I passed my university entrance examination with reasonable marks and enrolled at Auckland University. I was a year younger than everyone else and, not having a clue what I really wanted to do (other than ski and climb), I embarked upon a course in science with an aim to major in geology. Getting to university each day required transport, so my parents agreed to buy me a small 90cc motorcycle. Neither of them liked motorcycles but felt that providing I never went above 90cc I should survive the experience. My little Kawasaki 90 became yet another love and I rode with an aim to perfect my technique. There was a particularly windy section of road *en route* to the university and this became my daily training circuit.

University was a very different environment from the old English-style public school I had gone to. I made few friends, other than those involved in the university ski team and the odd motorcycle fanatic. Most of my old school friendships either disappeared or were moth-balled and I became very close to my mother as in a truly equitable friendship. I talked to her freely, there seemed to be no taboos for our conversation and so during my university years she took on the additional role of being my close friend and mentor.

At the end of my first year at university—a year when judging by the application given to various subjects you would assume I was majoring in ski-ology, mountaineering and motorcycle technique—I departed for the South Island with my climbing companion, Nigel Lewis. We had done a certain amount of scratching around on moderately steep ice at Ruapehu and rock climbing round the Auckland region and decided that we were going south to sort this Southern Alps business out. We had grandiose plans. We visited Nelson Lakes National Park and climbed Mount Traverse, we went to Mount Aspiring and succeeded in climbing it by the North-West Ridge while intending only a reconnaissance. Two days later we climbed the spectacular peak again in five hours by the steeper South-West Ridge and marched out of this notoriously bad-weather area having made two major ascents in three days.

By this stage we were beaming with confidence and we drove, harmonising our favourite Cat Stevens songs, to Mount Cook National Park. There seemed little point in wasting our time with 'the little stuff'. We planned to hire a skiplane and fly directly to the foot of Mount Tasman, New Zealand's second highest peak, which we would climb as a warm-up for its neighbour, Mount Cook itself. The skiplane lifted into the air with us and our gigantic packs aboard and droned its way up the massive Tasman valley. It's very difficult to interpret scale in the mountains and the Mount Cook region is a prime example, as everything is so very big—mountains, glaciers, moraine walls and ice cliffs. I don't think we registered the difference between Mount Aspiring and Mount Cook at all. We must have looked a prime pair of greenhorns to the pilot as we enthused about the grandeur and took multiple photographs. Because we planned to climb Mount Tasman we had asked him to fly us to Tasman hut. The hut near Tasman is in fact called Plateau hut and the nearest thing to a Tasman hut in the park is Tasman Saddle hut at the head of the Tasman Glacier and about fifteen miles of bone-jarring moraines and crevassed glacier ice from Mount Tasman itself. The plane flew past Mount Cook and then Mount Tasman. I asked the pilot where Tasman hut was, looking down at the foot of the great white mountain abeam us, expecting him to guide my line of sight to the hut. He pointed at an appropriate-looking hut which he announced was called Plateau hut. Perplexed, Nigel and I held an emergency mid-air meeting. We came to the astonishing conclusion that we didn't want to go to Tasman Saddle hut at all and that we wanted to go to Plateau hut. "We want to go down there," I said sheepishly to the pilot, pointing at Plateau hut. He mumbled something into his microphone and I have no doubt that both he and the chief pilot at the airport decided that, if we didn't know where we were going, there was a distinct possibility we didn't know what we were doing either, so we kept flying up the glacier to Tasman Saddle hut! It was almost certainly the best thing that could have happened to us as we learned a host of lessons over the ensuing days. Lessons learned included:

a) know where you are going
b) don't bring skis and boots on a strictly climbing trip
c) don't try to carry 100-pound packs
d) avoid carrying heavy canned foods
e) and over several exhausting and painful days we learned a little of the awesome scale of the Mount Cook region.

We became competent at gauging the heights of the moraine walls on the flanks of the Tasman Glacier. Our original estimates were in the vicinity of a hundred feet, but then we didn't realise the glacier was two miles wide. They were, in fact, 500 feet high and some even higher. In the end we did do some climbing in Mount Cook National Park and even visited Plateau hut, where the weather deteriorated and we spent five days hut-bound in the most atrocious conditions either of us had ever experienced. Having run out of food, we retreated down the hut's precarious access route to the Tasman Glacier, 3,000 feet below. Reaching the hut itself had proved a not inconsiderable mountaineering experience. Both Nigel and I came away from our adventures that summer with two things in mind: a hearty respect for the mountains and a love for them that has drawn us back to them ever since.

After two years at university I dropped my course in preference for the New Zealand ski-racing circuit. Dad had always wanted me to get a good professional qualification, so he was disappointed, but when I purchased a 750cc two-stroke Kawasaki he was furious. For two weeks we passed on the stairs of our home without a word being said. He was worried I would kill myself and when he found that Mum had unhappily signed a document to allow a nineteen-year-old to own such a motorcycle (at the time it was the most brutally powerful motorcycle model on the road) I think he became even less content. Because Mum's consent was also necessary for the hire-purchase agreement, we later joked that she was the only Remuera housewife who owned a Kawasaki 750 and we laughed about the idea of her appearing in the shopping centre upon it, all set to do her daily shopping. "Goodness me, Lady Hillary! This is an unorthodox mode of transport you have here!"

I worked long hours in several factories around Auckland to raise the money for the motorcycle payments before the onset of winter and my skiing plans. For four months I cruised around the South Island with skis tied to the side of the machine. I trained with other racers and skied in all the season's main events. My ambition was not so much to become a great ski racer as to become a strong and competent skier, able to ski any terrain. For in downhill skiing as well it was the mountains that attracted me—off the piste and on to difficult and challenging ground where the skier's skill was tantamount to being able to execute a descent and to survive it.

In January of 1975 the Hillary family left New Zealand to fulfil a dream of spending a year in Nepal. Mum and Belinda wanted to learn Nepalese and I wanted to try my hand at some photography and some writing, but our main objective was to build a hospital at 9,000 feet in the Solu region, south of Mount Everest. This was a big project and the largest building scheme Dad had undertaken in Nepal. All seemed set for a fabulous year. We moved into a comfortable bungalow in a pleasantly rural-cum-residential area of Kathmandu. The first month passed in a blur of Nepali language lessons, travels around the Kathmandu valley, meeting and socialising with Nepali friends and the massive logistics involved in despatching building materials and equipment from Kathmandu to the site for the hospital at Phaphlu. Simultaneously Dad was rebuilding the Phaphlu airstrip which had fallen into disrepair and disuse. An improved and enlarged airstrip he hoped would assist with the hospital construction project and provide an alternative means of transport from the Solu region to Kathmandu (the other means being the repetitive exercising of one's limbs!).

During February Sarah returned to New Zealand to university and I became more involved in helping my parents with the building project. Belinda attended a Nepalese girls' school as well as completing her correspondence school lessons and was as happy as I had ever seen her—and she was normally of an ebullient disposition! There were periods when I wondered if I shouldn't be getting on with some training myself and I scrutinised the people I found around me in the hope that their lives and accomplishments might give me some idea of what I should do. Although I was enjoying working with my parents on an aid project, I wished I could have had a specific skill to offer. My thoughts turned more and more to writing and to aviation. But before I could think too long on this question my friend Simon Maclaurin arrived in Kathmandu. We had planned to spend a month together travelling around northern India, visiting Kashmir and Assam, so early one morning in March, Mum drove the two of us to the Kathmandu bus depot. It was a clear, fresh morning and Simon and I were excited about the travels that lay ahead of us. Mum seemed happy about it too. I got the impression she was pleased I was heading off on an adventure and that I had something to 'get my teeth into'. We stood together chatting until the bus was ready to depart. It was a happy departure, for our elation was due not only to the impending journey but to the knowledge of our eventual return; of our all being together again, able to relate the stories of our travels to those we cared most about and who cared most about us. As I looked at my mother, that vivacious and loving personality, those bright eyes and smiling face, I could not have imagined that this was the last time I would see her.

Simon and I travelled to New Delhi and on to Srinagar in

Kashmir where we went skiing at the small ski resort of Gulmarg. Returning to the Gangetic plains, we travelled east on India's vast rail network to Assam. It proved a most thought-provoking and stimulating trip, one that we both enjoyed greatly. The train followed the banks of the Brahmaputra river, travelling north till it reached the town of Jorhat where we were met by a family friend, Bhanu Banerjee. Bhanu drove us to his house on the tea estate he managed for some relaxing days as his guest.

On April 4th I lay upon my bed, gasping in the mid-morning heat, watching the roof-fan whirring overhead. Bhanu and Simon came into the room and walked up to the bed. I immediately knew something had gone seriously wrong. I sat up. My diary reads: "Bhanu and Simon tell me that Belinda and Mum have been involved in the crash of a small aircraft. They are believed to be badly injured."

Bhanu drove us to the airport at Jorhat and at one thirty p.m. we took off for Calcutta. *En route* I wrote: "Emotionally I don't know what to think. I, at least, feel that I'm lucky having Phyl and Jim (my grandparents) and Dad in Kathmandu. I am lucky having Simon with me now."

In Calcutta we spent the night at the flat of a newspaperman friend, Desmond Doig. I was in the bathroom, washing the grime of the day's travel from my face, when Simon came in and stood beside me. He told me both Mum and Belinda had been killed instantly in a plane crash at Kathmandu on March 31st. They had been cremated that night.

Next day we flew on to Kathmandu. "I am dreading arriving in Kathmandu . . . I expect the full impact to hit me at Baluwatar, our Kathmandu home—empty—no Mum, no Belinda . . . I am constantly having to hold back tears . . . I am the top string of a violin being plucked in staccato fashion."

Landing at Kathmandu was an agony. It was like being plunged into a bath of cold, harsh reality. We took a taxi to Baluwatar. The house was deserted, it was eerie and silent. I made a telephone call to locate Dad. "Fifteen minutes later our little green car came bumping along the road. Sarah was driving, Phyl was in the passenger seat and Dad and Jim were in the back." The car stopped and the three remnants of the Hillary family reached for each other. We stood there on the road and wept. For me that meeting was the final affirmation of our loss.

Emotionally I felt demolished. We were all hanging on to threads. We existed, living in a hiatus, stunned and directionless. Slowly we began the long and painful business of salvaging what remained. Life would never be the same again but life would go on. I needed to grieve and think. I needed to get to know my father better, for we had always been bound through Mum. We needed to keep going, to persevere, although, right then, there seemed precious little point.

9

Skiing, flying, climbing

WE HAD BEEN cast reluctantly into a new chapter of our lives. And like it or not, the sun still rose in the mornings and set in the evenings. I found that we were still able to laugh and enjoy good company and that we still appreciated beautiful scenery, despite our pain.

For three months we travelled the world together, as Dad attended to various commitments—from Phaphlu to Kathmandu, Geneva, Paris, London, New York, Chicago and Toronto and, finally, home to Auckland. There we had to endure, for the first time, returning to our family home and the poignant reminders of the disaster. Slowly but surely we began to adjust to the new status quo, each of us coping as best we could and in our own way. During that first year our own personal dilemmas tended to retard our getting to know one another better in our new circumstances. Within each of us we carried a ball of emotion; one that had lost its *raison d'être*. Dad, Sarah and I had always been the least outgoing of the five of us; however, this had been amply offset by the personalities of my mother and Belinda. Now, we had to be the catalysts; to provide the binding forces for the family. As time went by we developed the necessary new relationships and I felt I got to know Dad better than ever before. Much of that, no doubt, was thanks to the process of 'growing old gracefully', a course that I had been pursuing ever since my twentieth birthday! We developed a pleasant little ritual of sitting in my father's study, once the sun was over the yard-arm, and imbibing a pre-dinner drink. I looked forward to this, as we would discuss whatever was topical at the time and especially the current projects and expeditions. Not infrequently, during these sessions, the telephone would ring and someone, somewhere in the world, would up-date us with news, developments or ideas. I found this tremendously exciting and most stimulating. Our conversations would then progress with a new slant. Life was certainly never dull around my father.

My grandparents, Jim and Phyl Rose, continued to be a comfort and a joy to us. They were always there and they gave us a sense of rock-solid permanence which made them a focal point for our more transient lives. We often had dinner with them, evenings that tended to be both cheerful and sumptuous. Every second weekend or so, when we were in Auckland, we drove out to Anawhata, our cliff-top holiday house, a magnificent retreat on the west coast of Auckland. I loved the wild beauty out there; the black-back gulls soaring above the cliffs, the rush of the westerly winds, the Tasman Sea crashing upon the rocks 300 feet below the house and the memories. I have been taken out to Anawhata ever since I can remember by my parents and by Jim and Phyl and, consequently, the place has left an indelible impression on me. I discovered that my fondness for Anawhata was not simply its untamed beauty but its association with key characters in my life. They had coloured the experiences and thus the location's significance was theirs also. After the accident much of the love of Anawhata had departed with my mother's passing. But as time went by I found other reasons to return there. Dad and I often walked the length of the Piha beach which lay to the south of the house. We didn't talk much as we marched along the two miles of that surf-swept sand but just I enjoyed his company. I also made frequent trips there with Jim and Phyl and enjoyed their time-practised ways of going about their daily chores: lighting the kerosene tilly lamps with a knowledgeable sensitivity, the preparation of good old-fashioned food and their reminiscences of the early days in the Auckland region. They had both been born in 1898 and a lot had happened in the world during their lives and that included improvements to the west-coast road that led to Anawhata. There were some enthralling stories of their having to help tow other cars out of ditches or through quagmires and, once, how their car had had to be dragged by horses through a sea of unfathomable mud. In those days while travelling along the Anawhata road there was always a necessity for chains on the tyres of their old Chevrolet. It sometimes took three hours to get to Anawhata then . . . if you were lucky! Nowadays the trip takes less than an hour and is usually devoid of untoward excitement.

Towards the end of 1975 the question of what I should do with myself raised its ugly head. A feeling of futility hung over me, chiefly due to my lack of a vocation. I wanted to get on with something in order to obtain some sense of accomplishment and after much thought decided to pursue a career in aviation. Although I had considered becoming a pilot on and off over the years, the accident reinforced my determination to succeed in this field and to overcome an invisible barrier. While Dad had returned to Nepal to complete the construction of Phaphlu hospital with my Uncle Rex, I began my lessons at Ardmore airport. I had tallied only seven hours when I was laid low with glandular fever and so the flying came, temporarily, to a grinding halt. I went through a period of total lack of confidence and resolved to throw myself into a season of climbing at Mount Cook. I desperately needed to do something that would engross my whole being, tax me totally.

"To climb well you've got to be hungry," philosophised Alex (and he didn't mean food). We had all been drinking vodka and verbosity reigned supreme with profound and philosophical statements being uttered left, right and centre. I have never forgotten that grand ·generalisation of the exceptional British mountaineer, Alex MacIntyre, and, in retrospect, consider that it summed up my climbing during the several years that followed 1975. I wasn't climbing that well but I was 'hungry' and I climbed with enthusiasm.

Still feeling a little drained by my sickness, I went south to Mount Cook with no concrete plans other than to climb some mountains. At Mount Cook village I met an Australian fellow called Fred From who had just completed an elementary climbing course and was fired with ambitious ideas that concurred admirably with my own. We went up the Tasman Glacier and climbed the precipitous Haast Ridge to Plateau hut. There we spent the best part of two frenetic weeks, a pair of ambitious, budding climbers in search of ever-more-challenging routes and the chance to prove ourselves to be a 'gun' or a 'heavy' in the climbing scene. We climbed the East Ridge of Dixon as a warm-up and then the East Face of Lendenfeld and the low peak of Haast. Then came our moment of truth and we nervously headed off across the Grand Plateau Glacier to the East Face of Mount Cook. We surprised ourselves. We climbed more quickly than anticipated and were soon over half-way up the 4,500-foot-high face. Moving off the snow and ice face we climbed a narrow rock rib which proved more difficult and slowed our progress, but by late morning we pulled ourselves over the lip of the face and on to the summit icecap. It was then that I realised just how big Mount Cook was. Climbing the East Face had demonstrated it, too, but then what lay below and that which lay above was foreshortened by the steepness of the face and the inability to stand back and absorb its vastness. As we climbed the few pitches that separated us from the summit I looked about me. The razor-sharp summit of Tasman rose to the north with the Balfour Face dropping abruptly to the south of its summit and, far below, the Tasman Glacier snaked its way amongst New Zealand's largest mountains. To the east lay Lake Pukaki, a great mass of water that seemed misplaced amongst the ruggedness that surrounded me, and to the west lay the Tasman Sea, 12,349 feet below. Next day we returned to Mount Cook village and the Tavern bar feeling like moderately accomplished 'heavies'. I called Dad in Auckland to tell him of my climbs. He is well known amongst his friends as one not overly disposed to spiels of superlatives, so his reaction seemed more an interested acknowledgement to me in my state of near euphoria.

The following season I joined forces with Merv English and we returned to Plateau hut, this time by skiplane. We took with us vast quantities of food—even fresh fruit, fresh meat and one of my grandmother's fruit cakes—and some photographs of the Balfour valley that we treated as classified information. One of these photographs had been on the lid of a cake tin which some unsuspecting commercial artist had assumed represented no more than a picture of pretty mountains and glistening white glaciers. To us, this cake-tin-lid illustration was a collection of new route ideas in one of the highest alpine valleys in the country.

From Plateau hut we crossed the glacier to the Silberhorn Ridge and ascended this moderately difficult and quite dangerous route to the summit of Silberhorn. Looking down we could see Plateau hut over 3,000 feet below and the Tasman Glacier another 3,000 feet below it. It was certainly an airy spot but magnificent as a vantage point. I enjoyed the thrill of being amongst such rugged and wild terrain and the excitement of making a fleeting visit to an environment so changeable and potentially hostile to humanity. We descended the western flank of Silberhorn into the head of the Balfour valley, a shrine of steep ice and rock; the seldom-visited Mecca of New Zealand's contemporary mountaineers. It must be one of the loneliest places in New Zealand as at the 8,000-foot level the valley makes an abrupt change in grade at a 1,000-foot-high bluff over which the glacier relentlessly drives itself, crashing to the second tier of the valley far below. It made me think of lemmings. If only snowflakes knew what they were in for! We made our way past the Balfour Face of Tasman and across towards the sheer greywacke rock face of Mount Magellan. At the foot of the peak we dug a snow cave and spent the remainder of the afternoon resting before consuming a nasty concoction that constituted our evening meal. As the sun sank below the western horizon of the Tasman Sea, the blue glow that filled the cave dimmed to near darkness and we both appeared as shadows against the background whiteness of the snow. The light gone, we nestled down in our sleeping-bags for a comfortable night in our tiny snow cave.

Next morning we climbed a red slab of rock that extended up for eight pitches (about 1,000 feet) on the north-east side of Mount Magellan. The rock was good and the climbing steep and enjoyable; the sun shone down upon us and it was easy to forget our isolation. We climbed rope-length after rope-length up the rock wall and as we got higher we noticed a bank of cloud over the Tasman Sea to the north-west. It moved progressively down the coast towards us. Not having a large quantity of rations, we could not afford to be caught by bad weather and once we had reached the top we hurriedly descended a gully back to the glacier. Collecting our gear from the ice-cave, we retraced our steps back up the glacier to the summit of Silberhorn from where we began our descent to the plateau far below. Cloud swirled around us and the light dimmed as we climbed down the ridge towards the refuge of Plateau hut. As we approached the base of the ridge it became dark and, since the snow conditions were unstable and there were crevasses and ice cliffs all around, we decided it would be prudent to bivouac. We dug a ledge in the slope, climbed into our sleeping-bags and sat on our sealed foam mats on the ledge. While I contemplated the discomfort of our predicament and the annoyance of being so close and yet so far from the hut, Merv lit our stove and proceeded to melt snow to make some soup. I had begun to nod off to sleep, snuggled in my down bag, when Merv nudged me and handed me a bowl of tomato soup. Still half-asleep, I slurped down the much-needed liquid and passed back the empty bowl.

"You bastard! You've drunk all the soup."

"Huh. Oh, sorry." Merv has never let me forget that incident and to this day drinks his share first, even when I'm wide awake.

My winters were spent on ski fields around New Zealand and my interest in racing turned to teaching the sport. I did my Stage I and Stage II ski instructor exams and worked both in the North Island and in the South Island. As much as I enjoyed the work, I found the opportunity to ski with world-class professional skiers one of the highlights of the job: those early morning ski runs with my fellow instructors before the field opened to the public and the opportunity to be first to leave rattle-snake lines of linked turns down the choice faces after a snow fall.

Learners tended to come in two broad groups: aggressive and brawny or fearful and lacking in confidence. The extreme examples of each generally succeeded in creating similar catastrophes, particularly in the beginner classes. The muscle-bound and aggressive types would hurl themselves into the fall-line and, straining from side to side, attempt to steer in one direction or the other. Refusing to accept failure they'd pick up speed and invariably veer off to one side and hurtle into another group of beginners carefully lined up by another instructor. If your runaway pupil happens to strike the top of this line of skiers the result is quite like dominoes. The second type, on the other hand, would turn his or her skis slightly downhill to the accompaniment of a barrage of squawks and squeals and verbal statements indicating the various states of apprehension. Having slithered no more than three feet they'd then collapse backwards on to their rearward landing pads and slide, shrieking all the while, as they drifted down the slope, colliding with all in their path, the net result being several entangled bodies and pairs of skis. It was enjoyable work though, and I loved the environment in which we were employed.

The intervals between climbing in the summer and skiing in the winter were devoted to my flying training. Along with about twenty others I spent an intensive six-month period studying, attending lectures, sitting exams and flying aeroplanes–compass turns, max. rate turns, side slipping, stalls and spins, aerobatics, short take-offs and landings, crosswind landings, forced landings, low flying and poor visibility procedures, night flying and elementary instrument flight training. My fellow students, like myself, aspired to fly anything from helicopters to 747s. Our lives revolved around flying. I originally thought I might enjoy working for a major airline but decided the flight schedule could become a little repetitive and that helicopters were for me. About the time I was going to have an introductory helicopter flight, after I had passed my commercial pilot exams, I realised that I was involved in three pursuits that independently demanded all my time and all my money. The ski season was on its way and I had a job arranged for the season at Mount Hutt. I had to make up my mind to what I was going to devote myself and be prepared to accept the other activities as holiday pastimes. Still undecided, I went south to Mount Hutt to work the ski season and on my free days hired a small plane from a local aero-club to fly around the winter-locked Southern Alps. I jokingly referred to these excursions as 'Hillary Wonderflites' because for me they were aerial journeys back into familiar alpine environments for a brief look-see. To complicate my decision-making further there was a major expedition to India in the offing, organised and led by my father who had always been my fount of exotic and imaginative adventures. I must be a sucker for such temptations but I certainly don't regret joining the Ocean to Sky jet-boat expedition up the River Ganges. It will stand in my memory as one of the most extraordinary experiences of my life. We drove three jet boats from the Bay of Bengal up the Ganges to the Himalayas where we negotiated colossal rapids and tall standing waves. When the boats could go no further we continued on foot to Badrinath, a Hindu holy place, at 10,000 feet amongst the snow-clad peaks. There we climbed two mountains and emptied on to their snows a tiny brass vessel of water we had collected from the river's mouth. As much as I enjoyed the jet boating and the climbing, the greatest impact was from the people of India. The expedition sparked an unanticipated reaction from the millions of people who live along the banks of the great river. At every refuelling site and in the evenings when we halted for the night we were besieged by thousands of enthusiastic local people. Initially I assumed it was simply curiosity but then I discovered our journey meant far more to them than that. The jet boats were certainly a draw-card and the stories that preceded us concerning the miraculous capabilities of the craft astonished even us. But more important was that we were making the pilgrimage that every Hindu would like to make but most will never be able. We were travelling the length of the River Ganges and so we were participating in an important religious rite. My father received tremendous approbation from the vast crowds, who would cheer his name. "Long live Edmund Hillary." The conqueror of Everest was making a pilgrimage up their beloved Ganges in three space-age boats. It was a superb combination and the public interest was enormous.

Like any subordinate I tended to find fault with the administration – in this case my father. But the differences were few and tended to be due to my youthful exuberance and impatience, for I genuinely admired his stamina and determination. He had to cope with a team of independent characters who frequently expressed their views. As well he had the demands of the crowds that thronged the riverside. Officials and dignitaries had to have their hands wrung and there were endless photographs and autographs. I myself found the Indian infatuation with the son of a family difficult at times. "Are you the son of Sir Hillary? . . . Ooooh! This is wonderful." The bombardment of interest for no other reason than that I was my father's son both annoyed and confused me. Acknowledgement seemed reasonable enough if you had accomplished something of note yourself, but a blood relationship alone seemed insufficient reason for so much attention. At times I swapped places with other expedition members and left them with the predicament of being 'Sir Hillary's son' in India. But when we were aboard the boats and racing up-river life was more relaxed, with the roar of the engines, the motion of the boats as they were manoeuvred past obstacles in the river and, all around us, the fascinating landscapes of India.

I returned home from the Ocean to Sky expedition inspired by what I had seen and experienced. Not only had it been a marvellous expedition, but it had been an important philosophical experience. I had been enormously impressed by the tolerance exhibited by so many of India's people and, while not ignoring their faults, I simply admired their strengths. I became increasingly aware of the foibles of my own society and, at times, despondent about them. I saw myself and so many others as new-world philistines living out the myth of egalitarianism. I became painfully aware that opportunities were not freely available for everybody, even in my own country, and I was thankful for the opportunities that I had had.

From Auckland I journeyed south to the mountains again. Mount Aspiring is an elegant peak that rises well above its neighbours to an acute summit. As I had climbed it before, I knew that it was a feasible and very attractive objective for a ski descent. Like most mountains in New Zealand, Aspiring had never been skied and, as I had heard a rumour on the mountaineering grape-vine that an attempt was imminent, I decided to nip it in the bud. Along with Nena Ritchie, whom I'd skied with the previous season, I left the road end in the Matukituki valley and we hiked up-valley beneath heavily laden packs. From the head of the valley we scrambled up the precipitous flanks following a vague track that led through the beech forests to the alpine scrub. Carrying skis proved most awkward on such steep terrain, for the ski tips would catch in the flora above as you strained to haul yourself over the more abrupt steps in the ridge. Cursing, I would lower myself sufficiently to disentangle the ski tips and with muscles screaming make a second attempt at climbing over the obstacle and maintaining clearance for my skis. We spent several days at French Ridge hut above the scrub line waiting for a spell of suitable weather for climbing Aspiring. Powder snow covered the ridge above the hut and, with blue skies overhead, we attached skins to our skis and headed up towards the Bonar Glacier. The ridge is like a rampart with huge cliffs lining both its sides, and the higher you climb the more it feels like a stairway to the heavens. The valleys shrink beneath you and your world becomes pristine and white. At the top of the ridge we removed the skins from our skis and skied down on to the Bonar Glacier with Aspiring rising spectacularly above us. We skied past the fluted South Face of the mountain and around the South-West Ridge to the North-West Ridge where we removed our skis and tied them to our packs. We roped up and climbed rope length after rope length up a snow ramp that led through a line of rock bluffs and on to the ridge proper. A strong southerly blew across the ridge and it became bitterly cold. I was still determined to attempt the ski descent, so we climbed on up the ridge with our parka-hoods protecting us from the onslaught of wind-carried spin-drift. As we approached the summit at just under 10,000 feet I wondered how the wind would affect me on skis and I worried it might gust strong enough to blow me off the ridge itself.

I stepped into my bindings, checked the buckles on my boots and the wrist loops on my poles and looked about me. This was it; something I had dreamed of doing for years and now here I was standing on Aspiring's narrow summit with skis on my feet. The Bonar Glacier was over 3,000 feet below me and the crowd of snow-clad peaks in the area seemed compressed against the green valleys far below. I had that sensation of being extremely exposed and vulnerable and I remember questioning my confidence in my ability to ski off the summit. I couldn't afford any mistakes; this was serious skiing, not a frivolous piste descent.

I turned the tips of my skis down the ridge. The speed built up rapidly as I slipped down the steep summit pyramid, my skis clattering over the tiny sastrugi; I planted my pole and drove my skis around and across the slope; again I planted the pole and, again, around I turned. It was as if all my apprehensions had been for nothing and I was soon speeding down the ridge in a rhythmic, gliding dance from side to side as I steered my skis around rocks and clumps of ice. It was magical. As the cold air rushed past my face I felt aware of my height above the other peaks, the glaciers below, the green valleys and the Tasman Sea to the west. It was exciting skiing and I enjoyed the variety of the snow conditions as much as the demanding nature of the skiing.

I didn't remove my skis that day until we reached French Ridge hut in the late evening. I had skied down from the summit, schussed across the Bonar Glacier from the foot of the mountain to the Breakaway pass and, there, traversed carefully across an unstable snowface below Mount French to the French Ridge and finally the haven of the little mountain hut. It had been a welcome refuge at the end of a long and strenuous day.

Over this period of my life I made many visits to Mount Cook and succeeded in doing a fair number of climbs. I learned that in the mountains, and especially in a region like Mount Cook, where the weather is fickle (to say the least), you cannot expect to do climbs every day, let alone every time you attempt one. We spent many days (the accumulated total would be months) awaiting a clearance in the weather, sitting in lonely mountain huts or sipping beers with the locals in Mount Cook Village or Fox Glacier township, telling progressively more outrageous mountain stories as the days ticked by. Fortunately, it does clear occasionally in the Southern Alps and there are, in fact, extended periods of superb weather. In one of my most energetic climbing sprees during a fine-weather spell I climbed the South Ridge of Dixon, the Balfour Face of Tasman and the West Face of Unicorn in one week of what felt like endless summer. (By the time we were descending off Unicorn that myth was being laid to rest by an impressive sky of mare's tails and lenticular clouds.)

The Balfour Face is still one of New Zealand's most prestigious routes and a fine technical climb. It was the hardest and most extending route I had climbed. We made our first bivouac with 3,000 feet of ridge below and darkness very nearly upon us, chopping a level platform in the snow and spending a cold, near-sleepless night beneath the stars. Next morning the eastern sky was painted in pale blues, greens and yellows as it heralded the rising sun. Fred From and I roped together and along with two other climbers, Nick Craddock and Nick Kaggan, set off upward. It wasn't long before we were standing on the summit of Mount Silberhorn. To the north the razor-sharp ridge leading to Mount Tasman swept upward and below us lay the forebidding and sunless Balfour valley. From where we stood Tasman looked like a shark's tooth with white vertical ice-bulges latched upon its super-steep southern side—a 2,000-foot face of spectacular ice and rock.

Leaving our sleeping-bags, cooker and some food in a small crevasse near the top of Mount Silberhorn, we climbed down into the frozen shadows of the valley. At the base of the face Fred set up a belay and I began climbing the steep, cold rock. In places the rock was coated with verglass which made progress slow but eventually I reached a tiny ledge where I prepared a belay for Fred. He climbed up to me and led on up a section of delicate, smooth rock. There were few holds and little possibility for placing protection. The higher we went on the face, the more shattered and broken the rock became. I led into a near-vertical gully and looking up I could see the ice-bulges a couple of hundred feet above me. They stood out from the rock; smooth, round and white, silhouetted against the sky. Continuing upward, I moved carefully, checking each hold before committing myself to it. When I reached the end of the rope I put in a belay and called down to Fred who began climbing up to me. I listened to the strange whirring sound of rocks that occasionally swished through the air a few feet out from the face as they rocketed towards the glacier below. I found it quite frightening and wondered if my helmet would protect me from a direct hit.

Fred reached my unpleasant little perch and was in the process of taking the gear sling from me when he accidentally dropped a few jam-nuts. They sailed down the face, their bright-coloured nylon slings twisting through the air. We watched in a stunned silence. I consoled myself that we needed mainly ice gear from here on so the loss shouldn't worry us. Fred began climbing the first ice-bulge. He kicked the front points of his crampons into the ice and, reaching up, whacked the picks of his axes in above him. Spread-eagled on the near vertical ice with 1,000 feet of air below, he clawed his way up the bulge to where the angle eased slightly. Here he placed three ice screws to secure himself and then it was my turn. I followed Fred's lead up the intimidatingly steep ice, my forearms were on fire with the pain of clutching my axes, and my legs were fatigued and jittery as I balanced out on the front points of my crampons. I looked up towards Fred, twenty feet above, and as I did so one of my crampons broke loose from the ice, setting off a chain reaction of dislodgements. I found myself dangling from one axe. In a frenzy of clawing crampons and a wildly swung ice-axe, I regained a more conventional and restful posture. Shaking from head to toe, I climbed up to Fred where I rested for a minute.

I climbed on up two more ice-bulges, placing my axes and crampons carefully, putting in ice screws for protection, making sure that each move I made was a good one. Then Fred led past up the final ice-bulge. I looked up at him past the soles of his boots, emblazoned with long, sharp crampon points, and was pleased to see concentration written on his face. He eventually went out of sight; a good sign, I realised, as the angle must have been easing off.

The sun had been on us since mid-afternoon and its effect on the ice was not proving helpful. By the time I reached Fred's belay stance, we were being engulfed by flurries of tiny pellets of ice, which swept the face with increasing frequency. I headed up the now only fifty- to fifty-five-degree ice slopes and discovered, much to my chagrin, that the stinging ice beads were not the only vexation the face had to offer us, but trickles of melt water as well. The freezing water tended to flow down my axes and hence down my arms until I was soaked to the skin. Five more rope lengths brought us to the summit, shivering in our wet clothes, as the sun rapidly sank on the western horizon. We changed into dry clothes which helped put a rosier perspective on life and we felt able to be pleased by our climb and enjoy what lay around us: mountains, glaciers, the long, arching coast of Westland with its towns, now just patches of flickering lights, the pastel greys and blues of the sea, and the sky broken by the darker, billowing shapes of clouds. To the east, in a pool of darkness, we could discern the faint glow of lights from a mountain hut and nearly 1,000 feet below us was the summit of Silberhorn, where our sleeping-bags, cooker and food awaited us.

"Only the upward climb is over when you're on the top," mumbled Fred as I set up a belay for the descent.

10

To the Himalayas

M Y MOUNTAINEERING AMBITIONS began to move beyond the shores of New Zealand. Although I had been on my father's expeditions, I realised I couldn't always leave the creation of adventures to him and I should start to organise my own. This seemed rather daunting, not so much because of differing alpine conditions or greater scale but because of the logistical and bureaucratic problems involved. There was also the considerably greater cost. I think my father hoped that the past few years of intensive climbing would come to an end and that I would now get on with a career. However, I had made up my mind about my climbing, skiing, aviation quandary. I planned to concentrate on climbing for the next three years and just keep abreast of flying and skiing in my spare time.

I discussed some of my ideas with Graeme Dingle, who had also been on the Ocean to Sky jet-boat expedition, and not long afterwards the two of us arrived in California *en route* to Yosemite National Park. Yosemite is one of the key destinations on the international climbing circuit. Climbers from all over the world live in a squalid little camp amongst the pines and traipse out each morning to the walls and rock slabs that fringe the valley. The climbing here is very specialised: big-wall techniques and a pre-dominance of cracks as features for the climber to find purchase upon. What I enjoyed was the fabled Californian weather, day after day of blue skies and no need to sit around, twiddling your thumbs, waiting for the weather to improve.

Graeme and I did a lot of free climbs, climbing cracks and slabs and a few aid routes. One of the more spectacular routes was the Leaning Tower, a 1,200-foot-high tower of granite that overhung from start to finish and involved some interesting problems along the way. Because it was a two-day climb, we brought a haul sack filled with food and water and sleeping-bags on an additional rope that hung below us. It also gave us an idea of how overhung the tower was as it indicated plumb vertical when it hung freely. After the first pitch of climbing it hung about forty feet from the wall. For this type of rock climbing you find yourself weighed down with technical paraphernalia and I felt more like an overworked technician involved in a most intimidating task in a very exposed place than a climber. Just to make things more enthralling on our first day on the wall, I found the occasional bolt in some of the bolt ladders was missing, completely sheared at the rock's surface. This necessitated using a handy tool, the cheating stick; simply a straightened wire clothes-hanger with a hook on the end and one of my etriers (small tape ladder) attached to it. With this contraption, I was able to reach the extra distance to the bolt above, place the hook through the hold in the bolt and then step gingerly into the etrier (feeling very like a monkey hanging at a great height from a piece of hot wire).

The sun was low and the sky already a brilliant gold as I crawled in an ungainly fashion on to the sloping guano-covered ledge with no rope to spare. Once Graeme had joined me on the ledge we traversed fifty feet to one side to a small but reasonably level area where we would spend the night. Here we sat in the darkness with our feet over the edge, drinking a can of beer each and nibbling at cheese and sardines. The roar of the traffic below filled the valley as the lights of cars and Winnebagos went to and fro the tunnel at the base of the valley. The contrasts in the valley were certainly marked and I found it difficult to believe, at times, that we were really in the mountains at all.

I belayed Graeme in the cool morning air as he pounded piton after piton into an awkward diagonal crack which led off to the right. From here on there were fewer bolts and we had to rely on placing our own pitons and nuts in the cracks. The diagonal traverse proved very strenuous, both for Graeme who led it and for me as I followed, removing the pitons by bashing them from side to side with my hammer. We moved slowly, as the climbing was difficult and very tiring. I watched Graeme climb over a six-foot overhang and asked him what he could see above. His reply didn't strike me as overly optimistic as far as reaching the top was concerned. I joined him in the dimming light under a giant twenty-foot overhang. I swallowed. It was my lead. I snapped an etrier on to a piton, climbed up it and leaned out placing my second etrier under the roof. Stepping into it, I swung from side to side as I hung, suspended, from the roof above me. With over 1,000 feet of air below me and my being twenty feet out from the face of the Leaning Tower itself, it meant I was displaced a long way, horizontally, from the start of the climb; I was out over the pine forests that stood near the foot of the wall! I struggled up the frighteningly exposed lip of the roof and on to a narrow sloping ledge above. Here I secured myself and called down to Graeme. We had one more pitch to climb before we were reunited with trees and streams and countryside that seemed cheerfully more amenable to support a flat-earth theory than did the Leaning Tower.

At the end of December 1978, I returned to New Zealand to work and raise funds for the Ama Dablam expedition in late 1979. Ama Dablam is an impressive 22,500-foot-high peak in the Mount Everest area of Nepal, and I think it was about this time that Dad resigned himself to the fact that I had become an incurable adventurer and climber with a propensity for pursuing outlandish projects whenever possible. It made life a lot easier, as I no longer felt I had to worry myself with such profound questions as to whether I should return to university and become a geologist or whether I should join Air New Zealand. I could allow myself to follow what meant most to me—the wilderness and the wide open spaces. Early in 1979 Dad and I went hiking in the South Island. It was a magnificent trip; we had no ambitious plans, only to cross a couple of high passes and descend the great valleys on the far sides. I think and discuss matters best while on foot, going somewhere, it doesn't matter where. From the Matuki valley we crossed into the Dart valley system and then to the Rees. We were on the march for hour after hour as we crossed the broad, green river-flats and passed through groves of native beech and matagouri and occasionally crossed the braided rivers. The water was always very cold as the rivers' sources lay amongst the snow fields above and it often took some time to warm our feet. At night we stopped at old musterers' huts and cooked a variety of simple meals over a compact petrol stove. I remember one evening when I produced a half-bottle of good red wine and we savoured every taste as we sat around the chuffing stove.

A few months later we were in Nepal. My father had an

intensive building programme in the Solu Khumbu region with schools, medical clinics and a bridge included in the programme. I helped with this work but also managed to fit in a reconnaissance trip to the foot of Ama Dablam. I wrote enthusiastically about the intended route on the mountain to my three expedition climbing companions back in New Zealand. The Ama Dablam expedition was to spark off another shattering and disorientating period of my life. The expedition was a fine one, we all got on well, we did some good climbing and we enjoyed ourselves while we were at it. It was just the tragedy that ended our adventure together that marred it. Suddenly everything that could possibly (or impossibly) go wrong, did go wrong . . . and in the most grave fashion.

The Mingbo Face of Ama Dablam (the West Face) has never been climbed and poses a magnificent objective. On such an attractive mountain a steep and technically demanding route becomes most compelling. I suppose it's one of those lines that make you dream of climbing it. Merv English, Geoff Gabites, Ken Hyslop and I made up our New Zealand team and in an air of excitement we set up Base Camp at Mingbo at the foot of the mountain. After a period of reconnaissance we erected two small tents as our Advance Base Camp at 17,500 feet on a small rock platform protruding from the lower slopes of the mountain. Over the ensuing days we established a route up the glacier to the bergschrund at the foot of the face and climbed the steep ice slope above it. One thousand feet up this slope rose a rock band that overhung in places and posed the first major difficulty. We considered that this would be worth fixing with rope so that when we came to make our summit attempt we could climb this section quickly.

At ten thirty at night on October 22nd 1979, we set off. We left the Advance Base Camp and ascended the glacier to the bergschrund and hence up the ice slope to our fixed ropes. As soon as all four of us had climbed the ropes to above the rock band we moved out into the moonlit central gully. It was an incredible feeling being up there in that broad, steep gully with bluffs, bulges of ice and the great Dablam ice cliff far above. We climbed on, hugging the side of the gully so as to be out of any avalanche danger and as we gained height the angle of the gully increased until we found ourselves on fifty-five to sixty-degree green ice. This meant slower progress and proved a great deal more strenuous. Across to the right side of the gully the face looked less fierce, so we traversed the green ice-bulges to some steep arêtes that we climbed for two pitches before stopping for the day. The sun had been on us for several hours and we were all tired and dehydrated. We cut narrow platforms, wide enough for one man each, in the sides of the snow arête and set up anchors on to which we could tie ourselves. We were ten rope lengths (pitches) above the rock band now and at over 20,000 feet on a steep and very serious face.

Below the ethereal silence of the heavens and the majestic summit of Ama Dablam we slept in fits and starts as waves of spin-drift wafted down the face, building up on our sleeping-bags and doing its damnedest to sneak in through the small gaps where our noses protruded from the bags. Frequently I had to rescue my feet and half the sleeping-bag from the dark void below the ledge so I tightened the rope to which I was tied in order to secure myself more effectively.

Little enthusiasm filled us that morning as we crawled out of our warm sleeping-bags into the cold. We traversed left from our bivouac ledges beneath a smooth rock bluff. The climbing involved some of the steepest ice on the route. It was as solid as the hobs of hell and at an angle of sixty to seventy degrees. At over 20,000 feet it proved hard work with only the front points of our crampons scratching tenuous little scars on the glassy surface and thousands of feet of air beneath our heels. Breathing deeply in the thin air we climbed an ice-choked crack system that led through the rock bluff and we emerged into the sunlight. The face above leaned back to fifty degrees and we could see the left-hand ice cliff a short distance above and to our left. We planned to bivouac on top of it, relax with the world at our feet, and climb the final 1,500 feet to Ama Dablam's summit the next day. I felt success was now a certainty as we had climbed the hardest section of the route and we all exuded a consequent contentment. We were no more than 200 feet from our proposed bivouac site when bang! There was a frightful cracking sound from above, then a dull roar that intensified to a deafening boom. It was an ice avalanche from the Dablam ice cliff and it was coming right for us. Giant armchairs of green ice bounded down towards us and a wave of smaller debris rumbled down the face itself. I grabbed hold of my

ice-axe and hammer above me, hugging close to the face, trying
to leave only my helmet and my pack exposed to what would
very soon be on me. I desperately wanted to believe it was only a
powder snow avalanche, but a horrible feeling inside refused to
oblige the fantasy. Ten strong men pulled on my legs, an angry
crowd beat on my helmet with sticks and stones and shouted in
my ears. I could hold on no longer and I fell, tumbling in a storm
of meteorites rushing across the heavens.

"This is it, this is it . . ."

I was hanging on a rope on some very steep, icy ground. I
groped about trying to reorientate myself and pull myself upright.
It was then that I discovered I had a severely broken arm. I
noticed some movement above me. It was Merv. I wasn't alone.
A short distance below me was Geoff; his rope had miraculously
caught between me and my rope. We looked down the face and
called to Ken. There was only silence in response. Ken was dead,
killed by the blocks of ice.

Merv descended the tatty remnants of our rope and put his arm
around me; we leaned our battered helmet-clad heads against the
ice and wept. What a nightmare had come to our happiness, our
success . . . and now this ghastly calamity at 21,000 feet on a
sunny day in the Himalayas. The loss of Ken still shocks and
haunts me. We were such an ebullient bunch of adventurers and
suddenly we were physically and emotionally devastated.

That same day we began to descend. I was fortunate my two
companions had sustained lesser injuries than mine as without
their help my chances of reaching the bottom were negligible. It
took us three days to return to our Advance Base Camp and they
were to be some of the most harrowing and uncertain days of my
life. The pain and grinding of bones was excruciating, but worst
of all was the hopelessness I felt due to shattered dreams and the
terrible death of a close friend. I remember looking down at our
two little tents at the Advance Base Camp 3,500 feet below.
I imagined their comfort, their security, their warmth and
remembered the good times we had all had there together . . . I
couldn't envisage ever returning there. The descent that lay
ahead of us seemed insuperable in our condition and I resolved to
devote all my energy to one theme, survival. For three days I was
lowered down the face and when it grew dark we stopped for the
night. Our first bivouac was on a ledge that the three of us could

A hilltop village near Pokhara.

Aid, ahead, and Paul negotiating the crevasses of the Everest Icefall.

Lhotse rises at the head of the Western Cwm. In the foreground,
Advance Base Camp at 21,500 feet.

The final camp at 25,700 feet.

Fred returns from the Geneva Spur, above the high speed wind clouds
over Lhotse's summit.

only just manage to sit upon with our feet hanging down the face and our backs against the wall behind. The second night was spent on the one-man-ledges we had cut in the face ourselves two days before. As darkness drew upon us on the third day we reached Advance Base Camp, thanks to the help we received that day from an Austrian expedition who had witnessed the avalanche and who had come to our aid. I thought it was all over when we reached the bottom of the face that evening but in reality the horror had only just begun.

The next morning I was bundled into a helicopter which lifted off, drifting past the Mingbo Face and descended into the Dudh Kosi valley. We flew below the summits of Kangtega and Tramserku and over the Thyangboche monastery nestled among rhododendron trees on its hilltop perch. Across to Khumjung village and, with a long, arching turn we touched down in an empty potato field below Khunde hospital. Dad was there. We looked at one another. There seemed to be nothing to say, just a feeling of love and concern. He climbed aboard and we were gone – to hospital in Kathmandu. It had all happened so suddenly: the climb with the summit so near, the nightmare, the descent, and then, from the lovely, fresh, alpine world to the pungency and clamour of Kathmandu.

I had never had serious injuries before and being immobilised took some getting used to. Just when I needed to walk and think, I was only able to lie on my back and watch the days drift by. With the urgency that encompassed our survival on the mountain being over, I was able to reflect on our experience, and the full impact of Ken's death hit me hard. Back in New Zealand I spent much of my time out at Anawhata, watching the black-back gulls soaring and the westerly squalls and the relentless rhythm of the sea. With my father, Sarah, and her husband Peter, I went to Great Barrier Island where we pitched tents by an idyllic shore and spent our days there swimming, fishing and diving in the crystal-clear water. During this time I began work on a book about our Ama Dablam experience and the year that I had spent in Nepal working on Himalayan Trust building projects.

During April 1980 I spent a strenuous week completing the final manuscript before flying back to Nepal. It was the first excursion since our harrowing experience on Ama Dablam and I was looking forward to it immensely. As well as participating in an aid project, I was to assist with the making of a film about my father's post-Everest activities in the Himalayas. I was anxious to see how my still-battered body would perform as we trekked through the mountains and additionally, for me, it would be a personal pilgrimage back to where our Ama Dablam venture had ended just six months before.

From Sydney I flew to Bangkok where I had a full day between flight connections before continuing on to Kathmandu. Suddenly my world seemed to collapse around me. I was arrested in broad daylight in a city street by two policemen whose interest in me initially confounded me but then, with the poignance of a Hollywood thriller in which I was an unwilling actor, the reality of the situation dawned on me. I was being extorted; they would drop their charges pertaining to the drugs they told me with a smile were mine, providing I co-operated with them. The day ended with me behind bars with about twenty miserable-looking Thais in a huge cell unfit for human occupation (we were out-numbered by the cockroaches). The only furnishings were two lazy fans overhead that rotated sluggishly in the 40°C heat. Over the ensuing three days I was to see with my own eyes what it must be like to be a heroin addict as most of the other inmates were indeed addicts and, thanks to the warders, had no need to interrupt their debilitating habit, providing they had the money.

I had been framed, and my simplistic, cut-and-dry ideas of justice had been shattered. Eventually my case was discharged and I returned home to New Zealand feeling disillusioned and bitter. I went south to the mountains, then returned to the North Island and worked on a ski field for the winter and all the time churned over in my mind the experiences of the past six months. I had been told while in Thailand that your twenty-fifth year had a habit of being a rough one, but all this seemed ridiculous. I felt that I could say I had endured, in one form or other, a broad range of life's woes. But I reasoned that it would do me no good to develop a giant chip on my shoulder or turn sullen and depressed, as that would only serve to show that I had lost the battle with the tribulations that had befallen me. I wrote: "Tomorrow, it's a new day and I have every intention to meet it and to make the most of it. Of all the things I have learned, I believe one is of particular importance: in life there is no time to waste."

I spent almost the duration of 1981 in the Himalayas making the first high-altitude traverse of that great mountain range with Graeme Dingle and Chewang Tashi, the Indian member of the expedition.

Crossing high glaciated passes we would descend into the valleys below, an alpine environment of azaleas and rhodo-dendrons, scattered with little villages. At these conglomerations of stone huts we halted to ask the way, purchase some of the very basic food the villagers survive upon, or even spend the night. I can remember so many nights when we huddled together with a group of high country villagers around a juniper fire, sitting cross-legged on the dusty floor, the firelight flickering on their hardy features. We were participants in a way of life that hasn't changed for centuries. When we embarked on the journey, we had anticipated an enormous mountaineering challenge, which it certainly was, but the cultural experience, a return to the grass roots of man's societies, and the challenge imposed by living so closely together, easily eclipsed it. Graeme, Tashi and I were walking and climbing together all day, cooking and eating together, and sleeping beneath the same dripping bivouac rock or shepherd's hut, or cramped tent, or beneath the same stars, for 265 days.

The traverse of the Himalayas was a Himalayan-scale marathon, an enormous challenge in mountaineering terms, and in endur-ance. For ten months we hiked across the alpine valleys and over passes, some of which were over 20,000 feet high, from the foot of Mount Kangchenjunga, the world's third-highest mountain, in Sikkim in the east, across the kingdom of Nepal, passing many of the world's greatest summits, including Mount Everest, to the Indian Himalayas, Kashmir and the Tibetan landscapes of Ladakh finally to reach the foot of K2, the world's second-highest mountain, in the desolation of Northern Pakistan—a region of extraordinarily spectacular geography.

Feeling like nomadic cavemen, we trudged the narrow paths and untracked mountainsides through a variety of cultures, races and lifestyles, passing by the world's most magnificent and gigantic mountains—as big as they are beautiful. I cannot imagine anywhere so multi-faceted in its peoples and geography. The collision of the Indian geological plate with that of the greater Asian plate, has brought to the world not merely the

Himalayas, the grandfather of mountain ranges, but a profusion of cultures, experiences and, to us, an enormous adventure.

It was an Indo–New Zealand expedition which was assisted by a small support team led by S. P. Chamoli and Doug Wilson with Ann Louise Mitcalfe, Corrina Gage and Shubash Roy making up the complement. They met us at prearranged rendezvous points along the way and restocked us with essential items.

As successful as the traverse had been, we all looked forward to returning home. To staying put for a while. Initially, on my return, I felt I slipped straight back into the Western way of life but I realised later that it took me some time to adjust. I wondered what all these lengthy and testing ventures might be doing to me as a person. I decided I needed to describe myself and in a light-hearted frame of mind I sat down and drafted an auto-definition:

"I would have to start by qualifying my answer. I imagine myself to be an *insouciant* character, born for the sixties but arriving too late to fill that mould. Still coining sixties' clichés, I marched into the seventies expecting it to be my developmental arena; somewhere to find my niche. Hey, man. The seventies were the pits! No one demonstrated for peace any more, they just cultivated paranoias. The intensity of this particular decade was quite bizarre and that really bugged me. Why? Why do you think? This was supposed to be my decade when I was supposed to flower . . . metaphorically speaking. The world was going to the dogs. David Bowie said it all with 'Diamond Dogs'. Confusion ruled, as I see it. So according to time's relentless plan, I was spat out at the end of the sinister seventies and into the awesome eighties, the decade of 1984. What now? I asked myself. I had dropped out of cricket and never really turned on to baseball. All these guys running around a paddock throwing a rock-hard ball at a defenceless soul with only a chunk of oddly shaped wood in his hands. The place was going to the pack. Our choices were few and the options were pretty dismal; that is, if it wasn't for the hills. Where a man could wander and think. He could perspire and enjoy it. He could stand tall without worrying if his body language was all wrong and some dude might come up and hit him for it. Yeh, it's a place where a bloke can still go to do heroic feats when nobody is around to watch and say you didn't do it right. The mountains have it all. Even with respect to your love life the hills are on target. In this day and age when promiscuity is rampant, you've got to take a good long look at yourself, preferably in a pool of a mountain stream. When it comes to women, or men as the case may be, 'one bird in the hand is worth two in the bush', that's what I tell those smooth-talking philanderers . . . Oh . . . Ah . . . So getting back to the . . . ah . . . question in hand, I generally consider myself to be a misplaced, however, gregarious and somewhat stultiloquent, sandy-haired dilettante with a passion for the salubrity of the hills."

11

Lhotse

PANDEMONIUM REIGNED AMID the clutter of high-altitude
clothing, food sachets and technical equipment. Lhotse,
Mount Everest's neighbour, is the world's fourth highest peak at
27,923 feet (8,511 metres) and the file of my Lhotse expedition
rose in similarly ominous proportions from the surface of my
desk. I found myself staring at it . . . incredulous . . . from where
I stood among the mounds of expedition paraphernalia.

"All I want to do is climb a bloody mountain," I pleaded with
myself. To do that it seems that I am to be, if not proficient, at
least vaguely competent at almost every business pursuit known
to man. I was bureaucrat, politician, diplomat, medic, typist,
dietician, businessman, public relations officer and had developed
a limited but effective ability to follow in the footsteps of Heath
Robinson, but most of all to be a tenacious optimist.

Remarkably my departure from New Zealand was accompanied by an almost disconcerting calm considering the previous
couple of weeks of feverish activity. I suddenly found myself at
the entrance to the departure lounge at the airport, struggling
with my forty-five-pound briefcase and preparing myself for
farewells. "Look after yourself," said my father as he wrung me
by the hand. I smiled. Language is quite incomplete when it
comes to expressing the feelings and emotions of people during
departures—especially in the sterile atmosphere of airports. I
marched for the departure lounge with tears welling in my eyes.

The well-intentioned, reasonably polite and mildly officious
airport security officer looked through my briefcase with obvious
delight. The assortment of camera equipment, film, climbing
hardware from pitons to ice screws and books and files was
apparently a little out of the ordinary.

The aircraft roared down the runway and lifted into the air

and my thoughts drifted to Nepal and my ultimate destination. I felt doubt . . . there was no doubt about that. Our objective was so gigantic and the agonies of altitude were frighteningly inescapable, or so it seemed as I remembered reading pages of such Himalayan heroics in books. I consoled myself. I had three partners who were competent and experienced, solid in every sense of the word, even body weight. Later on in Kathmandu, a French mountaineer labelled us the heaviest expedition he had ever seen. I was never quite sure how to take that quip. The expedition had been predominantly organised by post, over the telephone long distance to Scotland, Colorado and Queensland, and, in retrospect, with a little telepathic communication as well. I could only hope that our plans would proceed according to our arrangements and that the expedition members would duly appear at the appointed time from their various corners of the globe and thus form the Lhotse expedition. There was nothing I could do about it now, I told myself, I was on my way.

In Sydney I stayed with Michael Dillon who had filmed the Ocean to Sky jet-boat expedition in 1977. Together we rushed about the city obtaining items of food and equipment that I had arranged to procure here for the expedition. On July 29th Fred From was supposed to descend from the prickly heat of Brisbane to the hectic bustle of Sydney where he would join me for the flight to India. There were two contact numbers and I called them frequently during the day, but time and again I received a negative. No Fred Froms here. My mind began to play havoc! Had he broken his leg, or lost the Sydney addresses, or missed his flight (not impossible for Fred) or, worst of all, had he decided to finish his Ph.D. and withdraw from the expedition? I philosophised that at least this would benefit ionospheric physics, but it would not benefit the Lhotse expedition one iota! I tried to be rational: ionospheric physics was more important than the Lhotse expedition (although I didn't believe it) and I was sure a threesome could climb Lhotse.

Michael and I were sitting in his house sipping beer that evening and studiously avoiding the topic of Fred From, the Lhotse expedition and ionospheric physics. I looked at Michael, he was a reasonably strong-looking character, fit and had been to over 18,000 feet in the Himalayas. I wondered if he had a warm sleeping-bag and three months to spare?

There was a hesitant knock on the door. Michael's mother answered it.

"Excuse me," an Aussie voice began. "My name is Fred From," it said expectantly. "I'm trying to find Peter Hillary," it continued with a degree of vehemence.

Apparently Fred's taxi driver had never heard of the suburb let alone the street and consequently Fred had seen more of Australia's largest city than he had intended. I was mightily relieved that he had arrived, for we were due to depart early the following afternoon and, what is more, Fred had not yet paid for or procured his air ticket!

Fred is an old friend with whom I have done many alpine routes in New Zealand's Southern Alps. His unruly beard protrudes from the line of his jaw in an extraordinary array of tangles and his massive frame is certainly not a handicap in climbing. Adidas, who assisted the expedition and provided us all with running shoes and track suits, blinked twice when confronted with Fred's measurements. I had the feeling they thought he would be better off with rugby jerseys and boots with sprigs than athletic gear. Perhaps Fred's most well-known attribute is his love for climbing rock barefoot, using his large prehensile toes to balance his ninety-two-kilo bulk on minuscule rugosities. He had never been above Mount Cook's 12,000-odd feet and never beyond the boundaries of Australasia, so India and Nepal, with Lhotse's 27,900 feet as a final test-piece promised to be a very new experience for him.

Fred had joined the expedition only three weeks ago. Two other New Zealanders were to accompany me but they had had to withdraw just one month before we were due to leave. I was in Australia giving slide-shows. When I heard their decision I donned my thinking cap and pondered my dilemma. The chances of finding a suitable mountaineer with the inclination, the time and the money to join the expedition at such short notice seemed infinitesimal. A week later I was in Brisbane. I gave Fred a call and my problem was solved. Though I nearly lost him again when our Air India Jumbo, along with our 200 kilos of baggage, landed in Bombay. It was still not light when we disembarked and made our separate ways by bus across the tarmac to the immigration and customs hall. It was an hour before Fred and I were reunited amongst the throngs of people, the monsoon heat and humidity and our mountain of baggage. Fred had not been sure whether he was in transit or not and consequently went on a tour of Bombay airport in his efforts to ascertain where he should be and where I was. After waiting twenty minutes or so I decided I should go and search for him. I remained a couple of information counters, senior authorities and stairwells behind him until we both made our way to the baggage conveyor belts where I found Fred with consternation furrowing his brow.

Fred writes:

The customs queues were daunting, at least 100 people long and stationary. Our gear consisted of seven sinister-looking black drums which attracted the attention of a customs official. Pete opened his bag and produced a large poster of a mountain and a copy of the *National Geographic* with a picture of Lhotse, Nuptse and Everest in it. He managed to convey the idea that we weren't staying in India so we wouldn't have to pay duty, yet the Indian mountains were very special. While conducting an impromptu mountaineering lecture to one group of people, he offered to open one of the drums to show it really was mountaineering equipment, not that anyone could tell, even me.

Outside it looked like a giant cattle sale of people. I had a vision of having to walk across their heads like a sheep-dog to get anywhere. I stood beside our load of black drums and other bags, guarding them, while the sea of eyes peered in, inspecting a ginger-bearded man with huge feet and grey plastic boots who was nervously over-protecting a tall pile of very unusual baggage. Now I laugh at myself. If I could hardly lift the drums, they were probably safe from pickpockets.

We spent the day in Bombay sight-seeing before boarding another plane with our megatonnes of baggage and flying to New Delhi where we connected with our flight for Kathmandu.

The sky was filled with towering cumulus, a total layer of monsoon ebullience, and so, for the most part, the mountains were obscured. As the aircraft began its descent to Kathmandu a wave of relief came over me. Both Fred and I and our many bags and plastic drums of food and equipment had reached our destination. With a minimum of fuss we passed through the Nepalese immigration and customs hall and found ourselves ejected on to the street outside the airport building. The taxi-driver fraternity of Kathmandu besieged both us and our mountain of gear, quarrelling with us and with each other as to whom we were to patronise. It is times like these that a good pair of lungs, a healthy diaphragm and a powerful voice box, capable of distributing information at an intensity of more than 100 decibels, becomes invaluable.

We set off for the city in convoy with me in the front taxi, loaded to the gunnels with baggage, and Fred following similarly loaded. Before long I saw the familiar gateway that leads off the bumpy road to the Himalayan Trust flat, an apartment where we would stay for a week while we organised ourselves and our departure for the mountains. The taxi turned off the crowded street and into the comparative oasis of the garden in front of the flat. We carried our many bags of equipment inside and I staggered towards a bed where I sat and felt tempted to kick off my shoes and have a brief rest, but there was too much that had to be done. Adrian Burgess, another of the expedition members, was supposed to be in Kathmandu somewhere, so I wanted to locate him. We had to arrange meetings with the Ministry of Tourism's Mountaineering Section and be introduced to our liaison officer. There was food to be bought, equipment to be packed into thirty-kilo porter loads and a host of other tasks that swelled our intended seven-day stay in Kathmandu to ten. To complicate things further, we discovered a Government holiday which set us back another day.

As Fred said, "Nepal has a six-day working week with Saturday off, but more Government holidays than I could believe. What's more, I could find no calendar which predicted them all."

At twelve noon there was a 'tacker, tacker, tacker' sound outside as Elizabeth Hawley's blue Volkswagen pulled into the compound. Liz is Reuter's correspondent in Nepal and among her many other involvements she represents my father's Himalayan Trust in Kathmandu. But perhaps her most acknowledged contribution to a long succession of climbing expeditions has been in helping sort out the complexities of the bureaucracy that controls mountain climbing in Nepal. Liz is efficiency, orderliness, punctuality and thoroughness personified. I wondered what I had forgotten to do as I traipsed upstairs to her flat.

There was her usual warm welcome, beer and cashew nuts and a methodical up-date on local events, followed by a barrage of questions.

"So Fred's a replacement? Do the Ministry of Tourism know? Does Fred have an Alpine Club endorsement?"

Fred was looking perplexed and I tried to look casual.

"Ah, no."

"Well, he might as well go home then because he won't be allowed to go and climb Lhotse, will he?"

Oh, dear! I thought to myself, more work to do before we can depart for the serenity and peace of the mighty mountains.

Bells jingled downstairs at Liz's front door and I heard a Yorkshire voice. A minute later Adrian Burgess and his American lawyer wife, Lorna, appeared at the door of the room where Fred and I were sitting munching cashews. Adrian, or Aid as we called him, bounced in looking very fit. Terrifyingly fit I concluded as I considered trying to keep pace with him at 8,000 metres on Lhotse. We wrung each other by the hand and made all the appropriate introductions then returned to the task of consuming beer and cashews.

I had never climbed with Aid but knew his reputation. We had met periodically over the years in Kathmandu. I readily recognised his tolerant and amicable nature, his obvious physical strength and his impressive mountaineering repertoire. Originally I had invited both of the Burgess twins, Aid and Alan, to join the Lhotse expedition, but Alan had joined the Canadian Everest expedition with whom we would be sharing the Base Camp site. Paul Moores, a close friend of both Alan and Aid, was keen to join us and so we made up our four-man team, although Paul had not yet arrived in Kathmandu.

It gave me additional confidence having Aid on the team as his experience includes considerable high-altitude climbing. In the previous eighteen months he had attempted the West Ridge of Everest in winter, he and Alan had climbed Dhaulagiri, 26,795 feet (8,167 metres), and made the first winter ascent of Annapurna IV, 24,688 feet (7,525 metres). Aid is a one-time physical education teacher, more recently a carpenter and, as of now, is probably best described as a professional mountaineer. Before joining us, Aid and Lorna had been trekking the high and desolate regions of Northern Pakistan, Kashmir and Ladakh. So it was little wonder they both looked so lean and fit. However, Aid was a little concerned by his lack of extra condition (i.e. fat), as a certain amount can offset the natural weight loss experienced at altitude and serve as vital reserves during the final days leading to the summit. So he vowed to eat as much as he could over the ensuing few weeks and for the next ten days we pursued a vigorous campaign of eating out on the town in Kathmandu's many and varied restaurants.

Lorna was going to accompany us on the approach-march into the mountains, as was a friend of mine, Alex Witten-Hannah, from Auckland, who planned to arrive a few days later. He was a lawyer, like Lorna, and I hoped these two would help ensure a relaxed atmosphere during the trek to the Khumbu region where the four climbers would have to come to grips with the serious business of climbing Lhotse.

I felt decidedly run-of-the-mill beside the powerful physiques of Aid and Fred, and the arrival of six-foot-four Paul Moores from Scotland next day did nothing to help. However, such depressing observations on my part soon dissolved into an uproarious rapport in a motley of English accents. For the first few days I had the impression that none of us fully understood the other (particularly Paul's rapid Scottish slur), until a type of Commonwealth language was established.

I had only met Paul once some years before and he had established himself in my mind during that brief meeting as someone fun to party with. He is also a very experienced and competent mountaineer and had been to over 25,000 feet on Nanga Parbat a few years before. Paul works at Glencoe in Scotland as a climbing instructor for the military. He is a tough character both when it comes to difficult climbing and to bargaining with people, as many a Kathmandu shopkeeper discovered. When I think back I marvel at the four very different characters who made up our team and am sure that it was our diversity that made things always interesting, always exciting. Although I had my apprehensions about bringing together such a mixture of nationalities and, indeed, people who barely knew one another, we were to be a very happy team.

Though this was a Commonwealth expedition by nationality, the word would certainly be a misnomer for the financial status of the expedition. We were small and impecunious but we had big plans. Lhotse, as the world's fourth highest mountain, is a bit of a cloud piercer!

The monsoon manifested itself with lead-grey skies and cloudbursts of torrential rain as we rushed about the crowded streets of Kathmandu. We purchased pots and pans from retailers tucked away in narrow streets barely ten feet wide in the depths of the bazaars, and food from the colourful vegetable and grain markets. Then there were the hardware and second-hand equipment shops where we procured items that either we had forgotten to bring from home or Aid and I did not have in our inventories stored in Kathmandu. It was like trying to shop in sixteenth-century Europe for twentieth-century materialism. Frequently we had to make do with what approximated a required item and invariably this was more than satisfactory. At the end of each day the little Morris mini truck that my father has in Kathmandu would trundle back through the crowded bazaars to the flat, laden with food and equipment and weary, footsore sahibs. We had numerous meetings with His Majesty's Government of Nepal's Mountaineering Section of the Ministry of Tourism. We solved the problem of Fred's endorsement, were briefed by a very astute and pleasant Ministry official and finally introduced to our liaison officer, a slight, sinewy sub-inspector from the Nepalese Police Force. He was to accompany us as far as Base Camp, representing the Nepalese Government. Mahendra Bhattachan seemed a shy, fairly unassuming fellow when we first met him, but jovial enough and certainly agreeable to our plans. Later we learned he was a third *dan* black belt Karate expert and if that was not enough, a force to be reckoned with around the conference table, or in our case, around a cheap, plywood box that served as a table. Fortunately for us Mahendra's strengths were always on our side and we all became good friends.

Nepalese law requires every expedition to employ some staff to cook and care for the liaison officer, help deal with local porters, act as a mail-runner from Base Camp and so on. We had a sirdar, or Sherpa foreman, called Phu Tenzing who had worked with me before on Ama Dablam, a tough and experienced expedition Sherpa, not afraid of working hard. His job was to organise and control our porters during the approach-march to Base Camp and to assist us at Base Camp. Occasionally he would

descend to villages down-valley to deliver messages to the police
post there for our liaison officer.

An amicable man with a huge smile, also called Tenzing, was
our cook and continually surprised us with his ability to produce
haute cuisine in astonishing conditions. He proved to be quite a
character and made life in Base Camp a lot more fun and comfortable. To assist Tenzing we employed a young chap called
Krishna as cookboy. He too was light-hearted and hard-working.
All in all, these people meant that although life high on the
mountain would be fairly basic and, at times, our existence
would be harsh, we could descend to Base Camp and live well,
enjoying a touch of the 'pukka sahib'.

We left the city one surprising, sunny, monsoon morning. It
was August 9th. We would not return to Kathmandu until
October 16th. We found ourselves, along with fifty bamboo
porter baskets of food and equipment, each weighing thirty
kilos, bumping along on the back of a truck behind a driver who
was infatuated with his loud and piercing horn. He sounded it at
every available opportunity and, failing the opportunities, used
it to herald our imminent arrival at any village or bridge. The
journey proceeded in a series of fits and starts and police check-
posts. When we began travelling on some newly-made road that
snaked across the flanks of vast Himalayan hillsides, the ride
became most uncomfortable. With the utmost care our driver
insisted on easing only the front wheels of the truck across any
corrugations, culverts, ruts or washouts and would then accelerate
ferociously, causing the rear half of the vehicle, in which we
travelled, to be vaulted abruptly skywards. Then the dark ceiling
of cloud released its load with monsoon intensity and we huddled
beneath the canvas canopy trying to avoid drips as the truck
inched its way along the road.

At Kirantichap village beneath an expansive pipal tree the ride
came to a halt. We emerged bruised and sore and unloaded the
gear into a mud-floored house beside the clay path to Khumbu.
Phu Tenzing had arrived the day before to arrange local porters
to carry our loads and had had a great deal of difficulty obtaining
any. The monsoon of course was the time for cultivation and all
the villagers were busy tending their terraced fields, diverting
water through the paddies and planting seedlings. But he also
explained, rather sheepishly, that there were two large Everest

expeditions ahead of us on the trail and that they had absorbed a substantial proportion of the available porters. They had also inflated the wages and it seemed we would have to follow suit in order to get anyone to work for us.

The following morning we wandered around Kirantichap, pacing time, hoping Phu Tenzing would be more successful during this day's recruitment effort. We were all impatient to be on our way, get our teeth into the climb, and more important, to reach an altitude where we would begin to acclimatise. But for the moment Kirantichap was a beautiful place to·be. The great valleys yawning beneath us with the never-absent murmur of Himalayan-scale wind and river; the hillsides were speckled with villages, a patchwork quilt of terraced fields and paddies, worked by people who, despite our present porter inflation problem, still lived simple agricultural lives where cash-in-hand plays only a minor role. By midday the clouds were filling the sky and we retreated to eat lunch and discuss tactics. We decided we would depart the next day with what porters we had and would leave Phu Tenzing to bring up the rear and our remaining loads as soon as he could find the necessary porters.

It was during the walk-in and times like our stay in Kirantichap that the process of getting to know one another began. Paul and Aid already knew each other's strengths and weaknesses. They'd climbed together since 1972 and that included attempts on both Annapurna II and Nanga Parbat. To them Fred and I were the imponderables. Aid confided to his diary, "Although Peter had had an accident on Ama Dablam, I knew it was a very bold and pushy route, so I knew the psychology of his climbing was likewise." Understandably they both placed an initial unspoken question mark against Fred as the Himalayan novice on the team. But when it came to the point nobody needed to have worried. He went as strongly as any of us.

The walk-in was also a time of self-realisation: just how far we were from home and how long we were to be separated from our friends and families. In a way, it is the ultimate discipline, preventing one from tossing in the towel and rushing home to those you love and miss. But then the great goals, however obscure, were never meant to be easy, I am sure of that.

By seven a.m. we were marching along the slippery clay track, waving back at a rather forlorn looking Phu Tenzing and happy that we were on our way. The track descended steeply from Kirantichap's breezy knoll into the prickly heat of the valley. It led through pine forests and into broad-leaf jungle and then cut across the lush green of terraced paddies where groups of women in bright coloured saris toiled. At the base of the valley, truly in the banana belt, flowed the Bhota Kosi, a large grey river draining the Rolwaling valley and the Tibetan border. An ancient steel cable bridge spanned the river and I noticed the cast iron plaques at each end proclaiming '1913, Aberdeen Scotland'. We climbed the steep hillside on the far side of the bridge, and I pondered the anomaly of Scottish hardware in these hills.

We all perspired heavily in the already oppressive heat. Our porters, their sinewy, muscled legs straining beneath the burden of their thirty-kilo loads, had stopped for tea and food down by the bridge. It was to be a long slow journey into the Khumbu region. The porters needed cajoling periodically which proved a tedious and frustrating business. In these hills time is free. Certainly, they believe their time is. Consequently it did not matter to most of them whether we reached the day's destination . . . which, all in all, proved to be at considerable variance to the ideas of the more impatient sahibs.

In the late morning we would halt for a sizeable brunch and then stagger on, feeling distended, into the early afternoon. As the sky's grey turned to black and a double-bass concerto played above us, we would halt to pitch our tents or find accommodation in a house for the night. If we had timed it correctly then we missed the torrential downpours and the worst of the mud and the local annelid scourge, leeches. One day we saw hundreds of leeches, two inch-long yellow stems, protruding from the bushes along the track, and gyrating from side to side in a frenzy of anticipation for approaching sahibs' blood.

Dinners, just to change the topic, were a most relaxed affair. Having had a couple of hours to rest, read and write we would emerge to imbibe the local alcoholic brew. Tenzing would then serve soup, chicken stew with vegetables and rice followed by fresh fruit and a choice of tea, coffee or chocolate drink. Although our life was one of simplicity it was eminently liveable. We were like last century's British colonials making an intrepid sortie into the uncharted Himalayas. Umbrellas in hand and light haversacks on our backs, we strutted the mountain pathways and in the evenings were served by our faithful Sherpas.

For five days we climbed gigantic hillsides to cloud-besieged passes and descended slippery switchback tracks down through the mist-enshrouded rhododendron forests thousands of feet to the valley below. It was a type of geographical leapfrog. When we reached Junbesi we halted for a day to change some of our porters and wait for Phu Tenzing. While Fred and I went down-valley to visit Phaphlu hospital, the remainder of the team enjoyed a laid-back day which, on our return, appeared to have slipped by with the aid of the contents of several bottles of *rakshi*, the local distilled brew. Considerable porter problems had flared up during the day. Groups of porters we had were demanding more pay and we were still short of porters for some of our fifty loads of food and equipment. I found myself dreaming of my father's sirdar, and a close family friend, Mingma Tsering. If he'd been around our problems would have dissolved in minutes. But Mahendra, our liaison officer, was most helpful, sorting out grievances so that we could depart next morning. It was a relief when Phu Tenzing and the rest of our porters duly arrived.

The next day a somewhat unenthusiastic bunch of porters trudged out of Junbesi, cutting across the valley towards the Taksindu La, the pass which leads to the Dudh Kosi valley and the Khumbu region. By mid-afternoon we had descended from the pass to Manedingma village, nestled in the hillside jungle. Here further problems arose with a particularly awkward group of our porters whose ring-leader we did not trust. After a brief but volatile meeting we paid them off and much to our surprise the burly ring-leader with his Nepali cap tilted forward on his head came to say goodbye and to thank us. We were fortunate in obtaining more porters without too much difficulty and headed on next day, down to the foaming torrent of the Dudh Kosi river (translated it appropriately means milk river). From the stifling humidity of the bowels of the valley we climbed abruptly once more, up the broad hillsides, passing small villages and terraced fields until we again reached the rhododendrons and holly trees. It was raining when we halted at the tiny track-side teahouse of Karte and crammed our many loads and ourselves into the one large room that was available to us. I was attempting to count the loads stacked in the middle of the floor, and went outside to see if there were any more arriving, when I noticed a familiar face coming down the track. He was striding out with a purpose, a flannel hat on his head and a broad smile across his face. It was Mingma Tsering!

"Hello, Peter."

"Mingma! Where are you going?"

"Oh, I hearing you some trouble having. I nothing much doing so down coming. Some help giving."

We experienced no further porter problems and when we reached Khunde village, where Mingma lives in the heart of the Khumbu, we hired new porters and load-carrying animals for the standard rate, twenty-four rupees a day instead of thirty-five rupees. Mingma has a natural ability for managing people and motivating them. I watched him with our porters. When they stopped for a rest he would wait patiently with them and after five minutes or so he would crack a joke. They would all laugh and take up their loads and continue up the track. I'd known Mingma all my life, so was particularly pleased to see his special qualities immediately recognised by the others. Fred reckoned he would put many Australian businessmen to shame.

As we approached the upper limits of the leeches we passed a herd of cattle coming down the track. Fred and I noticed an obscenely large leech on the side of one cow's body and Fred tried to remove it with his fingers. We were all standing around ineffectually, but Mingma told us not to worry. He had just the thing. He reached into his pack and produced a large can of aerosol (Aeroguard I think it was) and promptly sprayed the slimy and bloated worm. It was an ideal solution! I have since added such an aerosol to my list of prerequisites for trekking during the monsoon.

After two weeks' trekking through the foothills we had reached Khunde, an idyllic alpine hamlet, at 13,000 feet. Here we halted for two days to acclimatise as per our careful acclimatisation programme, to change porters and to be reunited with many old friends that both Adrian and I have in the region. It turned out to be a very social period with an exhausting succession of luncheon and dinner engagements, not to mention mid-morning cocktails. (Sherpa beer, *chung*, is probably best described as a cocktail due to its many and varied contents.) Khunde is particularly beautiful at this time of year. The sacred rock peak, Khumbila, rises in a series of great bluffs to its summit directly behind the village and a low knoll lies on the south side, scattered with blue firs and yellow-blossomed rhododendron. The fields, divided off by precarious-looking stone walls, are green with potato plants and amongst these fertile gardens are the stone-walled houses with wood and slate tiled roofs and small, poky windows to retain the heat. On the green hillsides above the treeline we could see yaks grazing and across the valley rose the spectacle of snow-clad peaks; the classical serrated lines of Tramserku rising to a jagged summit, the sheer rock walls of Kangtega capped by a smooth glacier and the extraordinary form of Ama Dablam—a gigantic sphinx-like mountain with sweeping ridges and blocky summit well above all surrounding relief. I stared at the West Face, the familiar gullies and rock steps, the ice cliff that had halted us, causing disaster and sadness. Cloud rose out of the Dudh Kosi valley enveloping the peaks, the mountainsides, the yaks and even the village.

We had one more uproarious party at Mingma's house before the appointed day for departure when we continued up-valley towards Lhotse and to the Everest-Lhotse Base Camp on the Tibetan border. However, my head was anything but filled with such inspiring thoughts; it was sore and I felt rather poorly. Alex looked as if he had become a geriatric before his time and he complained of heart fibrilations.

"I'll never drink again," I moaned as I staggered along the mountainside' path. Aid later rationalised our indulgences. "Since altitude sickness is just like a hangover we are, in fact, already training!"

We climbed through rhododendron forests to Thyangboche monastery at 13,000 feet where we halted for the night. Our fifty loads of food, fuel, tents and climbing equipment were behind us, moving slowly upon the backs of large furry yaks that now carried most of our gear. As the light began to fade the ceiling of grey, monsoon cloud started to clear. We peered north . . . and upwards. A huge wall of rock and ice progressively appeared and as darkness began to fall we gazed at an awesome skyline. A jagged and imposing summit rose at the eastern end of a great wall of convoluted geology: Lhotse, a full 15,000 feet above us. "That's not it, is it, mate?" enquired an Australian voice. Aid wasn't sure whether it was the actual summit but there was no doubt that the colossal mountain before us, with the tip of Everest's summit appearing over the ridge-line, was Lhotse. A barrage of camera shutters recorded the brief clearance for posterity.

From Thyangboche our yak train ambled on to Pheriche, then Lobuche, along a track that wound its way ever higher into the mountains, beyond the rhododendrons and above the azalea scrub to the moraines and ice of the Khumbu Glacier at 16,000 feet. At the head of the glacier lay passes into Tibet and high above in the cloud our objective, Lhotse, alongside its big brother, Mount Everest.

12

Through the Icefall

I FOLLOWED THE YAKS over the glacier ice to some moraines below the chaotic staircase of the notoriously dangerous Khumbu Icefall. They were slow but surefooted, even beneath the sixty kilos of our equipment that each of them carried. I could see Adrian and Paul ahead, already levelling out tent platforms amongst the grey morainic rubble and expedition debris of the Everest Base Camp area. This would be our home, our base for the next two months. A magnificent place surrounded by jagged peaks and on one side the tumbling whiteness of the Icefall; however, you hardly feel you tread where no one else has trod before. For Everest Base Camp, the same Base Camp area used for climbing Mount Lhotse, our objective, is an appalling rubbish heap—or more correctly, a great number of rubbish heaps: rusting tin cans, empty gas cylinders, the remains of tents, glass bottles, paper and cardboard, broken crampons and twisted aluminium ladders. For myself, I found that my childhood memories of when I had first visited Base Camp at the age of twelve needed little amendment. It had been a cold anticlimactic rubbish heap then. It hadn't changed. And of course we were not alone. Two separate Everest expeditions, one Catalan, going for the West Ridge, and a multi-million dollar Canadian team attempting the South Pillar, were already established. So rather than feeling like a group of friends setting up camp in some gloriously pristine spot, we felt more like 'the new folks in town'.

Paul wrote: "Our neighbours made their own little town 200 yards away with all mod-cons, solar heated showers and many high radio antennas. With all the strange-shaped tents and colours it would have made a good sequence in a science fiction movie."

We could all feel the 17,500 feet altitude, we were lethargic and easily out of breath as we worked on building platforms for tents and counting the loads as they arrived. Aid and I, with Mahendra's help, paid off our porters and yak drivers. We sat on morainic boulders counting money from our aluminium money case, calling out Sherpa names and checking their respective loads. Before long the yaks and porters had gone, returning down the glacier, and we were left amidst a sea of bags and drums, and bamboo baskets.

Everest being Everest the mountain is 'booked' for years ahead, the Ministry of Tourism in Kathmandu marshalling expeditions by different routes like a remote control cop. Access to the West Face of Lhotse is up the same Khumbu Icefall which is also used by climbers attempting Everest via the Western Cwm, so Ministry regulations require any Lhotse expedition to have written agreement from the parallel Everest party that they will share a route through the Icefall. Accordingly, I wrote to the Canadian leader who agreed, with one stipulation, that we would leave them to fix the route. This suited us. The Canadians would proudly undertake the logistically difficult business of fixing rope and ladders up the Icefall, which though the most hazardous part of scaling either Everest or Lhotse, is certainly not an attractive mountaineering proposition in itself. We had no great desire to climb it for any other reason than it barred access to the mountain we wished to climb.

In fact, the original Everest route, climbed by my father twenty-nine years before, ascended the West Face of Lhotse first before cutting across on to the South Col, between Everest and Lhotse, from where they ascended the South-East Ridge to the Everest summit. But as the Canadian expedition were attempting a new version of the Polish route on the South Pillar we would only need to share the route through the Icefall into the Western Cwm.

For our first night at Base Camp, August 26th, we were invited to the Canadian camp for dinner. We trudged across the moraines from our partially erected quarters towards the multitude of tents above which a Canadian and Nepalese flag fluttered. I felt like a ghetto kid kicking a tin can into the air as I sauntered along, hands in pockets and eyes on the rubble ahead. The Base Camp area, I decided, was a high-altitude anachronism.

The Canadian camp was expansive with about sixty men living there and, as we found later, had a clearly delineated social structure . . . even suburbs. There was the Sherpa quarter with its own cook tent on the eastern side of town, the doctor's residence on the northern perimeter, the most senior members, including Bill March, the leader, and deputy leader, Kiwi Gallagher, in the western suburbs and all the Canadian 'young guns' dwelt in the south side. A long off-white tent was where we were bound – the sahibs' mess tent. Bending low we entered, feeling ravenous . . . and apprehensive. What first came to mind was a British Columbian lumberjacks' camp. Men sat down both sides of two long tables, but there was hardly a word being said.

"Reticent pack of Chinooks," thought I.

Adrian was in front and he shook hands with Bill March and introduced the rest of us. Before long the atmosphere had livened up and, I noted, several bottles of Canadian Club had appeared. We had a pleasant evening with the Canadians but it did impress upon us the problems inherent in a large expedition.

Over the next four days we settled in to life at Everest Base Camp. We made our own camp as comfortable as possible with a tent each, a cook tent and a mess tent where we stored equipment and spent the cold evenings. I had a pleasant chat with Bill March and Kiwi Gallagher about the route through the Icefall and confirmed our intention of ascending it on September 1st, the first day we were entitled to set foot on the mountain. During that time the Canadians established their Camp 1 above the Icefall and made a reconnaissance trip deep into the Western Cwm itself. On August 30th while we sat in our mess tent eating our dinner, we listened to the rumbling of avalanches in the Icefall area and across the valley near the beautiful, conical peak of Pumo Ri (23,200 feet). For the more resounding avalanches, we would go out and stare in the direction of the sound to get some idea of where they were most frequent. One thing was for sure, we would need to move quickly in the Icefall and planned to make our first trip up to the Western Cwm as fast as possible. Later that night as I lay in my sleeping-bag I listened to the thousands of tons of glacier ice beneath me, creaking and groaning and the occasional dull thud. We would not notice any appreciable change in the position of our Base Camp over the next two months but we were moving, albeit very slowly, down-valley aboard the Khumbu Glacier. As I began to doze around eleven p.m. there was a deep roar, the sound of falling ice . . . hundreds of tons of it . . . from across the glacier near Pumo Ri. This time the sound did not quickly fade but continued to intensify. The booming and crashing of falling ice reverberated around the head of the valley and as I lay there in the darkness I felt incredibly insignificant and a little fearful. Five minutes passed before the roar reduced to a faint rumble and I snuggled back into my sleeping-bag and dozed off to sleep.

As the sky became light there was another rumble from high above our cloud-besieged Base Camp. The rumbles grew to an intimidating roar and continued for several minutes. We all lay in our sleeping-bags inside our tents listening to the distant roar when a blast of wind struck the tents, shaking them wildly and deluged an inch of snow over the camp. The avalanche had been about a kilometre away and yet the ferocity of its wind blast had carried the snow down the Icefall to our camp . . . and beyond. Fred scrambled from his sleeping-bag and stumbled across to the Canadians, as we knew they intended to carry loads up the Icefall this particular morning. As he approached their camp in the overcast gloom of early morning, he could see several of their tents had collapsed in the onslaught of wind and snow. Fred continued to the centre of the camp where the Base radio set was kept. The walkie-talkies were jammed with the voices of pained and frightened men. Three Sherpas could not be accounted for and several other expedition members were being freed from tangles of rope and avalanche debris. It sounded like the most ghastly nightmare amidst the whiteness of ice and powder snow and thick cloud. It was hard for us to grasp that three men were dead.

Later one body was recovered and a depressed group returned from the Icefall with the victim. The other two Sherpas were never found. Several Canadians had spent that night at Camp 1 where eighteen inches of snow had fallen. At Base Camp we had had almost no precipitation whatsoever but were in a veil of cloud and consequently could not see whether there was fresh snow above or not. A combination of wind, forming wind slab snow, plus the fresh snow that had fallen during the night, had caused dangerous avalanche conditions on the West Shoulder of Everest (as it had on the surrounding peaks, judging by the considerable avalanche activity of the past twenty-four hours). It confirmed our fears of just how dangerous the Icefall was and made us all the more determined not to linger in it but to move rapidly. I remembered my father telling me of the most dangerous area of the Icefall during their expedition in 1953 being about two-thirds of the way up, a shelf they called the 'atom bomb area'. It had not changed in character only by name as the Canadians had given it a rather more blasé title, the 'Traverse'.

It was August 31st, the day before we had planned to make our first ascent of the Icefall. We discussed it together and concluded a delay of one or two days were in order. Several Canadians, including Bill March, were going down-valley with the body of the dead Sherpa and Mahendra decided to go with them to assist the Canadians' liaison officer with the formalities. I realised more than ever that we had been very fortunate to have a liaison officer like Mahendra Bhattachan. Difficult, often stressful, situations did not phase him and he was always willing to help, whether it be another liaison officer with major problems on his hands, or one of us moving rocks to build a toilet area.

One of the Canadians, 'Speedy' (Gordon) Smith, told us they intended to return to the Icefall on September 2nd to regain the route and to re-inhabit Camp 1. We decided we would leave early so that we could assist by plugging steps along the fresh snow-covered route and to ensure we would be clear of the Icefall by the time the sun reached it and stirred up more activity. Because we wanted to make as few journeys through the Icefall as possible our sirdar, Phu Tenzing, agreed to carry a load through. Phu Tenzing is a veteran of many high-altitude expeditions and had been to the South Col (26,000 feet) between Everest and Lhotse before, so I wasn't concerned about his being capable of it. My Auckland friend, Alex Witten-Hannah, had harboured a desire to reach the Western Cwm for some time and was very keen to assist us, so I agreed to let him take a load through the Icefall as well. He spent most of September 1st practising by climbing up and down the elegant shapes of the ice séracs in the Base Camp region. For Fred, the only one of us without previous Himalayan experience, it was a test-piece. How was he going to perform thousands of feet above the summit of Mount Cook?

We set out at three thirty a.m. on the 2nd. Phu Tenzing had juniper burning to the Sherpa deities on a moraine mound beside the camp and the rich aromatic scent filled the frosty air. He was

muttering copious '*om mani padme hum*s . . .' as we trudged off
into the darkness of the moraines beneath our thirty-pound packs
of fuel, tents and equipment. Adrian was in front with Paul close
behind and Fred, Phu Tenzing, Alex and I brought up the rear—
six specks of golden light from our headlamps moving steadily in
a sea of moonlit whiteness. For three hours we plugged steps
along the Canadians' Icefall route; across the low-angle ice, strewn
with the melted forms of the remnants of séracs, and on to the
steeper and more active Icefall where we clipped on to a fixed
rope. The higher we climbed, the more precarious the route
became. Twisted ladders spanning dark abysses and giant blocks
of ice the size of two-storeyed buildings slowly tipping over as
the Icefall progressed down-valley. The fixed rope led across
ladder after ladder spanning giant crevasses and wound its way
around the great blocks of ice until we reached the avalanche site.
An expansive tongue of ice blocks and snow extended across the
Icefall smothering all in its path. I pitied the two Sherpas who lay
there . . . an ignominious grave . . . we hurried on. None of us
wanted to linger in this section.

Far below we could see the lights of the Canadians and their
Sherpas leaving Base Camp and starting up the Icefall. By this
stage Alex had fallen behind us, as he was finding the strange,
debilitating effects of altitude difficult; however, he kept moving
steadily with his load. Phu Tenzing was tiring too but kept up
with Fred and me while Paul and Aid broke trail in front.

I clipped my jumar on to a steep section of rope and hauled
myself up the near-vertical face of an ice block. From the top I
could see into the Western Cwm and up towards Lhotse. Not far
off was a pile of equipment the Canadians had dumped from
earlier carries. As close as that depot looked, it took us another
half-hour to reach it as the hidden convolutions of the intervening
Icefall manifested themselves in deep valleys and complex mean-
dering. I hauled on my jumar, breathing deeply and thinking that
there was just not enough oxygen in the air to sustain my upward
plod when I reached the lip. Now I gazed directly into the
Western Cwm, to the head of the narrow Western Cwm Glacier
and towering above, huge and defiant, was Lhotse, still another
8,500 feet above where I stood. I was feeling tired as I plugged on
in the deep snow towards the depot where Aid and Paul were
already unloading their packs. But I was also feeling very pleased,

as I listened to Fred not far behind me. All four of us had gone well on our first day on the mountain. We had reached the top of the Icefall in three hours flat.

Already the sun had begun to rise and we could see the rays of its golden light on the West Shoulder of Everest. We wanted to be back in Base Camp when it hit the Icefall. We raced down the fixed ropes, rushing past groups of Canadians and Canadian Sherpas on their way up. I stopped and talked to Alex who was now not far from the top and, as he was happy to press on and come down a little later, I continued down. Some of the Canadians were working on the ladders that spanned large crevasses through the Traverse, the most active and potentially dangerous section of the Icefall. They all seemed very relaxed as they worked.

Shortly after eight a.m. we were down and feeling both satisfied with our effort and relieved. All of us had performed well, we had succeeded in getting a substantial proportion of our equipment above the Icefall and our adventure with Mount Lhotse was really under way.

It was nine thirty a.m. and we were all muddling about in the camp. Aid was reading and Paul was sorting equipment, Fred was putting his sleeping-bag outside to air in the sun and I was lying in my tent giving some thought to what I should do. There was a muffled rumble in the Icefall. Fred shouted to us. I poked my head out from the tent, and followed his gaze to a large cloud of snow that rose above the séracs of the Traverse. Fred told us it had appeared to be some sort of chain reaction as the puffs of airborne snow had appeared one after another along the line of the Traverse. Aid and Fred rushed across to the Canadian camp to find out what had happened. Our first anxiety was for Alex who still had to return to Base, and Aid was keen to check on his brother Al's whereabouts. The Canadians tried to make radio contact. Eventually they managed to call up a very shaken Rusty Baillie who talked of disaster.

As most of the Canadians were either in the Icefall already or down-valley at the Sherpa's cremation, we decided to help the rescue party. We were all apprehensive as the midday sun blasted down upon us and everywhere there was the sound of dripping water, a decaying glacier, a countdown to great danger. As we approached the fixed ropes we passed groups of Sherpas, all greatly shocked, who told us a range of conflicting stories as to what had happened and who had been killed. A short distance further into the white starkness of the Icefall, we met the main group of Canadians. They were returning to camp and said there was no more that could be done. The Traverse had completely collapsed, the route was in tatters, three people had miraculously escaped death, but one, Blair Griffiths, had been killed instantly by toppling blocks of ice. When would this spate of disasters cease? I wondered. The appalling loss of life shattered us all. All our high ideals and hopes for great adventure seemed dashed by tragedy. It had only been the evening before that I had spent an hour chatting with Blair, talking cameras and mountains. And now he was beyond retrieval. The past few days had been a nightmare.

Although we were safely back at Base Camp, Alex was still at large, supposedly above the Traverse area, as was Kiwi Gallagher. I only hoped they were together, as the thought of a tired Alex stumbling around alone in the Icefall during the middle of the day was alarming. We scanned the chaotic mass of ice and crevasses above until we located two tiny figures moving slowly back up the fixed ropes above the Traverse. With the aid of the Canadians' telescope, we were able to identify them as Alex and Kiwi. It transpired they had both reached the collapse area and found no one around, as they had expected. As the fixed ropes had been broken they decided to retreat to Camp 1 above and notify those who were ensconced there of what had happened. I was most relieved when Alex returned to Base Camp the next day after a night at the Canadian Camp 1. So was Alex.

That day we helped carry Blair's body down the Khumbu Glacier towards Lobuche where he would be cremated. As we struggled with the unwieldy sled that cradled the body, I found myself questioning our motives and our aims. Why go mountaineering? Was the Icefall worth the risk, even for a desirable summit? Perhaps the answer is to be found in the rationale for any endeavour which involves a challenge, and therefore risk, and the determination to succeed. The fact that mountaineers are attempting progressively more and more difficult objectives is to me a healthy sign . . . that society wishes to challenge itself, expand the parameters, to seek the ultimate. In a philosophical way, I suspect the day we are prepared to make do with the easy and assured route to a moderate success will be a sad day for our civilisation.

However, I found it difficult to reconcile such high-flown thoughts with the sacrifices that had been made. I suppose it reinforced my commitment to minimal logistics and reduced dangers, statistically, to the people involved.

As we started back up the glacier on our way to Base Camp, we were joined by Mahendra. He was returning from the cremation of the Sherpa who had perished a few days before. He was concerned by what had happened since his departure, and relieved when we remained in Base Camp over the following two weeks—well clear of the dreaded Icefall. During this time Alex left us, departing down-valley to Khunde.

After the second accident the Canadians and their Sherpas began talking of bad karma. Many of them felt the expedition should be abandoned. Rusty Baillie told Aid he would not return to the mountain. In both incidents he had narrowly escaped injury. "The letters at the end of the tunnel are ten feet high; I'd be a fool to ignore them," he said.

The expedition was in deep trouble, with abandonment high on the cards, and the Canadian decisions would affect us, due to our contractual agreement regarding the Icefall and our consequent dependence on them for this initial section. The next few days were strained. Seven Canadians marched out of camp on their way back to Canada which astonished the stalwart Catalan expedition, still camped nearby. "They should have made that decision before they left home," one senior expedition member told me when he learned of the defections and I suspect many of the Canadians who remained shared this view. I had a series of discussions with a demoralised Bill March and attempted to convince him of the worth of continuing. A number of compromises were mooted. They could no longer consider new and difficult routes on Everest and if they wished to put a Canadian on the summit they needed to repeat the 1953 South Col route. This, however, would involve using much of our route and under the strict Nepalese regulations they would have to receive our written agreement to share the route with them. Since the South Col route would take less time than their original objective, the South Pillar, it created a dilemma for our small expedition. In addition, the Canadians planned to climb Everest with oxygen and thus would not be restricted by as lengthy an acclimatisation period as we needed. This meant that we could, on agreeing to allow the Canadians to share our route, find ourselves 'high and dry' so to speak. If the Canadians pulled out of the Western Cwm while we were high on the mountain, not quite sufficiently acclimatised to try for the summit and without the means to maintain a path through the treacherous Icefall, we were simply cutting our own throats . . . or just doing ourselves out of a realistic attempt on Lhotse at all. Bill and the remaining Canadian climbers acknowledged that this posed a problem for us and said they admired our determination to persevere with the lightweight style of climb we had planned. The problem then boiled down to one of time. They obviously did not want to wait around for us while we carried our food and equipment up into the Western Cwm, which they had already done, for an extended period of inactivity could well be the straw that broke the camel's back as far as they were concerned. There was a renewed energy and even optimism being generated in the Canadian camp and they wanted, as did we, to get a move on.

We suggested a formula that Bill readily agreed to. To speed our progress by about one week he would provide us with food and tents from his depot above the Icefall. As the size of their expedition was now diminished, this would not endanger their own chances and it would mean virtually no more load-carrying trips through the Icefall. The second aspect of the agreement was that we had priority at leading the climbing on the Lhotse Face up to our Camp 4 in the vicinity of the South Col. Up to September 30th they agreed to remain behind us in order to give us the opportunity to climb the mountain in the style we had originally planned. (What transpired was that once we were all above the Icefall and the tensions of Base Camp—as if we had ascended beyond a 'worry line'—the two expeditions operated closely together.) This agreement seemed to everyone a fine compromise. It meant minimal delays for the large Canadian expedition, while allowing us, with no real disadvantage to them, to continue with our plans for climbing Lhotse without Sherpas and without the use of bottled oxygen.

The agreement brought a flush of relief and a refreshing *bonhomie* amongst us. Our expeditions were again on course for our respective summits and I think we all felt that the spirit of mountaineering as a sport had been upheld despite the complexities of bureaucracy. We were all climbers, and were in the

Himalayas to experience the ultimate in alpinism on a mammoth scale.

All we now needed was an improvement in the lingering monsoon weather conditions that plagued us. Every day the cloud rolled in obscuring all the peaks around us and dumping snow and sleet upon our camps. One morning there was a massive rock avalanche in the region of the Lho La. This route was being used by the Catalan expedition to the West Ridge of Everest and, they later told us, one hundred metres of near-vertical rock wall, up which their route had gone, had cleaved from the Lho La bluffs. The sound of hundreds of tons of rock crashing down towards the glacier unnerved us all, especially in the wake of what we had already experienced. Just the day before, the Catalans had made a third and successful attempt to take one of their Sherpa cooks up to their first camp, an extensive man-made snow cave above the Lho La. Apparently, he had grudgingly settled in to life at 20,000 feet on the Tibetan border and was coping with being separated from Base Camp by the 2,000-foot-high rock bluffs, when the huge rock avalanche occurred, cutting him off from the Base. He then said he would refuse to descend any new route that was put on to the rock wall, so on the radio schedule with Base Camp that evening, the Catalan hierarchy was informed of his concerns and requested to send the Sherpa cook a map of Tibet. He planned, we were told, to descend the Rongbuk Glacier into Tibet, head west along the border zone until he reached the Nangpa La, an old trading pass 19,000 feet high, by which he would return to Nepal and thence go home!

While the frustrating period of poor weather kept us camp-bound we waxed by turns lyrical, philosophical and even theological, as the glacier creaked and the avalanches roared. One evening we sallied forth in a blizzard to help the Catalans celebrate their national day with a banquet the like of which I had never anticipated sampling at 17,500 feet. There was Camembert and quails and Spanish beer chased with fine champagne and the Canadian liquor reserves. It proved a somewhat convulsive night and the morning after was one we all wished we could have 'skipped'. It was with a degree of relief that we greeted a change of weather for the better and made plans to return to the Western Cwm.

On September 16th we bade farewell to Mahendra and our
Sherpas and headed off into the darkness of the early morning to
make a second attempt to ascend the shambolic Icefall. We had
been forced back a few days before by bad weather and hoped
this time to regain the gear depot above. The route had fallen into
considerable disrepair and it was clear that the journey would
take us more than the three hours it had before. There were seven
of us—the four members of the Lhotse expedition and three
members of the Canadian Everest expedition: Aid's twin brother,
Al, Speedy Smith and Pat Morrow.

Some Canadian Sherpas accompanied us for the lower sections,
helping plug the route and drag the fixed ropes from beneath the
snow. The Traverse had changed completely. It was a nightmare
of tumbling blocks, gaping holes and tangled, snagged fixed line.
It was an awkward route now, involving a precarious scramble
over and around the gigantic and unstable obstacles. Moving on
such ground was unnerving. A mass of ice blocks temporarily
jammed across the mouths of great abysses was our only way
across many of the crevasses, so we all moved as quickly as we
could. Above the Traverse in the shallow basin where the
avalanche had been we found crevasses had opened up necessi-
tating wild leaps where before it had been just a stroll. In fact the
entire region seemed as if it was undermined, perhaps had even
hollowed out beneath the surface. Not wanting to spend much
time in the avalanche-prone area, we struggled on beneath our
heavy loads. In places the fixed ropes were as taut as violin
strings, in others they had gone. In one spot a double-ladder
bridge had dropped into a large crevasse as it had widened. We
could find no alternative route, so Paul tied a rope to the shaft of
his ice-axe, and lowered it like a fishing hook to lift the ladder
out. As the crevasse was now far wider than the two-ladder
bridge—it would have been about four ladders wide—we decided
to try descending thirty feet into the crevasse on to a snow
bridge. Al went first. With a good belay from Aid, he abseiled
into the crevasse and established that the snow bridge was
reasonably robust. He plugged steps across it to the other wall
of the crevasse and here positioned the remnants of the former
bridge as a vertical ladder. The higher we climbed up the Icefall
the deeper the fixed rope was beneath the snow. Sometimes we
had to dig up to four feet. Crusts had formed at various layers and

the task of pulling the submerged rope through the crusted snow proved exhausting at that altitude. Our progress was now much slower than we had anticipated and the sun was upon us. At least we were above the most dangerous part of the Icefall but the final section was proving more difficult than it had appeared before, and we more debilitated by our exertions, the intensity of the sun's heat reflected off the snow, and dehydration. Al, who was leading, found the old route to be impassable without a large number of ladders that we did not have and certainly had no intention of going to fetch. It was either bivouac where we were or keep moving. Aid led over to the left side and fortunately for us found an excellent route past the obstacles. It would obviously deteriorate fairly rapidly but by this stage longevity of the route to the depot was the last thing on our minds.

Eleven hours of plugging steps, pulling up the fixed rope, repairing the route and rerouting sections saw seven tired men above the Icefall, on the lip of the Western Cwm. We stumbled about erecting tents and locating food and stoves amongst the mountainous jumble of gear that lay at the depot. Within an hour the depot looked like, and was, our Camp 1. I felt badly dehydrated and decided to lie down in the large cook tent before moving into a small tent to spend the remainder of the afternoon. I rolled on to my side and bent my right knee. There was a sudden click somewhere in the knee joint and that unpleasant feeling of an injury deep inside. More a sickening discomfort than actual pain. A wave of nausea came over me. I couldn't think of a worse place to have cartilage problems. My knee was jammed in a bent position. It frightened me, for I was not at all sure I could descend the Icefall like that, let alone fast enough to ensure a reasonable safety margin. I crawled to the door of the tent and vomited. I clenched my teeth and growled as I kicked backwards with my right foot. My leg straightened to a point where it could either go no further or the cartilage would snap back into place and my leg could then straighten. A slight thud in my knee indicated the latter. Thank God it had gone back into place! I just lay where I was, with the others looking on aghast, feeling relief more than pain.

13

Into the Western Cwm

THAT EVENING WE discussed our plans for the next day. As more work was needed on the Icefall route, we decided to split up into two groups. One group would go further into the Western Cwm and reconnoitre the route, while the other would descend back into the Icefall, fix rope along the new route and repair damaged areas. Fred and I went back into the Icefall with Speedy and Pat. It was hard work and I felt a little depressed. My knee put a question-mark in my mind, I hadn't had any letters from the outside world for a while and I was feeling forgotten. The tragedies and delays were taking their toll; it was going to need a great deal of will-power to keep going.

A large number of Canadians and their Sherpas moved up to Camp 1 which began to sprawl, restricted only by the huge crevasses that lay around, marooning us like a deltaic remnant of the glacial chaos. We set up our own cooking facilities and began making preparations for the next few days. Paul and Aid said the route to Camp 2 looked all right, although they had only gone part of the way. We decided to make three carries of gear and food to 21,500 feet, the site of Camp 2 and our Advance Base Camp. This would assist our acclimatisation as we would return to Camp 1 each time until the third and final carry when we would establish our Advance Base Camp and remain up there.

At two a.m. on September 18th we rose and dressed. We lit the stoves and prepared breakfast and copious quantities of liquid. At three thirty a.m. we wandered off into the darkness following the golden arc of our headlamps. Not far behind came a group of Canadians and their Sherpas. The route took us backwards and forwards as we wound our way through the rows of crevasses across the Western Cwm. As it became light we passed beneath the expansive North Face of Nuptse, featured with flutings and

runnels and tiered by ice cliffs that leaned out from the great face
and left no illusions as to what would happen should they fracture.
The route ahead was uncertain as a huge crevasse stretched from
one side of the Western Cwm to the other. We divided into two
parties and set off to investigate the possibilities at either end. The
snow was crusted and quite deep, in places we sank up to our
calves. It made hard work and necessitated frequent halts to pant
in the thin air. The northern end of the crevasse afforded a satisfactory route although it did pass beneath some awesome ice
cliffs along the base of the West Shoulder, so once across we
moved quickly back towards the centre of the cwm.

We moved steadily, establishing our own rhythms of breathing
and pacing but co-ordinating the overall speed so as to accom-
modate a rope partner's pace. It was beginning to grow light and
I was enthralled by the dramatic scenery that lay around me. It
was also the feeling that I was entering an area where my father
had been twenty-nine years before. I imagined the feeling of
being amongst the first people into this shrine of the high altitudes.
It's an almost entirely enclosed amphitheatre on the greatest
scale. The South-West Face of Everest (29,000 feet) formed the
northern boundary and swinging around to the east rose our
objective, the West Face of Lhotse (27,900 feet) with the North
Wall of Nuptse (25,800 feet) completing the tight horseshoe
enclosure of the Western Cwm. The sun had still not risen and so
the lighting was flat and blue. The scene conjured thoughts of an
old, poorly exposed photograph, incredibly historical. I wondered
if Dad had been as excited when he first plugged a line of steps up
the cwm as I was. I suspected the answer was obvious! It was one
of the few times that I felt comparatively unleashed by the
debilitating effects of altitude and I plugged steps out in front
with enthusiasm – a high-altitude euphoria – or was it an hereditary
nostalgia!

We veered left towards a moraine that lay upon the ice at the
base of the South-West Face of Everest. Apparently this had been
the most popular site of Advance Base Camps in the cwm over
the past few years and the advantages of being camped on rocks
would be considerable. When the sun streams down on snow
you get almost total reflection and consequently the heat in a
concave reflecting surface such as the cwm is intense and most
unpleasant. Being camped on the moraine would reduce much of

this as the dark rocks would absorb the high concentrations of ultra-violet light experienced at these altitudes. And so it proved to be. I think the quality of our lives at Advance Base Camp was improved 100 per cent by being camped on the moraine as opposed to on the snowy surface of the glacier. We trudged up the moraine looking for a suitable camp site and I conducted a private competition for the lead with two Canadian Sherpas, one of whom was Sundare who had already climbed Everest twice and was renowned as an exceptional high-altitude performer. I was feeling in a sufficiently bloody-minded mood to maintain the lead – not wholly because of a mildly competitive streak but because the Canadian Sherpas, ignorant of the agreements we were bound by, felt we had taken unfair advantage of what was predominantly their work in creating the Icefall route. I wanted them to know that we were here to follow nobody. However, some of the Sherpa prejudice was more fundamental than that. We were a small Sherpaless climbing team and they saw us as heralding unemployment in what had been one of their most exclusive domains, the Western Cwm.

The gentle incline of the moraine eased further to a hummocky area littered with debris from Russian titanium oxygen bottles to damaged Japanese tents and American dried food wrappers. This was it. Our Advance Base Camp at 21,500 feet in what one would have assumed to be one of the most pristine settings was in fact another rubbish tip. It is a major problem in the Himalayas, for at the end of high-altitude expeditions everyone is physically and psychologically exhausted and carrying down rubbish is often out of the question, while the Sherpas consider burning rubbish too akin to cremation and a generally bad omen. The only alternative is to use a crevasse as the expedition cess-pit.

Despite our disillusion at the state of the place, it was a superb site. About an hour's walk from the bergschrund at the base of the West Face of Mount Lhotse, it was safe from the danger of avalanches and it afforded superb views of the cwm itself and the glacier leading back down to the Icefall. While we sat there, rays of sunlight shone over the South Col between Everest and Lhotse and touched the narrow summit of Nuptse, 4,000 feet above us. It was a hint to be back in Camp 1 before the sun reached into the cwm and fried us on the hoof.

Back at Camp 1, above the Icefall, we languished in our tents and I stripped off my fibrepile clothing in an effort to escape the heat. The temperatures were extreme, in excess of 30°C, when you were in the direct light of the sun or inside a light-coloured tent. The ideal tent for these conditions was one with a light-coloured fly and a dark-coloured liner. The combination afforded maximum insulation against the heat, although on cooler days a totally light-coloured tent proved more comfortable. We found ourselves feeling listless in these conditions and simply remained inactive until the sun dropped behind Pumo Ri and Cho Oyu to the west. Then it was cups of tea, dinner and preparations for the next day's carry to our Advance Base Camp.

Paul had suffered chest pains during the trip up to 21,500 feet and had had a lung infection for some time already. We were all concerned about this, not only for Paul's sake, but because he constituted a major force of our small team. The next day he decided to stay behind at Camp 1 to rest.

In all, we made three carries to Advance Base Camp, the third being a one-way trip with particularly heavy loads. Again Paul remained behind because, although he felt much better, we concurred he should convalesce as much as was possible before the climb proper. So for the first time when the sun's rays descended from the summit of Nuptse until they filled the cwm we were still at 21,500 feet working on the moraines, attempting to create platforms for our tents. We levelled the rock-strewn surface as best we could and gathered some of the camp site garbage to assist in the levelling process. Old cardboard boxes and tattered tent remains were ideal as a cushioning surface between the jagged rocks and the thin tent floors. Eventually we had our three tents pitched and we crawled, exhausted after our efforts, into the larger tent—Fred's bedroom and the expedition kitchen. (I was never quite sure how wise that combination was.) We made a billy of orange cordial and consumed some food. The remainder of the day was largely spent prostrate, recovering from the morning's exertions and the effects of remaining at 21,500 feet.

From my tent I watched the day go by; the sun casting shadows as it moved west, clouds forming over Base Camp, far below, and billowing up the Icefall to the vicinity of Camp 1 and I marvelled at the sheer immensity of the place. As evening drew on I went outside to admire the magnificent lighting. Below

Lhotse's craggy rock summit spread the expansive whiteness of its West Face (or, as it is more commonly called, the Lhotse Face) which at this time was turning a glorious pink. The succession of awesome rock walls of Everest's South-West Face loomed above us and Nuptse's dramatic flutings and cornices were splashed with colour. Down-valley, waning towering-cumulus contributed to the display . . . like an aerial garden of giant mushrooms. I turned towards our cook tent and there was Fred with an armful of old tin cans. He had fossicked about in the moraines and discovered a liberal assortment of canned meats and fish left by bygone expeditions. I wondered if we had really needed to bring any food with us at all.

That evening the three of us sat in the cook tent and munched on our dinners; eating becomes a terrible chore at altitude and you need to force-feed yourself, give yourself lots of encouragement, even some sort of reward . . . a bit like Pavlov's dog. If you didn't like something it was almost impossible to force down. I remember Aid commenting on the tea. "We found much of the tea we had was scented teabags, which isn't tea at all as far as I'm concerned."

We talked to Paul at Camp 1 using one of the Canadians' walkie-talkies. He said he was feeling fine and would arrive at Advance Base Camp in the morning. He added that the long-awaited mailbag had arrived. I eagerly asked him if I had any letters and if so from where. He told me there were a few but none of the ones I had hoped for. I felt quite despondent. What on earth was I going through all these deprivations, even miseries, up here for? All these ridiculously heroic feats in order to be forgotten and neglected by everybody. The glacier creaked and groaned beneath us and I decided that the sentiments were appropriate. With the radio schedule over we discussed our plans. We would have a rest day then begin work on the Lhotse Face. A route had to be found through the crevassed glacier that separated us from the bottom of the face; a suitable place for crossing the bergschrund was needed and then a route up the face itself. We had planned to fix rope up the steeper portions of the route on the face only as it was all we were logistically capable of and because we considered it all we would need. However, now that we had agreed to share the route with the Canadians it would be necessary to fix rope up the entire face because of their greater logistics and thus we planned to fix rope most of the way and use predominantly Canadian fixed line for the purpose. I think, even then, we realised that we would not be left to do all the leading of the face as the Canadians and their Sherpas would become impatient. For the most part I think our attitude was one of indifference as there would be two expeditions on the same route however you cared to view it. My own wish was that the larger Canadian expedition and their force of Sherpas remembered us and took our presence into account. I was confident we would do a large proportion of the leading on the face and that is certainly what came to pass.

At about seven a.m. the next morning I heard the slow and methodical sound of footsteps and heavy breathing approaching. Pat and Bill and Paul trudged into camp along with a group of Sherpas who were carrying double loads. It hadn't slowed them up. They were determined to get the climb over and done with. There was still bad karma hanging over the expedition and the sooner they went home, the better. Paul opened his pack and distributed letters to Aid, Fred and me. A hush settled on the camp as the serious business of catching-up with the lives of friends, family and loves was engaged in. I sifted through my letters. There was one from a friend and the rest were bank statements and business mail. I admired their tenacity in follow-ing me into the Western Cwm but since I had no intention of paying any bills or amending the status of my accounts at that particular juncture I stuffed them into a pocket in the side of the tent, and pondered the lack of mail from one person in particular. Perhaps she's grown tired of my globe-trotting and the succession of expeditions to the outlandish? There were footsteps coming around the side of the tent. Paul's red, sunburned face appeared at the entrance. He sported a very jolly grin. "Late delivery," he said and tossed five more letters into the tent. They were exactly the ones I'd been waiting for. What I said to him in reply would not make family reading.

14

Eight kilometres high

THE NEXT MORNING the four of us set out carrying fixed rope, ice screws and dead-men to attach the rope to the face with. We broke a trail up the glacier, winding through crevassed areas, marking the route with bamboo poles. Cones of avalanche debris and spin-drift led up to the bergschrund and above the erratic and brittle line of the bergschrund rose the face proper, a vast area of steep snow and ice, the size of a thousand football fields (and that in my estimation is no exaggeration), broken by ice cliffs and twisted rock outcrops.

We halted at the bergschrund and began preparing our gear for fixing on the face. It was miserable standing there uncoiling rope and racking equipment in the bitterly cold wind and the constant onslaught of spin-drift that showered down the face. If any of the tiny ice particles made contact with bared skin, and this tended to mean your face, it was most painful. Our hands were freezing and the altitude of over 22,000 feet made us slow. Fred dropped some gear he was handling and, as luck would have it, the equipment plummeted straight into the bergschrund. I confided to him my dissatisfaction at this act to which he responded with equal vigour. It was the only conflict or loss of tempers of the whole three-month-long expedition, which was just as well as I thought Fred was looking fantastically fierce and it occurred to me he presented a plausible argument for the existence of the fabled yeti. It demonstrated to me another of the effects of altitude: a greater propensity for flying off the handle. But as suddenly as that shouting match had begun, it was over, and we proceeded to work together in procuring the dropped climbing gear from the crevasse.

Paul led out 500 feet of rope over the bergschrund and up the steep, green ice at the base of the face. Once he had secured it in position he descended and we returned to camp feeling satisfied with the day's progress. When we reached the camp we found Alan, Pat and Speedy with five Sherpas setting up their tents alongside ours. It gave us an indication of just how large the Advance Base Camp was to become.

It is an extraordinary experience living at high altitude and we lived at 21,500 feet or above for three weeks. All physical activity is tiring and keeping your breath is not always easy even when all you are doing is walking from one tent to another or bending low to enter a tent. Hyperventilation is the norm rather than a potentially hazardous respiratory act. We couldn't rush our summit bid as we needed the three weeks for us all to acclimatise sufficiently to the high altitudes to make our attempt on Lhotse without oxygen bottles feasible. Each time we ascended the glacier to the foot of the Lhotse Face and there climbed the fixed ropes we had placed we felt stronger. We needed to monitor our physiological adaptation carefully for we would reach a point of optimum acclimatisation from where we would deteriorate. As we acclimatised, amongst other things, our blood was becoming thicker due to the increased concentration of red blood corpuscles. These additional cells assist by an improved absorption of oxygen which is important at high altitudes where the air is thinner and consequently there is less oxygen available. In fact the air is about half as thick at Base Camp as it is at sea level. So over the next two weeks we ascended the face, fixing rope and establishing camps and all the while we acclimatised. One thing that made life a great deal more pleasant, and in fact reasonably comfortable much of the time, was our specialised clothing. It has always been something that has fascinated me—and certainly not from a vogue point of view but from a pragmatic view. One needed something lightweight yet warm that required minimal changes of clothing; a system that complemented itself from your sleeping-bag through to your underwear. Based on my previous experiences and the gear already available, I worked with a New Zealand firm, Fairydown, to produce a one-piece down suit to satisfy the various criteria I had in mind. Wearing it I looked like an over-endowed gent in a boiler suit, but it proved ideal. With a moisture permeable (Entrant) nylon outer skin and goose down inside, the suit kept me insulated from the cold, the driving spin-drift and the wind while preventing condensation. On our feet we used plastic climbing boots with a sealed foam inner boot for extra insulation. Our whole outfits weighed very little and contributed to our ability to bring relatively little clothing with us. Our mainstay were our sleeping-bags into which we retreated when conditions became particularly cold and miserable.

Our evenings were generally spent with the Canadian team. Once we had finished our dinners, having forced as much food down our gullets as we could – all the while praising ourselves for such a sterling effort and looking forward to the increased performance we would experience – we sauntered across the moraines to their mess tent. It was no ordinary tent as it was in fact a carport suitable for a large Chevrolet station-wagon, used by the American expedition the previous year for their medical research expedition and afterwards they had sold it to the Canadians. What with Dave Read's hilarious repertoire of jokes and characterisations – I couldn't understand what he was doing on a mountain when he should be hosting his own television show – and the daily radio communication with Base Camp our evenings were a lot of fun. One of the Canadians, Dwayne Congdon, had his girlfriend arrive at Base Camp and naturally enough she wanted to speak to Dwayne. Dwayne was a beetroot colour as he conducted a self-conscious and tongue-tied conversation with his ladylove while his comrades and Sherpa companions roared with laughter, cracked a continuous series of bawdy jokes and generally conducted themselves in a manner exclusive to a group of males isolated from female company. Increasing desperation on this front led eventually to the altruistic reading aloud of romantic mail to the congregated population of Advance Base Camp. I had never realised how explicit some people become in their written communications!

On October 3rd there was a radio message from Base Camp for Aid, who recalls:

> When I answered, everyone at Base Camp started singing "Happy Anniversary to You". Then I was told someone there wanted to talk to me on this special day. Lorna came on the air and was obviously in high spirits. A light-hearted banter followed, with a good deal of laughter from everyone who was listening in. I told her I had been telling the Canadian Sherpas that in the West you don't have babies because you go

on expeditions and there is never any chance of conceiving one. Lorna replied that she had been giving this some thought herself, however, "even though you made me fly back from Bali and then up to Lukla airfield to join you after the Everest winter trip, and even though my uncle had to call up Sir Douglas Busk to get a reference before my father would let you marry me, and even though we did spend our honeymoon at your parents', and even though you did leave me immediately to go and climb a mountain in Nepal, and even though in the first year of our marriage you spent Christmas, my birthday, your birthday and our first wedding anniversary on a mountain in Nepal, I love you very much and there's no one else I'd rather be married to."

A rousing applause filled the night air, and Aid, I thought, looked quite speechless!

As the days passed the route was pushed higher on the Lhotse Face. Fred, Paul and I put in 500 feet in terribly windy conditions and Aid and Al fixed another 1,500 feet in similarly atrocious weather. Fred and Dwayne fixed the next 500 feet, while Paul, Laurie Skreslet and I established Camp 3 at over 23,000 feet. The conditions were appalling, we had great difficulty cutting a ledge in the hard ice for the tent and then preventing the tent from being blown away as we pitched it. Later two more tents were pitched at Camp 3. Aid and Al returned to the fray in the intensely cold and windy conditions and fixed a further 1,500 feet of rope from Camp 3 across the main gully on the face to below the yellow rock band that crosses the face at 24,000 feet. They were a superb team; strong and competent, willing to work on in the worst conditions.

Paul became feverish again and decided to descend to Base Camp, although Bill March had closed the Icefall because of its constantly deteriorating condition. Being cut off with no assured and maintained route through the Icefall concerned me. I tried not to think of contingencies. While Paul descended, Bill and Pat went up to Camp 3 and the following day Bill, using oxygen, led three more spools of fixed rope across the yellow band. Bill was ecstatic about the advantages of oxygen. He said his performance-increase had been dramatic. He kindly offered us the use of some of their oxygen, but in Fred's words it was like offering a bicycle to a runner. Fred and I ascended to Camp 3 the next morning with provisions for our final assault camp which we planned to site at about 25,500 feet. Sundare and Pemma, two of the Canadian Sherpas, descended via Camp 3 having fixed several more spools of rope above Bill's effort of the previous day. They said they had reached the Geneva Spur at over 25,500 feet. Fred and I were delighted with this news, as it meant that we could carry our provisions right to our proposed final camp site without having to lead and fix more rope on the face. From the high point on the fixed ropes, so Sundare told us, the Canadians would traverse left across the Geneva Spur and on to the South Col. There the Canadians would establish their final camp for their assault on Everest.

At four in the morning Fred and I began brewing cups of tea and preparing a little food. I talked to Bill at Camp 2 on the radio and he told me of the poor weather forecast which predicted high winds. That seemed ominous in the light of what we had already been subjected to. However, there was a lull in the strong winds and the falling debris that came down the face in waves, ricocheting off the roof of the precarious tent, so we elected to try our luck. With our loads on our backs we moved slowly up the fixed ropes above Camp 3 and out across the vast snow and ice face. There was the dull and rather terrifying roar of wind above us; the sound seldom faltered. A feeling of insignificance came over me as I struggled to breathe the freezing early morning air. Each step upward was a major effort, each time I slid my jumar further up the rope I felt I could not take another step. Breathing was not only difficult but painful, as we had all developed sore throats from the deep, rapid breathing in the cold, dry air. The pain of breathing and exertion at altitude faded into obscurity beside the simple necessity of functioning normally to live.

Life at altitude is often an uncomfortable business and as I climbed, concentrating on my breathing and climbing rhythms, I allowed my mind to drift just sufficiently to remember my rationale for being there in the first place. It's a pursuit that demands absolute determination to succeed, a strong grip of the psyche and the ability to switch-off and ignore the discomforts. I enjoy the excitement of making a serious commitment to such an extending challenge and to adopting a psychology that will carry you through. There is no doubt that the location and the dramatic scenery, the isolation, the feeling of self-reliance, all add to the experience and consequently the desire to climb, but much of the reasoning is inexplicable—some need to prove something to yourself (there is no audience) in the planet's potentially most hostile environment and conditions. To me, it's the ultimate challenge; a totally engrossing activity.

We climbed on for several hours, snapping our jumars on to the rope above each anchor and sliding them upward. We climbed across the yellow band and up on to the flank of the Geneva Spur. I looked down. The horseshoe of the Western Cwm lay below and I could just discern the tents of our Advance Base Camp far below. The summit of Nuptse (25,800 feet) lay to the left and was now only marginally above the level of the horizon. Turning towards the West Ridge of Everest I looked across the Nepal-Tibet border: on the south side the snow-clad jagged topography of the Himalayas with its deep valleys and gorges and on the northern side the brown barrenness and rolling geography of the sweeping Tibetan Plateau. The contrast is indisputably the most defined I have seen. It intrigued me, too, to think that I was peering across into the long-forbidden land of Tibet from a border pedestal upon which I was balancing at over 25,000 feet! I couldn't day-dream too much for fear of falling off. Suddenly an extraordinary high-pitched roar, like the blasts from a supersonic jet engine, flashed over the South Col, ripped across the South Pillar of Everest and over the crest of the Geneva Spur just 100 feet to my left. It made a curious cracking sound, like a whip; small pieces of ice were blasted off the Geneva Spur and flung across the face. I couldn't really comprehend what was happening. I looked back out over the Western Cwm foolishly expecting to see an airforce pilot playing silly-buggers amongst the giant peaks. I gripped the shaft of my ice-axe and held on. There could be no other explanation than a wind of exceptional speed. Later I gauged that gust to be in the vicinity of 200 mph. I could have been no more substantial than a leaf, plucked off the face by these mysterious high-speed gusts, and tossed out over the Western Cwm. I feared for my life. I began to feel that I was attempting to deal with a phenomenon for which I was not prepared.

For the remainder of the morning the wind roared overhead, past the summit pyramids of the peaks and through the narrow

South Col. The wind velocities were less than the mysterious gusts but still high. We were, fortunately, in some kind of wind shadow and despite the noise, the swirling snow further across the face and the vortices rising above Lhotse's summit, we remained in a region of comparative calm. The strange debilitating effects of 25,000 feet slowed our progress further and I, in particular, found myself having to halt in the ignominious 'ostrich posture' where you put your brow against the snow-clad face and gasp in a vain effort to get a decent lungful of air. We were both learning how to breathe and move at these high elevations and it took some experimentation. Fred was moving well and reached the top of the rope. Holding the fixed line in place he found a tenuous piton, placed by an exhausted Sundare the day before. Attending to this, he then watched me moving slowly up towards him. I wondered if I would ever make it and eventually left my twenty-pound load a short distance below the top of the rope. We dug a ledge and tied the gear into place. We estimated we were at 25,700 feet. There were some reasonable sites for a camp a short distance across the slope and the immediate route beyond looked straightforward. A broad, shallow gully would need to be crossed before ascending the snow face to the base of the summit gully which rose directly through the rock bluffs of Lhotse's summit cap. It was difficult to discern the features of this gully due to spiralling winds carrying spin-drift up it and high into the air above the peak. It was an incredible sight; an unharnessed inferno and I found it intimidating. After a while we saw what we wanted, the rock step half-way up the gully. For the most part it had ice on it and we decided it would not, under normal circumstances, prove a problem to us to climb but at about 27,000 feet it was hard to say. Certainly, the way I felt at that moment, at 25,700 feet, it was nothing short of an impossibility.

Leaving our gear, we descended off the Geneva Spur, down to the yellow band, back to Camp 3 where we stopped for a cup of tea before descending towards the cwm. We met Aid and Laurie on their way up for a night at Camp 3 from where they planned to ascend to our gear depot, Aid carrying more food for our final summit bid. Aid told us we were deemed heroes back in Base Camp. How can anyone climb in such fearful winds? We agreed about the conditions and reluctantly divulged the story of that miraculous wind shadow. Aid seemed pleased that Fred and I had gone reasonably well, as it meant we were now promising high-altitude material. I think he was relieved as it meant he definitely had company for the summit bid later.

Aid carried his load to 25,700 feet the next morning, while Laurie followed him up the ropes as far as the yellow band. Aid returned to the Advance Base Camp looking disconcertingly fresh, I thought. The same day Paul arrived back from Base Camp bringing Phu Tenzing, our sirdar, with him. Paul looked much better and wasted no time in boasting about the many washes with hot water and the sumptuous food he had enjoyed in the comparative luxury of Base Camp. The Icefall he said, was extremely dangerous.

Paul had brought Phu Tenzing up to increase the safety of his return journey to Advance Base Camp (otherwise he would have had to return alone) and to assist us with carrying down our equipment after our summit attempt, which we planned within the week. Poor old Phu Tenzing; he had come up to 21,500 feet too quickly and had three miserable days plagued by altitude sickness—nausea, insomnia, headaches.

The inclement weather was getting on our nerves. The almost incessant roar of the wind over the West Ridge of Everest was a monotone that was inescapable, the sound reverberated around the entire cwm. Great wind-carried plumes of snow rose from the summits, and spectacular sculptured clouds swirled over Lhotse and Everest in graduated pressure bands with acceleration curves from which whisps of cloud were jettisoned into nothingness. At times the cwm itself filled with cloud and the atmosphere became depressing. We crawled into our sleeping-bags still fully dressed (we never undressed!) with down booties on our feet and wool caps on our heads and listened to the wind. The tent walls flexed inward like drum skins, and sometimes I woke in the mornings with that penetrating headache, lack of breath, almost a desperation which I felt was as much altitude related as it was to the claustrophobia imposed by the weather. One day I saw a forlorn and displaced woodpecker fluttering about outside, blown off course by the winds, lost in the cloud and snow, doomed by the almighty elements. The weather ruled our lives. The cold was almost unbearable, not because we couldn't insulate against it but because it was unremitting; that is, until mid-morning on the better days when the sun baked the camp as if the refrigerator that contained us had switched roles with an oven. Large black plastic bags filled with snow produced plenty of water during these times and saved precious fuel, which helped compensate for the discomfort of the excessive heat. Some evenings the clouds would swirl in the sunset; a dance of irascible intent. Then the moon rose and filled the cwm with waxy light and a ghostly translucence; we all talked of yetis and demons. Only the Sherpas didn't talk in jest.

I admired the Sherpas. Singing as they worked, and cheerful when most of the foreigners could barely raise an excruciating grin, they were slow to complain about their lot. Fit and strong and small in stature, their high-altitude performance without oxygen is exceptional.

One day Emile Wick, that pilot *extraordinaire*, flew over in his Pilatus Porter with a Canadian photographer recording all he saw on film. Emile has worked for Royal Nepal Airlines for many years and must unquestionably be the most experienced STOL pilot in the Himalayas and, what's more, he seems to still love doing it. During the Canadian summit bids he flew over the summits of both Lhotse and Everest at a speed which, he later told me, was roughly equivalent to the aircraft's stall speed at that altitude! The aircraft appeared ludicrously small as it flew about these mountains.

At last the winds dropped and the skies were clear blue, wonderfully blue. There was a mad scramble for the mountains; Lhotse for us and Everest for the Canadians. Paul and Fred left Advance Base Camp early in the morning of October 4th. They planned to reach 25,700 feet, select a site for a camp and begin work excavating the necessary ledge for our tents. They moved steadily up the face, along with the Canadian Sherpas and several Canadians. Laurie had been selected as the first Canadian sum-miteer along with two Sherpas, Sundare and Lhakpa Dorji. Paul and Fred remained a constant distance behind Laurie all the way up the Lhotse Face. They breathed the air around them and Laurie was using a bottle of oxygen. Fred wrote, "We could see the Canadian member two lengths of rope above us. As the day wore on and the smaller peaks dropped below, he was still only two ropes ahead. Is oxygen worth its weight? I doubt it." Laurie's comment afterwards was, "I saw you coming up the rope behind me and thought you were gaining on me so I tried to go a little faster. You were going well, especially without juice."

Climbing at high altitudes without oxygen is very hard work but it did seem that the benefits of the oxygen were largely negated by the weight of the apparatus. More important for us was the aesthetic appeal of the simple approach; an acclimatised climber with minimal paraphernalia was an attractive concept and lent itself to a more enjoyable overall experience on the mountain. It also reduced logistics and meant there were fewer gadgets to malfunction.

Fred's diary:

> At this height [25,700 feet] there are only a score of peaks in the world higher and as we rested we could see out over the Lhotse-Nuptse Wall to the green of Nepal and over the Lho La to the brown of Tibet. The final gully which leads to the summit of Lhotse looked only a short distance away. The gully itself can't be seen from the floor of the Western Cwm so we looked at it carefully. Could we climb the critical rock step quickly? The aim of the day was not to examine the views but to find a camp site which was out of the wind and safe from avalanche. Two suitable looking white rocks protruded from the snow. I led out towards them but the snow lay over loose rock and after some scary moments, rocks even further left were chosen. Here the snow was tested and found to be deep enough for tent platforms and with an excellent consistency. I started to dig the platform while Paul fixed rope to the site of the camp. Starting down revealed how tired we really were, the snow was crusted and uneven. Going down is when fixed rope is really worthwhile. If we stumbled and fell it would only be a rope length, not thousands of feet to the bottom of the face. Dropping down was leaving behind height which hurt to gain, but this trip would trigger acclimatisation that was necessary for the summit.

While we prepared our evening meal and the temperature plummeted we watched the last members of the Canadian summit team moving slowly on the Lhotse Face. It was a puzzle to everyone why Dave Read and Kiwi Gallagher had not turned back. The light was growing dim and they were only just above the yellow band at about 24,500 feet. We diagnosed 'Everest fever' had broken out amongst the troops. There were food and sleeping-bags and shelter for only four at the Canadians' South Col camp and already ensconced were Laurie, Sundare and Lhakpa Dorji. But the two minuscule dots moved sluggishly up and out of sight behind the Geneva Spur. At Advance Base Lhotse and Everest expedition members alike speculated as to the outcome. Their oxygen would have run out. What would happen then? If they did get to the South Col, where would they all sleep . . . would there be enough oxygen left for the summit bid? I began to feel pity for Laurie as I felt there was a chance the summit attempt might have to be aborted in order to share round the oxygen.

Bill March decided a search was called for and over the radio Sundare and Lhakpa Dorji were given the task. We felt really sorry for these two and concerned about what they were about to do. It was now dark; after seven p.m., Laurie radioed when the Sherpas were ready to depart back down the fixed ropes. Just then Dave stumbled into the South Col camp. He was blue in the face, said Laurie, and had run out of oxygen. They put Dave on to a fresh bottle. Since he did not know what Kiwi was doing or where he was, Sundare and Lhakpa Dorji set off on their rescue mission. In the black of night these two hardy souls traversed the South Col at 26,000 feet, crossed the Geneva Spur and descended to our gear dump at 25,700 feet. From the cwm we watched the two specks of light from their headlamps moving slowly across the top of the face. It was an admirable effort, as not only had these two ascended to the South Col that very morning but they had assisted with establishing the camp there, and had been up and down the ropes like yoyos during the previous five or six days.

Lhakpa Dorji's cracked and tired voice came over the walkie-talkie; he was apologetic as they could not see Kiwi anywhere. We began to resign ourselves to finding him later, slumped on the face, hanging from his jumar. Bill told the Sherpas to return to the South Col and then over the air came another exhausted voice. It was Kiwi. He too had run out of oxygen and couldn't go on. He had tied his load to the fixed rope and left it there. "I'm just a stubborn old man," he mumbled. We watched his headlamp light move slowly, down the face and back to Camp 3 where he spent the night. We were all relieved that what had seemed certain disaster had been averted.

For the Canadians and their Sherpas it was now all-stations-go for their first attempt on the summit of Everest, for us it was a rest day for Paul and Fred before setting off up the face and our attempt on the summit of Lhotse. All we needed was for the weather to hold. I was sure, as sure as one can be, that we would make it to the top.

The next day Sundare, Lhakpa Dorji and Laurie climbed to the summit of Everest from the South Col. We were all delighted as the Canadians had suffered a great deal in the pursuit of this moment. They planned one more summit bid, again with two Sherpas to carry extra oxygen. We made preparations for our own climb. We would leave in the morning; on Wednesday, October 6th.

The sun was already filling the cwm with light but the heat did not seem as intense any more. The seasons were changing. Nevertheless I tied the top half of my down suit low around my waist and with twenty pounds of gear on my back set off across the glacier. We looked like the cast of a black and white minstrel show with the patches of ultra-violet block-out creams, contrasting with tanned or blistered skin. We crossed the glacier in a brisk but not uncomfortable wind and climbed up the fixed ropes on the face to Camp 3. We spent a remarkably comfortable night on those narrow ledges. The tents became quite warm inside as the gas stoves were almost constantly burning, producing drinks and food. Carbohydrates and sweet drinks were what we wanted, food we could metabolise at these altitudes.

On October 7th another fine day dawned and we climbed on up the broad, steep face, up the rutted wind-packed snow, clawing our way up the water ice and across the yellow band where we picked up another five or six pounds each of gear that was left there. For another 1,500 feet we climbed, breathing deeply in the thin, cold air. Each exhalation produced a draft of white, frozen condensate which caused a white frosting on our down hoods and collars and icicles formed in our beards. I felt eminently better than I had done on my first climb of the face. I was able to move steadily and I felt much stronger. I thought again of my father's climb up this same route on his way to the first ascent of Everest. As much as this was going to be an all-consuming adventure for us, there was one thing missing. Someone had been up here before. The route, the difficulties, even the feasibility of the climb were known factors. However, we were breaking ground in one area. We were attempting the first ascent of Lhotse by a small expedition and entirely without oxygen. From our top camp there would be no fixed ropes . . . no leeway. I needed to perpetuate the discipline that had got me this far, for this long. I needed it just to keep me going. The next day would probably be the most demanding day of my life in terms of endurance and determination.

At 25,700 feet on the flanks of the Geneva Spur we located our depot and moved across to Paul and Fred's small ledge. Taking turns we dug a platform in the precipitous flanks and erected two small tents. I plugged steps across the shallow gully opposite the ledge and up to a rock outcrop on the face. I was beginning to tire and was finding the climbing desperately difficult. I left a light hand line there to guide us in the morning and retraced my steps to the tents. We were exhausted and dehydrated by our exertions, so the remainder of the day drifted by with us taking turns to melt snow and make drinks. We needed eight litres of fluid to rehydrate at this altitude and it would take many hours to melt the necessary snow. While I rested I watched Fred cradling the stove. Every action had become a trial. For our climb we needed to be rehydrated and yet none of us felt the inclination to produce the drinks, let alone drink them. We had to discipline ourselves to work the stove, collect snow and ice for the billy, make the drinks and finally to consume them. I pondered on the following morning.

Aid writes:

The day before the summit day had been a very difficult one. The amount of digging needed to get the two tents pitched and the work of carrying loads up to the camp site, I knew would make us all feel poorly during the night with dehydration and fatigue.

Paul and I were restless all night and it was the first time I had taken a sleeping tablet on the entire expedition. I lay in a type of coma waiting for three o'clock in the morning when we would get up. The tent was frosted up and Paul said he didn't feel very well. As I crouched there with the little camping gas stove making hot chocolate, my head was throbbing with the lack of blood sugar caused by a night at high altitude and the lack of movement. I realised the headache would go when we began moving. It's like having a horrible hangover and knowing that only time will stop it. It was very cold that morning and everything seemed to take a long time. My crampons took forever to strap on to my boots and bending down brought blood into my head and made the throbs bigger, deeper.

With no more than a pocket camera and another pocket of our down suits filled with boiled sweets, we set off at six thirty a.m.

"I'll start moving, lads," said Aid quietly and one by one we moved off across the face following the route I had made the day before. It was a very cold morning and because we were on a West Face it would be ten o'clock before the warming rays of the sun reached us. Our fingers and toes were like wood and as we moved we constantly wriggled them in an attempt to warm them. At the top of the hand line, at over 26,000 feet, we roped up. Paul was moving very slowly, then he stopped and waved us on.

Paul wrote:

It was a breathless place taking all we gave and still coming back for more. After the sleepless and claustrophobic night we set out to climb the final 2,000 feet of Lhotse. Hands and toes with no feeling, numb with cold and early stages of frostbite can easily detract from the enjoyment of serious climbing at altitude. After some time I could not warm my hands at all, this made it very difficult for me, so I chose to return to Camp 4. I hoped this would give the others a better chance for the top, as I was becoming slow with the cold. It took me nearly two hours to get the feeling back into my hands and to rewarm my feet; the tears from pain and disappointment almost came trickling down my cheeks.

We moved together on the rope up the wind-rutted snow face until we reached some rock outcrops where the incline steepened. I was amazed at how well we were moving, how rapidly we were climbing. I think the lack of any superfluous weight made that difference. We were well acclimatised and with no packs or loads of any kind our performances were greatly improved. From the rock outcrop we continued with Fred, who was now in front, putting in rock protection as we moved and Aid, who was at the rear, taking it out. Above the snow and ice of the Lhotse Face rose the rock walls of the summit pyramid and through them lay the narrow summit gully. Here we paused to set up a belay. It was a magnificent position; so high and so far from anywhere, anyone and from the surface of the earth. We looked down on to the South Col at 26,000 feet and across at the South-East Ridge of Mount Everest wearing a gigantic plume of wind-blown snow. At first we seemed to be largely sheltered from the wind. Above the summit, scarves of white writhed in the blue sky. A veil of cloud was rapidly forming overhead and there was now a light, rather disquieting, wind in the gully. We climbed on swinging leads. First Fred, then I, then Aid leading the forty-five-degree snow gully till it veered right and steepened. A narrow rock step lay above us and now conditions were anything but clement. The wind had risen markedly and snow was falling. No longer could we look across at Everest and beyond at the broad Tibetan Plateau.

Aid writes: "It started to snow more heavily and I looked around me and had some doubts. I didn't say anything about my thoughts to the others."

We climbed on, becoming slower, it seemed, with every step upward. A couple of steps and then a bout of rapid, deep breathing; two more steps and more frantic hyperventilation. We were over 27,000 feet, in a storm cloud at this juncture—and climbing required every ounce of energy and determination that we could muster. On both sides rock walls rose steeply and the falling snow was settling here and there. If there was any avalanche it would funnel into the gully, collecting us on its way to the Western Cwm over 5,000 feet below. Our extremities were still very cold and along with the weather it made us apprehensive. We decided to keep going for a short distance.

Fred led on into the blizzard, climbing the narrow rock step and moving out of sight into the upper couloir. He could see up the snow-filled couloir to the summit. There was only 700 or 800 feet to go.

I didn't like the dramatic increase in the wind velocity. Aid and I discussed our predicament as we stood on the belay stance, shouting at each other in the howling wind and the constant sound of tiny pieces of ice plummeting down the gully. Snow swirled past us and we worried about the danger of avalanche. It was nearly midday and the sun was blotted out by cloud and falling snow, so we couldn't warm our fingers and toes, they were nearly frozen. It seemed to us prudent to turn back, to descend—if we continued there was the increasing avalanche risk, the high winds, the certainty of losing fingers and toes. We called to Fred somewhere above in the maelstrom. He down-climbed the rock step to where we were belaying him and we huddled there in the throes of making our decision. It had to be the right one.

Fred writes: "From our top point one can see up the gully through the cloud almost to the summit but at 500 feet an hour we would have been badly frostbitten by the time we got there and may have been swept out of the gully on the way down by fresh snow avalanches. We had reached perhaps 27,100 feet without oxygen and knew that there could be no second attempt."

We reluctantly agreed to turn back. It's never an easy decision but when it means survival, retaining all your fingers and toes and returning to the valleys below and to the people you love and care for, that's what it's all about. Posthumous heroism, we later agreed, had its limitations. We had ventured into a world that few others ever reach or ever know. An inhospitable environment where our presence could only ever be but fleeting. We had stood on solid ground, 8.3 kilometres above the surface of the earth! Now we began our descent.

Later I pondered on our expedition. We had ventured into an icy, oxygen-deprived environment and we had returned unharmed; however, not unchanged. As much as Lhotse was an adventure in physical terms, it was also one in terms of self-exploration. I had learnt a little of the frailty and of the strengths that are humanity and seen the ongoing metamorphosis of this earth where it is at its least benign. I had gained a better understanding of where my priorities lay and of what is really important in life—and I had shared that experience with friends. For me they had been powerful times.

Index